Methodism and Politics
in British Society
1750–1850

Methodism and Politics in British Society 1750–1850

David Hempton
Lecturer in History,
The Queen's University of Belfast

Hutchinson

London Melbourne Sydney Auckland Johannesburg

Hutchinson Education

An imprint of Century Hutchinson Ltd

62–65 Chandos Place, Covent Garden, London WC2N 4NW

Century Hutchinson Australia Pty Ltd
PO Box 496, 16–22 Church Street, Hawthorn, Melbourne, Victoria 3122, Australia

Century Hutchinson New Zealand Ltd
PO Box 40–086, Glenfield, Auckland 10, New Zealand

Century Hutchinson South Africa (Pty) Ltd
PO Box 337, Bergvlei 2012, South Africa

First published 1984
Reprinted 1985
First published in paperback 1987

Set in Times by BookEns, Saffron Walden, Essex

Printed and bound in Great Britain by
Anchor Brendon Ltd,
Tiptree, Essex

British Library Cataloguing in Publication Data

Hempton, David
  Methodism and politics in British society
  1750–1850.
  1. Methodist Church—Great Britain—
  History   2. Church and the world
  I. Title
  261.1′0941   BX8276

ISBN 0 09 173051 1

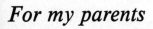

For my parents

Contents

Preface

In the preparation of this book I have accumulated an immense debt to a great number of people. My thanks go first to Professors Norman Gash, W. R. Ward and W. L. Warren. Professor Gash supervised my postgraduate research, and shared something of his incomparable knowledge of early nineteenth-century British politics. Professor Ward's monumental labours in English archives have taken our understanding of Methodist history on to a new level. I am specially grateful to him for taking the trouble to read the whole book in typescript, and for offering constructive criticisms. Without Professor Warren's practical help and advice over the past decade, this book would simply not have been written.

Several others have taken time from more valuable pursuits to read various drafts and to offer expert suggestions for its improvement. Dr Ian Green dealt with the manuscript in its most unpleasant form, and Dr David Bebbington gave freely of his wide knowledge of nineteenth-century Nonconformity. Dr Peter Jupp kindly made available to me his enormous collection of transcripts from the correspondence of British politicians in the period 1790–1830. This helped me to see the Methodists in a rather different light. John Prest gave me access to his family papers, and talked to me about early Victorian liberalism. Dr Martin Ingram stimulated some new thoughts, and rightly demolished some old ones.

My warmest thanks are due to my friend Sheridan Gilley who has been a constant source of encouragement and an indispensable supplier of information on all aspects of religious and social history in the modern period. This book is immeasurably better for his contribution.

I never cease to be impressed by the good humour and efficiency of librarians and archivists, when confronted by eccentric historians in search of 'crucial' information. In particular, I wish to thank those in the Queen's University of Belfast and in the John Rylands University Library of Manchester. I, in common with countless other students of Methodism, owe a special debt to Dr J. C. Bowmer who looked after the Methodist Church Archives when they were in City Road, London. I am also grateful to the Irish branch of the Wesley Historical Society for access to its fine library and manuscript collection.

I should never have been able to complete this book without the generosity of the Queen's University of Belfast and the helpfulness of my colleagues in the History Department. This high level of co-operation extended to the departmental secretaries Yvonne Smyth and Olivia Johnston, who were remarkably tolerant of my demands on their time.

My heaviest debt of all is to my wife who has cheerfully accepted the domestic consequences of having an historian in the house. Finally, I must apologize to Stephen, who should not have had to compete with the Methodists for his father's attention in the first year of his life. Mercifully, he is too young to read what follows.

David Hempton
Belfast 1983

1 Introduction

'The study of late-eighteenth and early-nineteenth century Methodism as a national movement has ceased to pay dividends, and references to Halévy should be sternly avoided.'[1]* Professor Kent's frustration with the seemingly endless debates inspired by Halévy was based on the premise that comprehensive social theories of Methodism had been superimposed on quite inadequate local research. This frustration was well founded, as anyone who has read undergraduate essays on Methodism and society can easily confirm. Students, and even professional historians engaged in works of synthesis, were forced by existing scholarship to confirm or reject the counter-revolution thesis, when many had little idea what Methodism, as a religious and social phenomenon, was really like.[2] What were considered to be secondary matters were hurriedly brushed aside to get at the big question of whether Methodism made men more radical or less. As with early modern Puritanism, however, regional studies soon made it clear that the dominant social theory was insufficiently subtle and flexible to embrace the diversity of local religious behaviour.

The Halévy thesis is, of course, far from buried – nor should it be – but other questions have at last received their share of historical attention. As a result much more is known about the numerical strength, social structure, geographical distribution and political significance of eighteenth- and early nineteenth-century Methodism. An increase in knowledge has inevitably led to an increase in complexity. There was after all not one Methodism, but 'many Methodisms in many places at many times'.[3] The much described 'chapel culture' was scarcely the same thing in rural Lincolnshire as it was in suburban Manchester. Similarly, the sermons of Conference dignitaries had little in common with those of Cornish folk preachers, and the political aspirations of Lancastrian manufacturers were poles apart from those of Durham trade unionists. But such variations should be used as a warning

*Superior figures refer to the References at the end of each chapter.

against inflexible analysis, not as an excuse for refusing to engage in it. For while it is true that all history is ultimately local history, Methodism, with all its diversity, made a profound impact on national life, especially in the nineteenth century. Interpreting that impact, albeit only in political terms, is the subject of this book, but first it is necessary to say something about the strength and distribution of Methodism in British society between 1750 and 1850.

Who were the Methodists?

A formidable array of statistical tables and graphs are now available to students of Methodism thanks to the efficiency of Methodist records and to the diligence of R. Currie *et al.*[4] It is now possible to find out, with a reasonable degree of accuracy, the numbers of members and preachers of all major Methodist denominations in the British Isles from the mid eighteenth century to the present. From these figures can be deduced the density of Methodism in relation to the total population, and patterns of church growth. The tables show that Methodism underwent a period of sustained rapid expansion from 1740 to about 1840 when its relative strength in English society was at its peak. Even then, a Methodist membership of 435,591 accounted for only 4.5 per cent of the adult English population. In assessing the social and political impact of Methodism on English society however, such figures are misleading. In the first place, Methodist membership figures are conventionally multiplied by three to find the number of adherents, but even this figure may turn out to be a low estimate. Second, Methodism was but the largest and most influential element in a much wider evangelical constituency. Third, Methodism was particularly strong among artisan occupational groups from whom most was feared in times of political excitement and public disorder. Thus Alan Gilbert concludes that 'the historian ought perhaps to think of something approaching 20 per cent of the most politicized section of the adult "lower orders" being associated with chapel communities' of one sort or another.[5]

Statistics, however well constructed, have their limitations. For example, Methodist local histories and biographies show that beyond the solid core of chapel communities there was a band of denominational gypsies of no fixed abode. Some were subject to the most dramatic denominational fluctuations. The historian of Cornish Methodism records the spiritual journeys of a Truro dressmaker who moved from Methodism to Quakerism via the parish church and the

Bible Christians.[6] Examples like this are legion.[7] Even when denominational allegiances were secure, there were wide variations in the level of religious commitment. Within Methodism important distinctions can be made between the respective commitments of full members, adherents, local preachers, class leaders, part-time officials and itinerant preachers. Moreover, while much has been written about the theology of Wesleyan Methodism, relatively little attention has been paid to how well it was understood and obeyed by those within the connexion. The disciplining of converts within Methodism was more rigorous than in any other denomination, but inevitably its results were limited by human nature. For example, Henry Abelove has shown how Wesley's preference for celibacy among Methodists was not only ignored by his followers, but could also be reinterpreted as a devaluation of marital and familial obligations.[8] Similarly, where a cultural pattern of dubious ethics had become established, as with smuggling in Cornwall, it proved remarkably resilient to moral transformation.[9] Thus the connection between evangelical teaching and practice, especially in sexual matters, could be a good deal more complicated than the dominant model of repression and release would allow.[10]

Research on other important aspects of Methodist belief and practice is still at an early stage. The role of women, apart from preachers' wives and colourful personalities, is virtually unrecorded, yet there were probably more women than men in eighteenth-century Methodism. A survey of 500 members in the Macclesfield area at the end of the century has shown that 56 per cent were women, half of whom were unmarried. If the high ratio of unmarried women to unmarried men in this sample were to be confirmed by other surveys, it would raise important questions about the social significance of chapel communities in a woman's life. Aside from their numerical strength, women played an important part in the expansion of early Methodism, especially in remote areas where they had more opportunities. In the nineteenth century the well known institutionalization of Methodism brought the movement more firmly into the male world of professional ministry, chapel finance, business meetings and local courts.[11]

The influence of Methodism on family life is also underresearched. On one level families could be useful in recruitment, as converted parents or children shared their faith within the household. Moreover, local studies show that the Methodist community expanded through natural succession, at least to the second and third generations.[12] On another level, however, the austerity of Methodist religion could be a source of tension within families. Serious Methodists could be recognized by their dress, hairstyles and physical detachment from the world of revelry, sports and dancing.[13] Such religious expression was too serious a matter to allow much breathing space for deviance within the household. At its best, however, it was also a religion of family commitment, thrift and charity.

If the re-creation of Methodism as a religious and social experience is still at the pioneer stage, much more is known about its social structure. The picture of a great discontinuity between a predominantly working-class Methodism of Wesley's day and its bourgeois successor has been considerably modified, even if the upward social mobility of mainstream Wesleyanism is still accepted. Although the size, geographical range and occupational classification of his sample is too narrow to be conclusive, Clive Field's admirable survey of eighteenth-century Methodism shows that

The nascent movement commanded relatively little support amongst the professional farming, and trading communities, and it could only effectively reach the labouring element in mining districts like West Cornwall. There was a marginal overrepresentation of gentry, but the most outstanding feature was the preponderance of manufacturers [craftsmen], they being more than twice as numerous (47 per cent) as in the country as a whole.[14]

Occupational surveys of nineteenth-century Methodism show that the ascendancy of the craftsman was even more marked, but there is an enormous range of jobs and wages covered by the umbrella term artisan.[15] All are agreed however that Wesleyanism made little impact on the unskilled masses. Even Primitive Methodists and Bible Christians were more likely to be semi-skilled than unskilled. Nevertheless, both the leadership and the rank-and-file of Primitive Methodism was on average from a lower social constituency than their equivalents in the parent connexion.

The geographical location of Methodists

Wesley's meticulously kept *Journal* gives an accurate impression of the geographical distribution of early Methodism. By the end of the eighteenth century it had been particularly successful in the manufacturing districts of the north-east, the north Midlands, the West Riding, and the Potteries. It was strong too in mining areas, especially Cornwall, in seaports and fishing villages, and in rural areas where squire and parson control was weak. Little impression was made on London, the Home Counties and Scotland.[16] As England's industrial pace quickened, Methodism grew strongly in factory villages, railhead and canal settlements, and areas in which economic expansion attracted a migratory labour force.[17] By the time of the Census of Religious Worship (1851) it was recorded that Methodists were 'found in greatest force in Cornwall, Yorkshire, Lincolnshire, Derbyshire, Durham and Nottinghamshire'.[18] The census also showed that while Methodism was far from being a purely urban religion, it had a better record than any other Nonconformist denomination in large manufacturing towns.[19] One other area of Methodist strength that has been virtually ignored by historians is Ireland; yet at the beginning of the nineteenth century Irish Wesleyans accounted for 23 per cent of the British Isles' total. Irish Methodism grew particularly quickly in the 'linen triangle' of Ulster between 1790–1810, when the development of outwork and a wage system produced the same kind of environment as occasioned Methodist success in parts of England.[20]

Anyone explaining the geographical pattern of Methodist growth in the countryside must, of course, be indebted to Professor Everitt's study of rural Dissent in Northamptonshire, Leicestershire, Lincolnshire and Kent, which has served as a model for local historians.[21] Without minimizing personal factors, he shows how the pattern of religious adherence is related to the social and economic structure of local communities. Thus rural Nonconformity was strong in market towns,[22] boundary settlements, industrial villages and in parishes where land had been subdivided. All were characterized by an unusual degree of freedom from paternalistic control. In Lincolnshire in particular the contrast between the Anglican 'estate' parishes and the Dissenting 'freeholders' ' parishes was exceptionally sharp, which no doubt accounts, in part at least, for the anti-Anglican radicalism of Methodist chapel culture in that county.

Everitt concluded also that whereas Old Dissent was strongest in the scattered settlements of forest and wood-pasture regions, Methodism predominated in smaller and more arable parishes. Although this pattern has been detected elsewhere, Methodism in general thrived in areas of Anglican parochial weakness, whether in the rural tracts of Durham or in the large towns and cities of Yorkshire and South Lancashire.[23] Depending on local circumstances therefore, Methodism could be either a more lively religious alternative to established Anglicanism, or, more commonly, a beneficiary of

Anglican and Dissenting weakness. To put it crudely, Methodism of all denominations gained most from the expansion of the English population and economy between 1750 and 1850. Although theories of Methodist growth based on social, economic and ecclesiastical structures have helped our understanding, they should not detract from the importance of the Methodist community itself. Without its deep sense of religious commitment and conversionist zeal, no expansion would have taken place. In Nottinghamshire, for example, Methodist growth followed a regular pattern, regardless of environmental peculiarities.[24] Thus Methodist revivalism had an internal dynamic of its own, and was based more on religious zeal than on social determinants. A helpful environment facilitated growth, but it did not produce it.

Methodism and politics

It is exactly fifty years since E. R. Taylor wrote the last book dealing specifically with Methodism and politics on a national scale.[25] That it was recently reissued is a sign both of the quality of the book and the paucity of its competitors. Because his ideas are usually painted in primary colours with bold strokes of the brush, the strengths and weaknesses of the book are not hard to pick out. Particularly admirable is his appreciation of the religious foundations of many Methodist political attitudes, and the way in which they could find expression in denominational conflict. Equally impressive are his insights into the nature of Wesleyan Conservatism and evangelical social ethics. But the weaknesses of the book are serious. Its social context is always poor and sometimes it becomes dangerously misleading.[26] Even more problematic is his main argument that 'the history of Methodism's relation to politics has been the story of a Liberal displacement of a strong Tory sentiment'.[27] In essence, Taylor's view of nineteenth-century Methodism is the same as the Whig analysis of the eighteenth-century constitution. Bunting is the king, the metropolitan committees are Burke's double cabinets, Conference is the House of Lords, and the great Methodist laity is the House of Commons. Methodist secessions served the same function as Reform Acts, except that Methodist preachers proved to be more insensitive to popular demands than English aristocrats. As a result the Wesleyan polity fractured, and the 'manifest destiny' of Methodist Liberalism was borne by the secessionists. Rather like eighteenth-century Whig theorists, Taylor stated quite categorically that he was not interested in treating any specific example of Methodism and politics in action between 1790 and 1850.[28] This, along with the limited use of primary sources, leaves Taylor's picture lacking in realistic detail and subtlety of expression.

The half century since Taylor's prize-winning essay has brought a remarkable increase in the knowledge of English social history and a proliferation of Methodist local studies.[29] Until recently, however, the most reputable historians of Methodism have confined themselves to the exorcism of Halévy's ghost. But in the past decade pioneering works by Ward, Gilbert, Obelkevich, Moore, Colls, Gowland, and others have lifted our knowledge of Methodism on to a new plane. By comparison, this study has only a few objectives. The first is to make accessible to students of Methodism a range of material that might otherwise elude them. The second is to follow the single theme of politics by using the widest possible range of sources, including the huge volume of private correspondence in the Methodist Church Archives in both England and Ireland. A liberal definition of politics has been used to include the struggle for power and control within Methodism, as well as the relationship between it and its surrounding environment. Where possible political issues have been placed in a proper social and, if necessary, theological context; but the book is not intended to be a social history of Methodism as such. The third objective is to contribute a new angle to the debate on Methodism and politics by paying more attention to Ireland, and to the contest between popular evangelicalism and Irish Catholicism, than others have done. This study is therefore a mixture of synthesis and original research. Inevitably the style of presentation has varied to suit what is already known on each theme. My hope is that the resultant changes of gear are not unacceptably rough, and that scholars upon whose work I have built are not too shocked by my representation of their ideas.

Above all the aim is to look at political problems from as many directions as possible in order to understand, if not condone, the actions of the main participants. Even the historically unloved Bunting had reasons for his policies, and like most men he believed he was right. In the generations after the French Revolution churchmen of all persuasions were operating in uncharted social territory. Not surprisingly, they made errors of judgement, often through fear or under pressure. Occasionally in Methodist correspondence one trips over regrets about past behaviour or the way problems were handled, but history is remarkably unforgiving. All one can do is to restore the colour and texture of religious debates and personalities at a time when religion was important to people, and to reapply Edward Thompson's words, to rescue the Methodists 'from the enormous condescension of posterity', not least of its historians.

References

1   J. H. S. Kent, book review in *Proceedings of the Wesley Historical Society*, **39**, part 6 (1974), p. 180.
2   See, for example, M. I. Thomis, *The Town Labourer and the Industrial Revolution* (London 1974), pp. 165–83.
3   Raphael Samuel (ed.), *People's History and Socialist Theory* (London 1981), p. 357.
4   R. Currie, A. Gilbert and L. Horsley, *Churches and Churchgoers: Patterns of Church growth in the British Isles since 1700* (Oxford 1977). A. D. Gilbert, *Religion and Society in Industrial England* (London 1976).
5   A. D. Gilbert, 'Methodism, Dissent and political stability in early industrial England', *Journal of Religious History*, **10** (1978–9), pp. 381–99.
6   Thomas Shaw, *A History of Cornish Methodism* (Truro 1967), p. 24.
7   See J. Burgess, 'The growth and development of Methodism in Cumbria: the local history of a denomination from its inception to the union of 1932 and after', *Northern History*, **17** (1981), p. 137; and R. W. Unwin, 'Tradition and transition: market towns of the Vale of York 1660–1830', *Northern History*, **17** (1981), p. 92.
8   H. D. Abelove, 'John Wesley's influence during his lifetime on the Methodists' (unpublished PhD thesis, Yale University 1978). I am grateful to Dr Abelove for his paper on the sexual politics of early Wesleyan Methodism at the History Workshop, London 1983.
9   Shaw, pp. 29–31.
10 See Lawrence Stone, *The family, sex and marriage in England 1500–1800* (London 1977); and E. P. Thompson, *The Making of the English Working Class*, 2nd edn (London 1968).
11 For this section I am indebted to Gail Malmgreen. See also H. F. Thomas and R. S. Keller (eds.), *Women in New Worlds* (Nashville 1981).
12 Shaw, p. 64.
13 ibid., pp. 26–8.
14 C. D. Field, 'The social structure of English Methodism: eighteenth–twentieth centuries', *British Journal of Sociology*, **28** no. 2 (1977), p. 202.

15 Gilbert, p. 63, and Unwin, pp. 93–5. Gilbert estimates that 62.7 per cent of Wesleyans were artisans, and Unwin concludes that 70 per cent were craftsmen or tradesmen.
16 Scottish Methodists never accounted for more than 1 per cent of the British total. For reasons why, see A. J. Hayes and D. A. Gowland (eds.), *Scottish Methodism in the Early Victorian Period* (Edinburgh 1981); and W. R. Ward, 'Scottish Methodism in the age of Jabez Bunting', *Records of the Scottish Church History Society*, **20** (1978).
17 Burgess, pp. 133–52.
18 An extract from the Census reproduced by D. M. Thompson, *Nonconformity in the Nineteenth Century* (London 1972), p. 148. For a table of Nonconformist strength in English counties see Alan Everitt, *The Pattern of Rural Dissent: the Nineteenth Century* (Leicester 1972), p. 69.
19 K. S. Inglis, 'Patterns of religious worship in 1851', *Journal of Ecclesiastical History*, **11** (1960), pp. 74–86.
20 This point is made by D. W. Miller, 'Presbyterianism and "modernization" in Ulster', *Past and Present*, no. 80 (1978), p. 75. A full series of membership figures bearing out his point is available in *Irish Conference Minutes*. See also Raymond Gillespie, *Wild as Colts Untamed* (Lurgan 1977).
21 Everitt, in which the statistical appendix is particularly illuminating.
22 For the importance of market towns in Methodist growth see Unwin, p. 88.
23 Robert Currie, 'A micro-theory of Methodist growth', *Proceedings of the Wesley Historical Society*, **36** (1967), pp. 65–73; and Gilbert, pp. 94–115.
24 B. J. Biggs, 'Methodism in a rural society: North Nottinghamshire, 1740–1815' (unpublished PhD thesis, University of Nottingham 1975), pp. 204–20.
25 E. R. Taylor, *Methodism and Politics 1791–1851*, first published in 1935, 2nd edn (New York 1975).
26 ibid., p. 88, where the pace of change is quite unrealistic.
27 ibid., p. 13.
28 ibid., pp. 134–7.
29 Many of these can be found in the extremely useful bibliography of Methodist historical literature compiled annually for the *Proceedings of the Wesley Historical Society* by Clive Field.

2 The Wesleyan heritage

Now nothing is more unworldly than enthusiasm in every form: in Art, in Science, in Politics, in Trade, it is an inveterate Antagonist of selfishness: nor is there any character for whom the worldly (or selfish) man feels so much contemptuous pity, as for an enthusiast, until some undeniably great result forces him to confess that enthusiasm is a powerful reality.[1]

Enthusiasm became such a powerful reality in eighteenth- and nineteenth-century England, that the comparative decline of spiritual excitement in the twentieth century (at least in advanced Western countries) has forced many theologians into an historical pilgrimage to discover the secret elixir of earlier Protestant success. This pilgrimage has inevitably centred on Wesley, whose 'radical Protestantism' is now seen as an important model for contemporary church renewal movements.[2] In fact Wesley's emphasis on a functional approach to church order, lay participation, the importance of Spirit and Word as against traditions and creeds, and his concern for stern discipline have been eagerly seized upon by a new generation of anti-institutional pietists. Moreover, twentieth-century experience has confirmed an old ecclesiastical history paradox – the more popular the movement, the more authoritarian is its discipline. But perhaps this is not so much a paradox as the predictable consequence of weakening old control mechanisms while at the same time laying greater emphasis on the experiences of quite humble people. This unstable compound can be rendered safe only by the imposition of a new authority, which because it rejects prescriptions must be based on personality. Hence, any attempt to come to terms with Methodism, either theologically or socially, must first grapple with the influence of Wesley himself.

In dealing with the evolution of Methodist political attitudes therefore, it is difficult to know what approach can be taken other than concentrating on Wesley and on the social characteristics of the pre-political Methodist community. Because, while Professor Bradley has rightly challenged the Whiggish historiographical tradition which deals with eighteenth-century Dissenting politics in terms of what a selection of leaders thought, it is impossible to apply his conclusions to Methodism.[3] They are that the so called libertarian ideals of Dissenting politics (parliamentary reform and repeal of the Test and Corporation Acts) have been grossly exaggerated. By contrast he sees the political importance of eighteenth-century Dissent in its links with Whig patronage networks, its concentration on local corporation politics (often for economic reasons), and its apparent lack of protest about Anglican privileges. But Methodism, because of its low social milieu and its formal position within the Established Church, was insulated from these concerns.[4] It is not until the social changes wrought by urbanization and industrialization were in full swing that one can talk about Methodist politics in a more collective sense.[5] It would, however, be wrong to infer from this, as some historians of Methodist politics have to their cost, that the period 1740–80 was unimportant. Religious organizations, like plants, can have their distinctive characteristics strongly developed before they become visible to the outside world.

The purpose of this chapter then is to place Methodism in a wider eighteenth-century social setting, to explore its unique role in English religious life, and to assess Wesley's response to the major sociopolitical issues of his time. Many of Methodism's nineteenth-century political characteristics are here in embryo, especially its anti-radicalism, anti-Catholicism, humanitarianism, and its ambivalent relationship with the Church of England. Above all it shows that one of the principal results of the Evangelical Revival – a heightened sectarianism – had its origins deep within the eighteenth century. It is to this period that we must now turn.

With the projected publication of a new thirty-four volume collection of *The Works of John Wesley*, an historical journal specifically devoted to Methodism, and recent works of first-class scholarship on popular religion, the importance of Methodism in modern British history has been secured; even if some of this work has been occasioned by an expansionist denomination becoming sensitive to its own decline. Though the importance of Methodism has been established, its role is still the subject of much debate. Whereas historians in the 1960s and 1970s still seemed dazzled by Halévy's thesis and Thompson's polemical brilliance,[6] the focus has now shifted from Methodism and revolution to Methodism and the Enlightenment; for, as one historian states, 'if the eighteenth century was an age of reason, it was even more an age of enthusiasm, with its German pietists and Moravians, its camisards and convulsionaries, with the Methodist and Evangelical revivals in England and the Great Awakening in America'.[7] Methodism, as the major religious catalyst of eighteenth-century England is now at the centre of ingenious attempts to reconcile enthusiasm and enlightenment, or at least to explain their essential differences.

Bernard Semmel argues that whereas Wesley had no affinity with the ideas of the leading *philosophes* there are, nevertheless, important links between Wesleyan Arminianism and Enlightenment liberalism.[8] Thus, Wesley is a man of the Enlightenment in his concern for religious toleration, his hatred of persecution and violence, his desire that all men should be saved (not just the Calvinist elect), his strenuous advocacy of slavery abolition, and his doctrines of perfection and assurance which could be seen as the theological equivalents of enlightenment optimism. Moreover, in rejecting the twin elements of religious and political instability in seventeenth-century England, Calvinistic antinomianism and Catholic absolutism, Wesley was firmly in the tradition of John Locke, the apostle of English liberalism. Even conversion and an austere lifestyle can be given an enlightened gloss by using the more liberal concepts of freedom of choice and self-improvement through personal discipline. Semmel can, therefore, conclude with Halévy that Methodism was an essential element in England's transition from a 'traditional' society characterized by collective behaviour under authority to a 'modern' democracy based on individual freedom. This was England's distinctively democratic and peaceful revolution. Illiberal elements in Methodist ecclesiology and in Wesley's political views can be explained by his High Church Arminian fear of Puritan revolutionaries. For Wesley this fear was renewed by the participation of American Calvinists in the War of Independence, which appeared to be yet another manifestation of the anarchic antinomianism of Calvinism – the unrestrained elect at play.

Semmel's conclusion that Methodist conversion and self-help, even if frequently clothed in primitive and irrational garb, promised more for the poor than revolutionary violence has received some support. R. W. Malcolmson reluctantly concedes that the early Methodist preachers brought to the unruly Kingswood colliers 'not only a compelling personal dynamism, but also a message of concern and compassion and personal salvation to people who had stood alone'.[9]

Semmel's picture of Methodism as a popular religious vehicle for Enlightenment liberalism is at once stimulating and problematic. Concepts of 'attitudinal modernization' on the one hand, and of the difference between 'traditional' and 'modern' societies on the other, depend, in the last analysis, on one's personal views of Western cultural development. Enlightenment is such a slippery term, especially when used beyond the ideology of articulate élites, that one is well warned not to 'carve up the century with the knife of moral prejudices or anachronistic categories, or be deafened by illuminati rhetoric'.[10]

Professor Ward's recent work on Continental Protestantism is more securely earthed.[11] He states that the roots of eighteenth-century pan-revivalism can be traced to the displaced and persecuted Protestant minorities of Habsburg-dominated Central Europe, in Silesia, Moravia and Bohemia. This revival was partly a reaction against the confessional absolutism of much of early eighteenth-century Europe, and was also an attempt to express religious interest outside the stranglehold of politically manipulated established churches. The social background of these displaced minorities was low and their idea of religion fitted well into the dominant motif of the German Enlightenment, that is religion 'as the means and way to a better life'. Revivalistic religion and pietism (according to Ward they are substantially the same thing, the former was simply more urgent than the latter) survived on a diet of Bible study, Reformation classics and a cell structure pastored by itinerant ministers. Even camp meetings originated in religious provision for the large Swedish army in Silesia. This Continental Protestantism influenced English religious development through its meeting with the Wesley brothers in Georgia. When John Wesley emerged from the religious crisis provoked by his encounter with the Salzburgers and Moravians, he became one of the most eclectic churchmen in history. Weary of the entrenched theological and ecclesiological divisions of the past, Wesley was distinctive in his theology (evangelical Arminianism), his flexibility (willingness to use laymen), his optimism (Methodists unlike the Reformed churches refused to give way to apocalyptic speculations), his tolerance (men and women of all denominations were accepted for class membership), and his commitment to self-help through discipline and the sharing of resources. Moreover, like other European Protestants, he was reacting against the pastoral inefficiency and political chicanery of a mediocre establishment. Professor Ward asserts that most of what Wesley achieved was forfeited by the nineteenth-century Wesleyan leadership, because of its increasing rigidity, sectarianism and ministerial professionalism.

There is a deliberate paradox in Ward's argument which is worthy of comment. Although stating that eighteenth-century revivalism can only be understood in the widest possible geographical area 'between the Russian and American frontiers of the European world', he also demonstrates the need for particularity in tracing the social and political characteristics of popular religion.

The political and social ambiguities which are usually discussed on an absurdly narrow basis in relation to Halévy and Methodism were there from the beginning. The religion which was a tool of state policy at Halle was that of a country opposition to a baroque court in Wurttemberg much as the earliest Methodism seems to have been related to the opposition to Walpole. The same Lusatian Pietist gentry who incited the Czechs to rise against serfdom proposed to enserf them as soon as they got over the border. Germans and Czechs from adjacent Bohemian villages went opposite ways; the one into universal evangelism and a forswearing of politics, the other into the defence of a national tradition by a mixture of intense trade unionism and political intrigue.[12]

This gives the lie to the kind of ecclesiastical scholarship that assumes there is an unrefracted ray travelling from the theology to the politics of a religious movement regardless of the social, regional and temporal context.

While the writings of Semmel and Ward have been the most stimulating attempts to enlighten eighteenth-century enthusiasm, many others have concentrated on the progressive and rational elements in Wesley's theology. Frederick Dreyer, for example, has drawn attention to the relationship between Wesley's insistence on the perceptibility of the fruits of faith and Lockean empiricism. Wesley, unlike the mystics and speculative thinkers, was a man who brought hard evidence to bear on matters of faith and conduct, even if the evidence of witnesses pointed to improbable supernatural occurrences. Dreyer concludes that Wesley's empiricism and epistemology owed more to the intellectual climate of the eighteenth century than to Reformation ideas. Moving from philosophy to theology, A. C. Outler, editor of the Wesley volume in the Library of Protestant Thought, turns his grudging admission that Wesley was hardly a theologian's theologian into an unexpected triumph by describing his subject as a great folk theologian. Unlike the arid systematizers of the reformed tradition Wesley wrote his theology to help plain men cope with practical problems of Christian living. Thus, if his theology was not as intellectually polished as that of some Puritans, it at least had the virtue of arising from, and speaking to, ordinary people. Such theological pragmatism enabled Wesley to transcend the stark doctrinal confrontations that bedevilled European post-Reformation theology and society.

In their stead he proceeded to develop a theological fusion of faith and good works, Scripture and tradition, revelation and reason, God's sovereignty and human freedom, universal redemption and conditional election, Christian liberty and an ordered polity, the assurance of pardon and the risks of falling from Grace, original sin and Christian perfection.[13]

Outler christens him an 'evangelical catholic', a theological eclectic who picked his way through the minefield of doctrinal polarization and arrived at a popular and dynamic synthesis. Outler's own fusion of editorial enthusiasm and valuable insight has done much to redeem Wesley's reputation from the damage inflicted on it by unsympathetic theologians, but there is now an equal and opposite danger of creating a Wesley whose ecumenical and theological importance outstrips his historical credibility. One is tempted to conclude with John Kent that 'to concentrate on Wesley as the theologian of the ecumenical future will tell us very little that is useful about the past'.[14]

Finally to Gordon Rupp who makes an earnest attempt to place Wesley's theology in its historical setting.[15] While unwilling to overstate Wesley's rationalism and his theological scholarship, Professor Rupp draws attention to Wesley's writings against militant zeal, intolerance, the charismatic excesses of revivalism, and faulty logic in all matters of faith and conduct. But he admits that Wesley was prone to quirky interpretations of history and that he delighted in the extravagant religious experiences of others, even if he was more cautious with himself. Above all, he is impressed by the sense of balance in Wesley's theology and his inculcation of decency and compassion into his followers in the cruel environment of semi-industrial England.

Though divergent in detail and emphasis, these historians are united in their view of Methodism as a 'progressive' force in popular religion, if only because it rejected the seventeenth-century extremes of predestinarian fanaticism and the Catholic confessional state. This view is not accepted by two rather different historiographical traditions: the one concerned with the Church of England and its theological development, and the other with the application of marxist

presuppositions and/or sociological techniques to the study of popular religious behaviour. Norman Sykes in his magisterial book
Church and State in England in the eighteenth century admits that
Methodism and the Evangelical Revival 'supplied the new leaven to
quicken and revivify the religion of the nation', but that they also had a
retrograde intellectual influence.

Owing its origin and strength largely to a reaction against the rationalistic and
Socinian tendencies which had developed from the Latitudinarian movement
in theology, it went to extremes in depreciation of the intellectual study and
criticism of the Bible. Even John Wesley, despite his academic training and
scholarly attitude, was almost superstitious in his notions of the special interventions of Providence. . . .[16]

Sykes saw little of value in the theological and literary production of
evangelicals by comparison with the evidential and philosophical
writers of the Hanoverian period. Indeed, it would be difficult to
demonstrate Wesley's long-term influence on Anglican theology,
although Methodist competition did improve Anglican pastoral
efficiency.

   The most impressive attack on the idea that Methodism was a 'progressive' religious movement comes from E. P. Thompson. The
framework for his interpretation of eighteenth-century Methodism
can be seen clearly in his review article of Keith Thomas's book
Religion and the Decline of Magic. Thompson disagrees with two of
the author's supposed assumptions. Why should the 'sophisticated
magic of theology' be regarded as more reputable than 'the symbolic
magic of the poor'? Why should the irrational and superstitious elements in popular culture be written out of English history from the
mid seventeenth century onwards? Instead, Thompson states that,
despite the theological pretensions of churches, the role of religion in
popular culture was entirely negative, because it did not help men
cope with practical problems, but merely reinforced the social and
political dominance of a paternalistic establishment. He argues here,
and elsewhere, that in eighteenth-century England there was an
increasing dissociation between patrician and plebeian cultures
which was solidified by the theatrical materialism of the rich and the
erastianism of the Church. Methodism was, therefore, a 'psy-
chologically compelling' attempt to bridge this cultural gap.

Moreover, this might help us to understand the true character of Wesleyanism
as explicitly a movement of counter-enlightenment. In returning to his pas-

toral duties to the poor, Wesley perforce must leap a gap of sensibility between two cultures, even though leaping that gap meant reaffirming scores of
superstitions which Thomas confidently describes as being in 'decline'.
Among these were bibliomancy, old wives' medical remedies, the casting of
lots, the belief in diabolical possession and in exorcism by prayer, in the hand
of providence, in the punishment (by lightning-stroke or epilepsy or cholera)
of ill-livers and reprobates. Dr J. G. Rule, in an unpublished study of the
Cornish tinners (University of Warwick Ph.D., 1970) has shown exactly this
process at work: Wesleyan superstition matched the indigenous superstitions
of tinners and fishermen who, for occupational reasons which are examined,
were dependent upon chance and luck in their daily lives. The match was so
perfect that it consolidated one of the strongest of Methodist congregations.[17]

Rule's work is indeed significant in showing how 'Methodism did not
so much replace folk-beliefs as translate them into a religious idiom'.
Thus, Cornish Methodists declared holy war on drink, hurling,
wrestling, bull-baiting, cock-fighting, and folk superstitions, but
replaced them with revivals, Love Feasts, watch-nights, hymn singing,
providential interventions and colourful local versions of the cosmic
drama between god and the devil. Furthermore, Rule concludes that
this cultural transmutation was not necessarily a product of social
control from above, but was to some extent a genuine expression of
alternative working-class values. One of the most useful aspects of
Rule's work on Methodism and popular culture is his concern to treat
the subject within a proper regional and chronological setting, and to
avoid imposing inflexible models on the relationship between religion
and social change.

The opposition of Thompson and Rule to the idea of a unilinear
decline of 'irrationality' in popular culture has been vindicated by
James Obelkevich's book *Religion and Rural Society: South Lindsey
1825–75*. Obelkevich's vivid re-creation of Lincolnshire rural culture
is almost the film of Thomas's book: religious holidays and rites are
given quasi-magical interpretations; God, the devil, ministers and
nature are the local spiritual agents; and there is the familiar kaleidoscope of witches, wise men, oracles, divinations, dreams, folk
medicine, portents of death and luck. Even within popular religion the
author concludes that 'paganism was dominant and Christianity
recessive'.[18] While Obelkevich has confirmed Thompson's scepticism about the decline of a superstitious popular culture, he does not
interpret Methodism in the same way (though the difference of a century
makes comparisons problematic). Rather than matching Methodist

irrationality with cultural irrationality, Obelkevich states that Methodism 'consistently promoted "modern" attitudes towards life and work' by de-parochializing villagers (unlike the Church of England), stimulating a sober sociability, developing talents of self-expression and organization, and acknowledging the individual worth of each person both in theology and in practice.[19] He does concede, however, that Methodist economic networks reversed the modern trend to differentiate the economic from other areas of life, and that the community aspect of Methodism delayed the advent of class conflict.[20] Obelkevich concludes that Methodism had its maximum appeal in the period of transition from community to class, and from a period of traditional folk recreations to one of mass leisure. In that respect Methodism, far from accommodating traditional popular culture, helped to channel it in a more modern direction.

The relationship between Methodism and popular culture is clearly more complicated than some would allow. Consider, for example, the whole area of folk healing, popular medicine and supernatural cures. Wesley believed in miraculous healing, even if it occurred at a Roman Catholic shrine, although it facilitated his anti-Catholic prejudice if the Catholic shrine in question was a Jansenist one.[21]

In January 1750 Wesley made this entry in his *Journal*.

I read, to my no small amazement, the account given by Monsieur Montgeron, both of his own conversion and of the other miracles wrought at the tomb of Abbé Pâris. I had always looked upon the whole affair as a mere legend, as I suppose most Protestants do, but I see no possible way to deny these facts without invalidating all human testimony. I may full as reasonably deny that there is such a person as Mr Montgeron or such a city as Paris in the world. . . . If it be said, 'But will not the admitting of these miracles establish Popery?' Just the reverse. Abbé Pâris lived and died in open opposition to the grossest errors of Popery, and in particular, to that diabolical bull *Unigenitus*, which destroys the very foundations of Christianity.[22]

Wesley also believed that psychological and physical illnesses could sometimes be attributed to sin and the need for spiritual repentance. Therefore, healing, based on group prayer and intercession, could have all the elements of a community-based morality play.[23] But Wesley, sensitive as usual to popular needs and to his own empirical observations, introduced basic medical visitation schemes and published a collection of old wives' medical remedies under the engaging title of *Primitive Physic*. Eighteenth-century medical and ecclesiastical élites thought all this was bunkum, but there are good grounds for arguing that popular pragmatism was at least as effective as the sophisticated theories of a rudimentary medical establishment. Rationally based scientific medicine has not even won its final victory in our own time, and only in so far as it can actually deliver the goods. Wesley in his electric shock experiments, primitive visitation schemes, small-scale dispensaries and folk remedies combined the 'modern' notion that bodily health was of prime importance in the spiritual life with more traditional methods. This is another example of how Methodism established deep roots in popular culture but did not surrender to a purely magical framework.

The relationship of Methodism and popular culture is two-sided. On the one hand Methodism did chime in with popular culture in its conversionist theology (the age-old desire to make a fresh start), providential interventions, religious entertainment on a cosmic scale, underlying anti-Catholicism, and in its function as a religious association in the age of associations. On the other hand Methodism confronted popular culture in its opposition to drunkenness, bawdiness, rough music, wife sales, popular sports and race-meetings. On balance, Methodism provided enough to maintain a slow, steady growth until changing social and economic circumstances opened up new opportunities at the end of the eighteenth century. Nevertheless, in both the eighteenth and the nineteenth centuries, Methodist opposition to all manner of entertainments, for both rich and poor, was probably its biggest millstone in the passionate quest for more members. Sydney Smith attacked Methodism for two main reasons. Its frequent providential interventions took the fun out of Anglicanism's occasional providential interventions and

The Methodists hate pleasure and amusements; no theatre, no cards, no dancing, no punchinello, no dancing dogs, no blind fiddlers; – all the amusements of the rich and of the poor must disappear, wherever these gloomy people get a footing. It is not the abuse of pleasure which they attack, but the interspersion of pleasure, however much it is guarded by good sense and moderation.[24]

Gloom and boom were almost, but not quite, incompatible.

This attempt to get to the heart of Methodism in its social setting has obvious weaknesses, not least because the harder one looks for the essence of Methodism the more one is convinced that there is no essence, apart from inspired innovation based on biblical ideas. Moreover, its pragmatism and eclecticism brought short-term benefits at the expense of long-term consistency. The consequences had to be faced by Wesley's successors, who for various reasons, not all of their own making, were unable to reproduce his flexibility and spiritual urgency. Clearly the extension of a concept like enlightenment from an intellectual coterie to the collective mentality of a religious movement has obvious difficulties, but hopefully it has helped to expose the genuine ambiguities at the heart of Methodism. Moreover, the development of Methodism's political consciousness, as distinct from its social impact, owes much to those enlightenment preoccupations of religious toleration and the nature of good government. These will be our main themes. Wesley's faltering and sometimes inconsistent response to these two issues formed the basis of Methodist political views, even after his death. That principles worked out in the more tranquil waters of the Whig Ascendancy might not apply to the turbulent conditions of nineteenth-century England did not occur to many of Wesley's followers. Jabez Bunting, the much-maligned Pope of nineteenth-century Methodism, appreciated more than most that a Wesleyan precedent sanctified a political viewpoint.

In eighteenth-century England the intellectual formulation of religious toleration and its constitutional reality were broadly similar. Locke's *Letters on Toleration*, though neither radically liberal nor particularly original, argued persuasively for individual liberty of conscience and no state compulsion in religious affairs. Of course the civil power had the right to control religious opinions that threatened 'the peace, safety and security' of the state. Locke followed in the tradition of Milton and Marvell in excluding Roman Catholics from toleration, because of the maxim that no faith was to be kept with heretics and the recognition by Catholics of an authority overriding that of their own civil government. Besides why should toleration be extended to Catholics when 'they think themselves bound to deny it to others'? With typical philosophical licence Locke never clarified the sort of coercion which the civil power could legitimately use against Catholics and atheists. But, according to Philip Hughes, Locke gave the 'highest philosophical sanction' to 'the traditional prejudice and careless ignorance' of English anti-Catholicism.[25]

In political affairs religion was a major element in England's 'divided society' in the period 1689–1714, when the old fears of popery, arbitrary government and Puritan resurgence inflamed party divisions. At times of national emergency anti-Catholic penal legislation was enforced and occasionally extended, while Tories used their moments of ascendancy to restrict Dissenters' political and educational opportunities.[26] With a Hanoverian safely on the throne, and the Whigs in control of a comprehensive patronage system, religion played its part in restoring stability to Walpole's England. Annual Indemnity Acts for Dissenters after 1727 and lax administration of penal laws on English, if not Irish, Catholics further reduced religious temperatures. Wesley began his preaching ministry in a religious climate dominated by intellectual recognition for toleration, if ambiguous about Catholics for supposedly liberal reasons, and by political quiescence. The grand old Church of England seemed in danger from nothing but its own inertia.

Since Wesley was too busy for speculative writing, his view of religious toleration did not develop from a systematic philosophy but from a series of responses to historical circumstances. Ironically, the first was the accusation that Methodists were papists. This most persistent criticism of early Methodism had both theological and social foundations. Wesley's evangelical Arminianism was clearly distinct from the pervading Calvinism of evangelical Protestants in eighteenth-century England. In fact, only Fletcher of Madeley supported Wesley in a controversy with Calvinists that raged spasmodically until his death. Calvinists like Toplady and Whitefield argued that Wesley was virtually Catholic in the role he gave to good works in his doctrines of justification and sanctification. So vindictive were the disputes that Wesley launched his own *Arminian Magazine* in 1778 to counter the theological propaganda of the Calvinistic *Gospel Magazine*. The strand of mysticism in Wesley's religion, particularly strong before 1738 and again after 1765, also brought forth accusations of popery. Wesley's doctrine of sanctification clearly had its origins in the writings of Catholic mystics like Thomas à Kempis, François de Sales, Monsieur de Renty and Fénelon. Even more than the contemplative mysticism of Law, Wesley admired the Catholic mystics for their 'religion of the heart', their ideal of perfection and their emphasis on holy charity.[27] G. C. Cell suggests that Wesley developed a 'synthesis of the Protestant ethic of grace and the Catholic ethic of holiness'.[28] This had too little grace for Calvinists and too much holiness for latitudinarian Anglicans.

It was as enthusiasts that Methodists and Roman Catholics were most often bracketed together. George Lavington, Bishop of Exeter from 1747 to 1762 and author of the infamous *Enthusiasm of Methodists and Papists Compared*, stated that the 'whole conduct of the Methodists is but a counterpart of the most wild fanaticism of Popery'.[29] Moved by personal resentment, Lavington argued that

Methodists imitated the worst excesses of medieval Catholicism in their special providences, revelations, apparitions, visions, ecstasies, healings and exorcisms. The Anglican establishment rejoiced in the content and objective of Lavington's attack on the Methodists, even if it was sceptical of the Bishop's literary skill. With Anglican minds still scarred by memories of seventeenth-century sectarianism, the charge of antinomianism was added to that of enthusiasm. This was the substance of Edmund Gibson's *Observations upon the Conduct and Behaviour of a Certain Sect, usually distinguished by the name of Methodists*, published anonymously in 1744.[30] He asked 'whether notions in religion may not be heighten'd to such extremes, as to lead *some* into a disregard and disesteem of the *common* duties and offices of life'? Only a new movement could be attacked by one side (Calvinists) for being Catholic in its emphasis on good works and by another (Anglican Bishops) for being antinomian in its view of religious experience.

Theological attempts to damn Methodism with Catholic abuse focused on Wesley's Arminianism, mysticism, enthusiasm and doctrine of sanctification. But there were powerful social and political reasons for giving a Catholic label to a revived popular Protestantism. John Walsh describes how Methodists were attacked by the gentry, who suspected them of levelling notions, by clergymen, who detected danger to the Church, by Dissenters, who feared new competition, by alehouse keepers and actors, who were incensed by Methodist charges of ungodliness, and by general ruffians who sensed easy prey.[31] Further, Methodists were attacked by Catholic mobs in Ireland for being ultra-Protestant and by Protestant mobs in England for being papists. Methodism was unfortunate in making 'its first, well-publicised appearance in many areas during the Jacobite scare of the 1740s', and there were all sorts of fanciful rumours linking Methodists with Jacobites. 'In 1741 the rumour was going round London that Wesley kept two popish priests in his home, and was being paid by Spain (which country had been at war with England for two years) to raise an army of 20,000 in support of an intended Spanish invasion.'[32] In February 1744 the threat of a Jacobite invasion and open war with France heightened anti-Jacobite feeling in England. Wesley recorded in his *Journal* that 'Mon. 27 was the day I had appointed to go out of town; but understanding a proclamation was just published, requiring all Papists to go out of London before the Friday following, I was determined to stay another week, that I might cut off all occasion of reproach'.[33] On 2 March Wesley had to confront a JP, parish officers and an unfriendly mob in Spitalfields, and three weeks later Surrey JPs asked him to take oaths of loyalty to the king and to sign the declaration against popery. Tales of persecution up and down the country forced Wesley to draft a letter to George II assuring him of Methodist prayers, money and loyalty.[34] The letter also contained anti-Catholic comments which were expanded a year later in Wesley's *Word to a Protestant*. The eighth edition of this pamphlet contained three bitterly anti-Catholic hymns, probably written by Charles Wesley.[35] Anti-Jacobite scaremongering, based on the expression of popular loyalty and no popery, provoked the same sentiments in its Methodist victims. Although the failure of the '45 rebellion did not result in a withdrawal of such allegations against Methodists, the charge of Jacobitism became less important as Jacobitism itself declined. The stigma of disloyalty was lost, but at a price.

If Methodism was suspected of popery in its theology and politics, John Bossy's study of the English Catholic community in the eighteenth century invites broader comparisons. Consider, for example, his description of the priest's role in the community.

We can now be fairly sure that most priests in the early decades of the mission were peripatetic; the wholly travelling priest did not disappear until about 1700, and the partially travelling or 'riding' missioner succeeded him. The secular clergy tended to find this condition irregular, as it was natural they should; but a degree of mobility was as appropriate to the missionary state, as a certain blurring of the distinction between clergy and laity, and between one sort of priest and another.[36]

With a slight change of clerical terminology this statement could equally apply to the Methodist itinerancy. The fact that both communities used itinerant rather than parish- or congregation-based clergy possibly accounts for the lack of discernment in popular hostility.[37] Without stretching Professor Bossy's analysis too far, other similarities are apparent. The separatist tendencies of Catholic rites of passage and religious ceremonies have obvious parallels in Methodist Love Feasts, society tickets and class meetings. Moreover, increasing clerical self-consciousness, internal property squabbles and an expansionist ideology characterized both groups.[38] These conclusions are fairly predictable if one accepts two premises: that the primary division in post-Reformation English religion is between the Established Church and all others; and that Methodism and Catholicism expanded at roughly the same time for roughly the same reasons. That is, both adjusted successfully to the new economic and social structures of an industrializing Britain.[39] Therefore, despite their different theologies and traditions, they were both expanding movements within religious Dissent with sufficient national organization and financial resources to challenge a becalmed Church of England.

Although Wesley's theological admiration for some Catholic writers, his sincere belief in religious toleration and the fact that Methodists and Catholics were fellow sufferers might have led to harmonious relations between them, this was not to be the case. There were three reasons for this: the polarizing impact of theological controversy, Wesley's experiences in Ireland, and the particular events of the years 1778–80 – from Savile's Relief Act to the Gordon Riots. It is evident that controversy, especially in theological matters, drives disputants into more rigid positions than would otherwise be the case. Methodists in the eighteenth century, and to a greater extent in the nineteenth, engaged in theological and political polemic with Roman Catholic authors. Richard Challoner, once Professor of Divinity at Douai and Vicar-Apostolic of the London district from 1758, was the most eminent eighteenth-century Catholic to confront the Methodists. In 1760 he wrote *A Caveat against the Methodists*, which was designed to show that 'Methodists are not the people of God, nor is their new raised Society the true Church of Christ or any part of it'. He stated that Methodist teachers could not be true ministers of Christ because they did not 'come down from the Apostles of Christ'. Consequently Methodist doctrine must also be in error since there was no proper authority to validate it. In fact, Challoner's anti-Methodism, like his anti-Deism, was an appeal to religious conservatism over anarchistic novelty. Both were departures from the true faith.[40] Wesley replied to this attack in a letter to the *London Chronicle* by pointing out that, although Challoner singled out the Methodists, the same argument could apply to all Protestant denominations. Wesley rebutted the charges by publicly renouncing, for the first time, the idea of an uninterrupted Apostolical Succession.

I deny that Romish bishops came down by uninterrupted succession from the Apostles. I never could see it proved; and I am persuaded I never shall. But unless this is proved, your own pastors on your own principles are no pastors at all.[41]

Wesley devoted much time to other writings showing the superiority of Protestantism over Catholicism and carefully delineating opposing doctrines.[42] Although there are traces of a more tolerant approach in Wesley's personal letters,[43] this type of close definition in public sets up obstacles that are difficult to overcome.

Wesley's attitude to Roman Catholicism was also strongly influenced by his twenty-one visits to Ireland, that great 'mission field' which so fascinated eighteenth- and nineteenth-century evangelicals. On his first two visits Wesley equipped himself with an ultra-Protestant account of the 1641 rebellion,[44] reflected on the inadequacy of penal laws in making Ireland Protestant,[45] and was repeatedly opposed by Catholic priests who were jealous of their flocks.[46] In Ireland Wesley was rejected by both the Protestant establishment and the Catholic priesthood. In the early days, at least, the Methodist message appealed most to a motley crew of Irish Catholic poor, English soldiers and Palatine refugees. On Wesley's third visit opposition hardened into the most severe rioting that Methodism ever encountered, in England or in Ireland. A Cork mob, led by an eccentric ballad singer called Nicholas Butler and winked at by mayor, corporation and clergy, went on the rampage for ten days in May 1749. Wesley, no doubt sensing that the future of Methodism in Ireland was at stake, wrote his *Letter to a Roman Catholic* in July.[47] Not surprisingly, it has excited more attention from twentieth-century ecumenists than it did from eighteenth-century Catholics. Augustin Cardinal Bea, President of the Vatican Secretariat for Christian unity, states that

Because it expresses so simply and so effectively the main features of the ecumenical movement as recommended by Church leaders today and, as far as Roman Catholics are concerned, by the Second Vatican Council and Pope Paul VI, John Wesley's Letter to a Roman Catholic cannot but be a welcome source of inspiration and encouragement to all, both the ecumenically committed and the ecumenically diffident . . . .[48]

The aim of Wesley's letter was to remove common misunderstandings about the Methodists and also to make a plea for mutual love and toleration. The letter begins by setting the boundaries within which such toleration should exist.

3.   I do not suppose all the bitterness is on your side. I know there is too much on our side also; so much, that I fear many Protestants (so called) will be angry at me too, for writing to you in this manner; and will say, 'It is showing you too much favour; you deserve no such treatment at our hands.'

4. But I think you do. I think you deserve the tenderest regard I can show, were it only because the same God hath raised you and me from the dust of the earth, and has made us both capable of loving and enjoying him to eternity; were it only because the Son of God has bought you and me with his own blood. How much more, if you are a person fearing God, (as without question many of you are), and studying to have a conscience void of offence towards God and towards man?

Wesley then gave a brief statement of Christian belief, a lowest common denominator that both Protestant and Roman Catholic could accept. The letter reached its climax in four resolutions: 'not to hurt one another'; 'to speak nothing harsh or unkind of each other'; 'to harbour no unkind thought'; and 'to endeavour to help each other on in whatever we are agreed leads to the kingdom'. Although this letter is more favourable to Roman Catholics than anything else in the whole corpus of Wesley's works (all the more reason for placing it in a proper historical setting), one thing is crystal clear; throughout his life, even during the religious excitement of the Gordon Riots, Wesley consistently opposed religious persecution and violence.[49]

Wesley's *Letter to a Roman Catholic* was not typical of his views on Catholicism, but it is difficult to establish what was, because his *Journal* is a series of random comments occasioned by particular historical circumstances. Nevertheless, a number of assumptions about Irish Catholicism do emerge from his writings. First, Wesley believed that the Catholic Church was chronologically and geographically unchanging in its teaching and influence. Thus, Hus's execution at the Council of Constance, details of Continental Protestant persecutions, the Marian executions, the St Bartholomew's Day Massacre and the Irish rebellion of 1641 merely testified to the immutable persecuting spirit of the Church.[50] This selective history was reinforced by Wesley's journeys through one of the poorest and most isolated Catholic countries in Europe. Near Castlebar he wrote that he was 'surprised to find how little the Irish Papists are changed in a hundred years. Most of them retain the same bitterness, yea, and thirst for blood, as ever, and would as freely now cut the throats of all the Protestants, as they did in the last century'.[51]

Second, most of Wesley's hostility was directed at the priesthood and not at the native population. This was part of the traditional evangelical distinction between hatred of a theological system and hatred of its adherents. Wesley looked upon the inhabitants of Ireland as victims of a delusion perpetrated by the Roman priesthood. Ignoring the irrational elements in this attitude, one can detect two reasons for it. The Methodists could understand that an illiterate and ignorant peasantry would be strangers to the truth, but they could not understand or forgive their educated representatives continuing in error. More significantly, the control by priests of their flocks was a barrier to the Methodist missionary enterprise. In 1762 Wesley preached at Ahascragh, 'but their priests would not suffer the Papists to come. What could a magistrate do in this case? Doubtless he might tell the priest: "Sir, as you enjoy liberty of conscience, you shall allow it to others. You are not persecuted yourself; you shall not persecute them" '.[52] Primitive English liberalism was thereby invoked to sanction missionary competition in Ireland.

Third, one can notice a conviction beginning with Wesley, but held more strongly by later Methodists, that Roman Catholicism not only caused the religious and political problems of Ireland but also the economic distress of the country. In 1776 Wesley recorded the dramatic difference in living conditions between the Roman Catholic south and the more densely Protestant province of Ulster. 'No sooner did we enter Ulster than we observed the difference. The ground was cultivated just as in England, and the cottages not only neat, but with doors, chimneys and windows.'[53] When the economic condition of Ireland became a major concern in the years preceding the famine, the Methodists in England and Ireland were convinced that the propagation of the Gospel was the best solution. This was not purely wishful thinking since the English Methodists were not slow to take credit for the improvement of the living conditions of working-class Methodists during the early stages of the Industrial Revolution.

Fourth, Wesley was convinced from his selective reading of seventeenth-century Irish history that given the opportunity Catholics in Ireland would be disloyal to the British Crown. The demands of the American War resulted in a reduced military presence in Ireland and the militia was too inadequate to take up the strain. The entry of France into the war and the activities of the American privateer Paul Jones were powerful stimuli to a growing Protestant Volunteer movement. The predominantly Protestant Volunteers, though initially suspicious of Catholics, were by no means anti-Catholic, especially when the movement developed politically. Nevertheless, when Wesley saw them marching in Cork in 1778 he wrote, 'at least they keep the Papists in order, who are exceedingly alert ever since the army moved to America'.[54]

These examples of Wesley's anti-Catholic prejudice need to be balanced with the many favourable comments on Catholic congregations and individuals that are to be found in the *Journal*. For if Wesley was undeniably anti-Catholic, at least he was no bigot. His reasoning, if not his prejudice, was based on standard liberal philosophers.

Wesley's opposition to Catholicism was given a political direction by the introduction of Savile's Relief Act in 1778. The act was designed to remove the disabilities that had been imposed on Catholics by Parliament in 1700. This meant easing the persecution of Catholic priests and schoolmasters, and enabling Catholics to buy and transfer land. For these clauses to take effect, Catholics had to take a special oath abjuring the Pretender, the temporal jurisdiction and deposing power of the Pope, and the doctrine that faith should not be kept with heretics. Having earlier stated that politics were out of his province, Wesley made no public response to Savile's Act, although he did publish *Popery Calmly Considered* a year later. The real crisis came in 1780 and it is important to understand Wesley's motives for becoming publicly involved. In January 'receiving more and more accounts of the increase of Popery, I believed it my duty to write a letter concerning it, which was afterwards inserted in the public papers'.[55] Wesley had noticed the remarkable growth in Catholic numbers that predated the large-scale Irish immigration of the early nineteenth century.[56] In fact Catholic numbers in England in 1780 probably exceeded those in Wesley's own societies. It was because Catholics were 'increasing daily' that Wesley wrote to the *Public Advertiser* on 21 January.

Some time ago a pamphlet was sent me, entitled 'An Appeal from the Protestant Association, to the People of Great Britain'. A day or two since, a kind of answer to this was put into my hand, which pronounces its style contemptible, its reasoning futile, and its objects malicious. On the contrary, I think the style of it is clear, easy and natural; the reasoning, in general, strong and conclusive; the object or design, kind and benevolent. And in pursuance of the same kind and benevolent design, namely, to preserve our happy constitution, I shall endeavour to confirm the substance of this tract, by a few plain arguments.[57]

For Wesley, the crux of the debate was that the oath in Savile's Act would not give the required assurance because of the old Catholic maxim that 'no faith was to be kept with heretics'. His information was derived from the Council of Constance in 1414, when John Hus was executed in spite of a pledge of safe conduct. Wesley also affirmed that Catholic recognition of the spiritual and dispensing power of the Pope, and of the priesthood's right to absolve sins, precluded them from giving absolute allegiance to any government. If it had simply been the oath with which Wesley took issue, then his objections would have been more understandable, but he was also opposed to the actual measures of toleration themselves. There is a real contradiction between the two paragraphs in his letter.

Let there be as 'boundless a freedom in religion' as any man can conceive.

'But the late Act', you say, 'does not either tolerate or encourage Roman Catholics'. I appeal to matter of fact. Do not the Romanists themselves understand it as a toleration? You know they do. And does it not already (let alone what it may do by and by) encourage them to preach openly, to build chapels (at Bath and elsewhere) to raise seminaries, and to make numerous converts day by day to their intolerant, persecuting principles?

Wesley was prepared to concede 'freedom in religion' to anyone who knew what freedom meant. He did not accept that the Roman Church, with its 'intolerant, persecuting principles', deserved freedom because it was not prepared to grant it. Wesley might well have emerged unscathed from this brief foray into religious politics but for three circumstances. The first was the absolute delight with which the Protestant Association heralded its recently acquired and well-known supporter.[58] The second was the outbreak of the most serious rioting in eighteenth-century England at the instigation of Lord George Gordon and the Protestant Association. The third was a lengthy controversy between Wesley and an Irish Capuchin named Father O'Leary in the Dublin press. This debate has had an extraordinary historiographical legacy.

The dark deeds of the London mob in June 1780 have been portrayed in a new light by George Rudé and John Stevenson.[59] Rudé has shown that the rioters were not socially destitute, and that they attacked wealthy Catholics and symbols of authority rather than the wretched Irish of St Giles in the Field, Whitechapel and Holborn. No doubt the traditional xenophobia and irrationality of popular anti-Catholicism played their part, but there was also 'the ritual humiliation of the wealthy and a certain degree of "levelling" rhetoric'. Above all, the forces of order both winked at, and retreated from, the forces of disorder. The importance of Methodism in inflaming popular Protestantism, though vigorously maintained by Catholic controversialists ever since, is difficult to estimate. E. C. Black states that 'the undoubted

misdirected religious zeal of the Methodists' was a contributory factor
to the riots. This conclusion is based on episodic comments by
Samuel Romilly and Horace Walpole, and a contemporary pamphlet
by David Williams, which asserts that Scottish Presbyterians and
English Methodists were Gordon's principal supporters.[60] The most
substantial modern accounts of the riots by J. Paul de Castro[61] and
Rudé do not single out the Methodists. It is likely that Wesley's support for the Protestant Association's objectives (but not methods)
encouraged some Methodists to participate in Gordon's theatrical
march on Parliament, but the drunkenness, violence, theft and destruction that followed would not have made good confessions in
Methodist class meetings. The Wesley brothers, who were out of
London in June 1780, later repudiated the violence of the Gordon
Riots in the Methodist vernacular of sermons and hymns.

I preached at new chapel, on Luke ix 55, 'ye know not what manner of spirit
ye are of'; and showed, that supposing the Papists to be heretics, schismatics,
wicked men, enemies to us and to our church and nation; yet we ought not to
persecute, to kill, hurt or grieve them, but barely to prevent their doing
hurt.[62]

> As in religion's cause they join,
> And blasphemously call it thine,
> The cause of persecuting Zeal,
> Of treason, anarchy and hell,
>
> 'Havoc', the infernal leader cries!
> 'Havoc', the associate host replies!
> The rabble shouts – the torrent pours –
> The city sinks – the flame devours!
>
> Our arm of flesh entirely fails,
> The many-headed beast prevails;
> Conspiracy the State o'erturns,
> Gallia exults – and London burns![63]

The Methodist contribution to the Gordon Riots passed into history through the filter of Wesley's dispute with Father O'Leary. This
dispute not only shows the importance of Ireland in the growing hostility between Methodists and Catholics, but also demonstrates the
difficulty of Wesley's distinction between religious and political matters. The controversy is not without intrinsic interest, if only for the
contrasting polemical style of an Oxford logician and an Irish lyricist.
Wesley, following Locke, monotonously maintained that Catholics

could not give security of conduct because of their doctrines, and tried to prove it by focusing on the fifteenth-century Council of Constance. O'Leary denied his interpretation of that Council, but even if it was true surely 'it is vain to ransack old councils, imperial constitutions and ecclesiastical canons, whether genuine or spurious, against heretics, in order to brand the present generation of Catholics'.[64] Wesley wanted hard evidence that an unchanging Roman Catholicism had changed. In reply O'Leary could only offer wit, common sense, and the observation that Roman Catholic civil liberties ought not to be restricted 'because Mr Wesley puts on his spectacles to read old Latin'.

More important than the debate about what was written in 1780 was the dispute about what was not written. For, by cleverly manipulating his title pages, O'Leary made it appear that Wesley not only wrote the letters to the *Public Advertiser* and the *Freeman's Journal*, but was also responsible for the *Defence of the Protestant Association*.[65] By extension, O'Leary alleged that Wesley was the publicist for the Association in the build-up to the Gordon Riots. Wesley denied writing on behalf of the Protestant Association and rhetorically inquired whether O'Leary's title page was the result of negligence or design. O'Leary's more accurate but scarcely less machiavellian alteration in the title page for the second edition of his works answered Wesley's question, but the damage had already been done.

Remarkably, Catholic scholars up to the First World War accepted O'Leary's allegation that Wesley was the scribe for the Protestant Association. O'Leary's biographer, T. R. England, accused Wesley of writing the *Defence* and of trying to exterminate popery 'by physical force'.[66] More public and more serious accusations were made by Daniel O'Connell in two letters opposing Wesleyan educational policy in 1839. O'Connell was piqued by Methodist opposition to the Whig proposals of that year and stated that Wesley was 'the great instigator of the Protestant Association' and that 'the first page of your political history is stained with the plunderings, the burnings, the destruction of property, the bloodshed, and the fearful insurrection of June, 1780'.[67] O'Connell's attack caused George Cubitt, a Wesleyan preacher, to scurry off to the British Museum to prepare a defence. Cubitt kept in regular contact with Jabez Bunting and finally published a pamphlet entitled *Strictures on Mr O'Connell's Letters to the Wesleyan Methodists*.[68] Cubitt soon discovered O'Leary's sleight of hand, but more important was the impact of the controversy on relations between Methodist and Catholics in the early Victorian period. Cubitt wrote that the 'result of the whole inquiry is a deepened, strengthened conviction, that, for the perpetuation of liberty in this country . . . it is absolutely necessary that a political power should be possessed by Protestantism which ought not be conceded to Romanism'.[69] The polarizing effect of the Gordon Riots therefore did not end with Lord George Gordon's committal to the Tower of London. As late as 1883 Alexius Mills, in a Catholic history of the Gordon Riots, gave the most florid picture of all.

The pulpit, no less than the platform had resounded with every kind of menace, and, at the moment of which we are speaking, the one hundred thousand members of the Association represented a power ready disciplined for evil, and taught, by the founder of Methodism, to consider the chastisement of the Papists a work decreed by heaven.[70]

Even more remarkable than this tradition of nineteenth-century Catholic scholarship has been the way twentieth-century ecumenical writers have transformed Wesley from an 'enthusiast' and a 'firebrand'[71] into a significant precursor of the ecumenical movement.[72] It seems that the quest for the historical Wesley must continue!

Wesley's attitude to religious toleration fits quite well into Semmel's chancy ideological interpretation of Methodism as a bridge between a 'traditional' society and a more 'modern' one. Wesley shared the anti-Catholic prejudice of his day, but much of his opposition to Catholicism stemmed from his quasi-liberal impulses. In the economic deprivation of Ireland and in the close ties between Irish Catholics and their priests, Wesley thought he saw a church that did not promote individual self-improvement and freedom of choice. Since his view of the world was fundamentally religious, it did not occur to him to look for answers to these problems in English commercial policy and in the social function of the priest in a peasant society. His early olive branch was understandably not reciprocated, and by the 1770s competition between two expanding and opposed religious movements was likely to result in conflict. The fact that Methodism was gaining a foothold in Ireland while an already growing English Catholicism was about to receive its Irish immigrants merely expanded the theatre of conflict. If toleration really is the child of indifference, then the outlook was bleak. The irony is that Wesley, who pioneered the formation of a non-sectarian religious association, should have been instrumental in heightening sectarian rivalries at the end of the eighteenth century. Indeed, Wesley's anti-Catholicism was one of his profound and enduring legacies to the Wesleyan connexion, and the connexion's vigorous anti-Catholicism – in which it genuinely reflected its following – was a most important determinant of Wesleyan political attitudes during the nineteenth century.

Apart from the political dimension of religious conflict, Wesley's other contributions to public affairs came in the decade 1768–78 in response to increasing radicalism at home and troubles in America. To these overtly political concerns Wesley brought a series of religious assumptions. He accepted that politics were out of his province and stated that Christian ministers should comment on political matters only to counter malicious rumours against king and government.[73] Wesley wrote like this not just to support establishmentarian ideals, but also because he recognized his own ignorance of high politics. In his *Free Thoughts on the Present State of Public Affairs* (1768), Wesley rejected the notion of the politically sophisticated freeborn Englishman. He agreed that 'every cobbler, tinker, porter and hackney-coachman' had political opinions, but 'while they are sure of everything, I am in a manner sure of nothing', with the exception of his own empirical observations on the state of the country. Empiricism bred scepticism about popular politics when Wesley came up against petitioning. 'I was not long since at a town in Kent, when one of these petitions was carrying about. I asked one another, "Have you signed the petition?" and found none that had refused it. And yet not one single person to whom I spoke had either read it or heard it read.'[74] Wesley's distrust of popular participation in politics was based primarily on a deep-seated fear of civil war and disorder on a mid seventeenth-century scale. Indeed, it is remarkable how often Wesley analysed contemporary politics within the framework of the 1640s. Above all, Wesley thought of politics as an extension of his religious faith: God establishes governments;[75] the political discontent of the 1760s was based on such moral failings as covetousness, ambition, pride and resentment;[76] the popular clamour for liberty was inspired by Satan;[77] and God put a curse on the nation because of the moral blight of slavery.[78] However, Wesley was no mere providentialist, since he always took account of human agency in his explanation of events.

It has been noted that Wesley's early public ministry coincided with a period of political stability characterized by single-party government, a comprehensive patronage network, a shrinking electorate, and harmonious relations between king and Parliament over the choice of ministers.[79] Indeed, it could be argued that a man of

Wesley's conservative views could only have embarked on a comparatively radical religious movement against the background of a wider political stability. In contrast, the 1760s was one of the most volatile decades of the century due to a combination of ministerial instability and popular discontent. John Brewer has shown that there were many aspects to this growing instability. Partly because Tories were no longer a threat, George III was unwilling to conduct politics under the rules devised by court Whigs in the previous two reigns. A new king, new issues and a new configuration of politics forced changes in party alignments and in party ideology. As a result 'under George II oppositions were anti-party, and administrations favoured party divisions', whereas 'under George III this position was very largely reversed'.[80] Moreover, popular political culture (to be found in alehouses, clubs, the press, etc.), which had been easily contained by the old Whig hegemony, now developed a sharper focus over issues like Wilkes, America and parliamentary reform. An expanding press, periods of economic recession after 1763, and the exploitation of public opinion by opposition politicians added further elements to an unstable chemical mixture. Although they varied widely in their interpretation of what was happening, as historians have done since, contemporaries were agreed that English politics had entered a more unstable period. Governments blamed factious oppositions while oppositions condemned administrative tyranny, but all could see that oligarchy interspersed with infrequent elections was finding it difficult to contain political expression. Politics were being widened, and popular forces which had been relatively inert since the Civil War period were once more coming into play.

Wesley knew little of the dimension in high politics to the growing instability of the 1760s. The political machinations of the king, Rockingham, Newcastle and Pitt were beyond him. Instead he focused on what he could see for himself: English society was becoming more divided, only this time religion was a peripheral matter.[81] As for Wilkes, Wesley did not come down firmly on one side or the other on the main issues of general warrants and the Middlesex elections. On balance he appears to have been against general warrants, and in favour of the House of Commons determining its own electoral privileges. What really upset him was the way in which contentious issues were used by the radical press and popular orators to foment discontent.

By this means the flame spreads wider and wider; it runs as fire among the stubble. The madness becomes epidemic, and no medicine has availed against it. The whole nation sees the State in danger, as they did the Church sixty years ago; and the world now wanders after Mr Wilkes as it did after Dr Sacheverell.[82]

Anyone who could speak of Sacheverell and Wilkes in the same breath was certainly not a Tory of the old school. It was not just the extent, but also the content, of Wilkite propaganda that disturbed Wesley. It was often bawdy, blasphemous and anti-authority, so that Wilkes seemed to be a mixture of court jesture and Lord of Misrule.[83] For Wesley the issues themselves were less important than the cultural context in which they were expressed. The conflict between Wilkes and Wesley was more about ethics than politics. It was therefore unfortunate for subsequent Methodist relations with popular radicalism, 'that the first extra-parliamentary organization devoted to a programme of reform should have started life in an attempt to pay off the accumulated debts (incurred more through riotous living than political commitment) of a mercurial elusive rake, John Wilkes'.[84]

In the 1770s, with the popular clamour for liberty slowly abating and with American disputes dominating political debate, Wesley wrote in a more philosophical vein. He published pamphlets on the nature of civil and religious liberty and on the origin of political power.[85] He rejected Lockean notions of popular sovereignty on historical and pragmatic grounds, and stated with typical Wesleyan bluntness that universal adult suffrage was the only logical deduction from natural rights theories. On the growing conflict with the American colonies, Wesley was more ambivalent than his oft-quoted *Calm Address* would indicate. There were times when his sense of justice overcame his fear of rebellion. In 1768 he wrote that 'I do not defend the measures which have been taken with regard to America: I doubt whether any man can defend them, either on the part of law, equity or prudence.'[86] Wesley admitted to Lord North that all his High Church ideas of passive obedience and non-resistance went against the Americans, and yet 'I cannot avoid thinking (if I think at all) that these an oppressed people asked for nothing more than their legal rights; and that in the most modest and inoffensive manner which the nature of things would allow.'[87] Whatever his private feelings about America, in public Wesley repeated Dr Johnson's arguments about Britain's right to tax the colonies and of the validity of virtual representation. The real cause of the conflict, according to Wesley, was the dissemination of anti-monarchical propaganda in England and America by evilly-disposed men.

Bernard Semmel has shown how America acted as catalyst for a wider controversy between Wesley and the Unitarian, Dr Price, on the one hand, and between Wesley and the English Calvinists, Toplady and Evans, on the other.[88] In reply to Price's *Observations on the Nature of Civil Liberty*, Wesley used roughly the same arguments that Burke employed against Price in his *Reflections on the Revolution in France*. Wesley countered Price's statement that government originated from the people and was dependent on their consent by showing historically that there was 'not a single instance, in above seven hundred years, of the people of England's conveying the supreme power either to one or more persons'.[89] Displaying the English preference for mixed government, Wesley stated that democracy, of all governmental systems, was least likely to secure liberty and that Price's ideas could only fuel the flames of discontent at home and abroad.

Toplady and Evans detected in Wesley's American writings the 'old Jacobite doctrines of hereditary, indefeasible, divine right and of passive obedience and non-resistance'. Wesley replied with equal force that English liberty stemmed from the Revolution, certainly not from the Cromwellian protectorate, and that Dissenters had better watch their language lest they provoke an eighteenth-century High Church reaction.[90] It says much for the psychological impact of the English Civil War and the Revolution of 1688 that late eighteenth-century religious polemicists could still pour their political perceptions through a seventeenth-century filter. Moreover, Wesley was convinced that Price's Unitarianism was merely a modern manifestation of Civil War radicalism, and that Calvinism had not yet shed its antinomian coat. With evidence like this, Semmel concludes that Evangelical Arminianism, 'the ideology of the Methodist Revolution', was a dynamic new theological and political synthesis made up of loyalty to king and country, an authoritarian ecclesiology, High Church charity, gospel fervour, unlimited salvation and individual freedom. However, Evangelical Arminianism was also a divisive force, not only because it was opposed by Catholics, Calvinists, Anglicans and radical Dissenters, but also because growth inexorably produced conflict. Nineteenth-century sectarianism had at least some of its roots in the response of religious groups to the turbulent decades of the 1760s and 1770s, from John Wilkes to Lord George Gordon. In the eighteenth century these roots can be detected in polemical pamphlets by religious leaders. For this to be converted into a more widespread sectarianism churches had to develop stronger institutional characteristics, such as a professionalized ministry, substantial property holdings, political and financial structures, and a more sophisticated communications system. When that sectarianism did develop in the nineteenth century, it did so on principles that had already been broadly defined. This was also true of Methodist attitudes to political radicalism.

Wesley's other political interventions were less important and less controversial. He repeatedly urged electors not to accept 'entertainment, meat or drink', but to vote for those who feared God and honoured the king.[91] He advised Pitt not to introduce new taxes until the old ones had been properly assessed and collected, and asked him to introduce draconian measures against distillers and suicide victims.[92] More compassionately, he advocated prison reform,[93] and encouraged Wilberforce and others in their campaign against slavery.[94] This is a familiar Wesleyan recipe of honesty, justice, prejudice and homespun morality. As with Baxter in the seventeenth century, Wesley was more concerned with the religious quality of men than with the more abstract world of measures.

Wesley's political legacy to his followers was determined more by reactions to events than by a clear ideology – apart from what was biblically explicit. As such the design and coherence that Semmel portrays in the 'Methodist revolution' must be matched with less harmonious factors like bad luck, irony, stupidity and over-confidence. It was bad luck for Methodist leaders to have to begin public life by refuting wild accusations of popery and Jacobitism. Wesley was unfortunate in writing a few lines in support of the Protestant Association several months before the most serious outbreak of anti-Catholic rioting in the eighteenth century. It was unlucky that Wesley's growing self-confidence in public affairs should have coincided with two of the most complex decades in British political history. It is ironic that Wesley, who wrote so eloquently in favour of civil and religious liberty against slave-owners and persecutors, should have been castigated by Catholics and radicals for contributing to neither. It is equally ironic that Wesley, who was impatient of sectarian and dogmatic conflicts, should have contributed to their return in the later eighteenth century.

Wesley's political directives, though wanting nothing in firmness, often lacked discernment. This was true of his 'no politics' rule. He merely meant by it that religion was of paramount concern to Methodists, and that party politics, and politics with which he disagreed, deflected the movement from spiritual objectives. But he did not consider the implications of the rule. What happened when religious and political issues were inseparable, and how could the argument be met that this rule simply reinforced the status quo? More fundamentally, the operation of the rule conferred enormous political power on its operator. Wesley would not have been troubled by these objections, but his followers were.

To talk of Wesley's politics in party terms is not particularly helpful. He loved his king, his country and the constitution. He grew to accept with gladness the defence of liberty and property by predominantly Whig aristocrats and philosophers. He hated discontent, violence, injustice and corruption. He never lost his High Church belief in passive obedience and non-resistance. No doubt one could detect in all this a mixture of Tory and country ideology, but Wesley's politics developed naturally from two sources, the Bible, and his own observations on the state of the country. Like Burke, Wesley was more concerned with duties than with rights, and with God's providential ordering of society than with the collective wisdom of democracy. If the Bible taught Wesley about human sinfulness, then his experience merely confirmed it. Therefore, an emphasis on obedience to established authorities and on reciprocal duties in all human relationships promised greater rewards of happiness and security for humankind than could be guaranteed by 'revolutionary liberalism' and secular idealism.[95]

There were, however, many unresolved tensions in Wesley's view of politics and society. Though opposed in principle to revolutionary change, he retrospectively endorsed the Dutch revolt against Catholic Spain in the sixteenth century, and by 1784 he had accepted as *fait accompli* the American repudiation of British authority. But Wesley's position was no mere adaptation of Pope's phrase that 'whatever is, is right', because his approval went only to changes that resulted in more, not less, civil and religious liberty. A similar concern for religious freedom moderated Wesley's customary adherence to the established order in Church and State in Britain when Methodists were themselves victims of mild persecution. For example, when the registration of Methodist chapels in 1787 failed to stop prosecutions under the Conventicles Act, Wesley gave full vent to his frustration in a letter to Wilberforce.

Now, sir, what can the Methodists do? They are liable to be ruined by the Conventicle Act, and they have no relief from the Act of Toleration! If this is not oppression, what is? Where, then, is English liberty? the liberty of Christians?

yea, of every rational creature, who as such has a right to worship God according to his own conscience?[96]

Wesley's concern for Methodism's vested interests, regardless of political parties or ideologies was perhaps his most important legacy to Bunting's generation.

Thus, Wesleyan Methodism entered the 1790s with a developing political consciousness, not so much based on a coherent party ideology, as on a series of episodic and religious responses to the major issues of religious and civil liberty, and the nature of good government. But its role was modified by even more profound factors. It was in, but not of, the Church of England. Its fervent support for establishments in Church and State was not reciprocated. It changed, and was changed by, popular culture, but it never fully harmonized with it. Methodism demanded so much more from its cultural constituency than did the alehouse or the coffee shop. Above all, its remarkable growth changed the political, religious, and social setting in which it was trying to find its place.

References

1   F. W. Newman, *The Soul* (London 1849), p. 248.
2   See, for example, H. A. Snyder, *The Radical Wesley and Patterns for Church Renewal* (Illinois 1980); and R. F. Lovelace, *Dynamics of Spritual Life: an Evangelical Theology of Renewal* (Exeter 1981).
3   J. E. Bradley, 'Whigs and Nonconformists: "Slumbering Radicalism" in English politics, 1739–1789', *Eighteenth Century Studies*, **9** no. 1 (1975), pp. 1–27.
4   For further information on the economic basis of much Church and Dissent conflict in the corporations see Lewis Namier and John Brooke (eds.), *The History of Parliament: The House of Commons, 1754–1790* (London 1964), pp. 113–18; P. J. Jupp, 'Urban politics in Ireland 1801–31', in D. W. Harkness and M. O'Dowd (eds.), *The Town in Ireland* (Belfast 1981); and E. N. Williams, *The Eighteenth Century Constitution* (Cambridge 1960), pp. 155–6. The sections of the community from which Methodism drew its members had no vested interests to protect in corporation politics.
5   J. Money, 'Birmingham and the West Midlands, 1760–1793: politics and regional identity in the English provinces in the later eighteenth century', *Midland History*, **1** no. 1 (1971), pp. 1–19.
6   Elie Halévy, *A History of the English People in 1815* (London 1924). E. P. Thompson, *The Making of the English Working Class* (London 1963). See also, E. J. Hobsbawm, *Labouring Men* (London 1964), and

the recent summary of the debate by E. S. Itzkin, 'The Halévy Thesis – a working hypothesis?', *Church History*, **44** no. 1 (1975), pp. 47–56.

7   Sheridan Gilley, 'Christianity and Enlightenment: an historical survey', *History of European Ideas*, **1** no. 2 (1981), pp. 103–21.

8   Bernard Semmel, *The Methodist Revolution* (London 1974).

9   R. W. Malcolmson, ' "A set of ungovernable people": the Kingswood colliers in the eighteenth century', in John Brewer and John Styles (eds.), *An Ungovernable People: the English and their law in the seventeenth and eighteenth centuries* (London 1980).

10   Roy Porter and Mikulas Teich (eds.) *The Enlightenment in National Context* (Cambridge 1981), p. 7.

11   W. R. Ward, 'The relations of enlightenment and religious revival in central Europe and in the English-speaking world', *Studies in Church History*, Subsidia 2 (1979), pp. 281–305. See also, W. R. Ward, 'Power and Piety: the origins of religious revival in the early eighteenth century', *Bulletin of the John Rylands University Library of Manchester*, **63** no. 1 (1980), pp. 231–52.

12   Ward, 'Power and Piety', p. 252.

13   A. C. Outler (ed.), *John Wesley* (A Library of Protestant Thought) (New York 1964), p. viii. Frederick Dreyer, 'Faith and experience in the thought of John Wesley', *American Historical Review*, **88** no. 1 (1983), pp. 12–30.

14   J. H. S. Kent, book notice in *Proceedings of the Wesley Historical Society*, **41**, part 2 (1977), p. 63.

15   Gordon Rupp, 'Son to Samuel: John Wesley, Church of England Man', in *Just Men* (London 1977).

16   Norman Sykes, *Church and State in England in the Eighteenth Century* (London 1934), p. 398.

17   E. P. Thompson, 'Anthropology and the discipline of historical context', *Midland History*, **1** no. 3 (1972), pp. 41–55, and 'Patrician society, Plebeian culture', *Journal of Social History*, **7** no. 4 (1974), pp. 382–405. John Rule, 'Methodism, popular beliefs and village culture in Cornwall, 1800–50', in R. D. Storch (ed.), *Popular Culture and Custom in Nineteenth-Century England* (London 1982).

18   James Obelkevich, *Religion and Rural Society: South Lindsey 1825–1875* (Oxford 1976), p. 305.

19   ibid., p. 203.

20   This is also the argument of Robert Moore in *Pit-Men, Preachers and Politics. The effects of Methodism in a Durham Mining Community* (Cambridge 1974).

21   See B. R. Kreiser, *Miracles, Convulsions, and Ecclesiastical Politics in Early Eighteenth Century Paris* (Princeton 1978), p. 398.

22   *Journal*, 11 January 1750.

23   For this idea and others in this section I am indebted to those who gave papers at the 1981 Ecclesiastical History Society conference on the theme 'The Church and Healing'. Some of the papers have been published in W. J. Sheil (ed.), *Studies in Church History* (1982), vol. 19.

24   *The Works of the Rev. Sydney Smith* (London 1840), vol. 1, p. 105.

25   Philip Hughes, *The Catholic Question 1688–1829, a study in political history* (London 1929), p. 77.

26   See Geoffrey Holmes, *Religion and Party in Late Stuart England* (London 1975), and E. N. Williams, pp. 325–40.

27   For a fuller discussion of this see Jean Orcibal, 'The theological originality of John Wesley and continental theology', in Rupert Davies and Gordon Rupp (eds.), *A History of the Methodist Church in Great Britain* (London 1965), vol. 1, pp. 81–111; and also R. G. Tuttle, *John Wesley: His Life and Theology* (Michigan 1978).

28   G. C. Cell, *John Wesley's Theology* (Cokesbury 1950), p. 361.

29   George Lavington, *The Enthusiasm of Methodists and Papists Compar'd* (published in three parts 1749–51), p. 3 of the preface to part one. For the full text of Wesley's reply see G. R. Cragg (ed.), *The Works of John Wesley* (Oxford 1975), vol. 11, pp. 353–436.

30   See Norman Sykes, *Edmund Gibson* (London 1926), pp. 304–21; and Cragg (ed.), *Works of Wesley*, pp. 327–51.

31   John Walsh, 'Methodism and the mob in the eighteenth century', *Studies in Church History*, **8** (1972), pp. 213–27.

32   Frank Baker, 'Methodism and the '45 Rebellion', *The London Quarterly and Holborn Review* (October 1947), pp. 325–33.

33   *Journal*, 27 February 1744.

34   The letter was never sent: see *Journal*, 5 March 1744.

35   John Wesley, *A Word to a Protestant*, 8th edn (London 1745), pp. 7–12.

36   John Bossy, *The English Catholic Community 1570–1850* (London 1975), pp. 251–2.

37   *Journal*, 27 August 1739.

38   See J. M. Turner, 'Of Methodists and Papists compar'd', *Proceedings of the Wesley Historical Society*, **41** part 2 (1977), pp. 37–8.

39   See Bossy, pp. 278–92. See also, G. P. Connolly, 'The secular missioner of the North in the evangelical age of the English mission', *North West Catholic History*, **10** (1983), pp. 8–31.

40   Richard Challoner, *A Caveat against the Methodists* (London 1760). For a fuller discussion see E. H. Burton, *The Life and Times of Bishop Challoner* (London 1909), vol. 2, pp. 15–17; and Sheridan Gilley, 'Challoner as Controversialist', in Eamon Duffy (ed.), *Challoner and His Church* (London 1981), pp. 90–111.

41   *Letters*, vol. 4, p. 140.

42   See, *A Roman Catechism, Works* vol. X, pp. 86–128. *The advantage of the members of the Church of England over those of the Church of Rome, Works*, vol. X, pp. 133–40, and *Popery Calmly Considered, Works*, vol. X, pp. 140–58.

43   See Wesley's letters to his nephew Samuel who joined the Roman Catholic Church. *Letters*, vol. 7, pp. 230–1, and vol. 8, pp. 218–19.

44   *Journal*, 14 August 1747.

45   *Journal*, 15 August 1747.

46   *Journal*, 3 April 1748 and 10 April 1748.

47   *Works*, vol. X, pp. 80–6.

48   Augustin Cardinal Bea in the Preface to Michael Hurley SJ (ed.), *John Wesley's Letter to a Roman Catholic* (London 1968), p. 21.

49   Wesley, *A Word to a Protestant*, p. 2, *Works*, vol. X, p. 159, and *Sermons*, vol. 1, XXXIX on *Catholic Spirit*, pp. 490–501.

50   *Sermons*, vol. 2, XCVII, *On Zeal*, pp. 462–71.

51   *Journal*, 3 June 1758.

52   *Journal*, 17 May 1762.

53   *Journal*, 19 July 1756.

54   *Journal*, 26 April 1778.

55   *Journal*, 18 January 1780.

56   See the graph in Bossy, p. 422.

57   John Wesley, *A letter to the printer of the 'Public Advertiser'* (London 21 January 1780). *Works*, vol. X, pp. 159–61.

58   *Protestant Magazine*, 1 (1780), p. 28.

59   George Rudé, 'The Gordon Riots: a study of the rioters and their victims', in *Paris and London in the eighteenth century* (London 1952), and John Stevenson, *Popular Disturbances in England 1700–1870* (London 1979), pp. 76–90.

60   E. C. Black, *The Association: British Extraparliamentary Political Organization 1769–1793* (Harvard 1963), p. 158.

61   J. Paul de Castro, *The Gordon Riots* (London 1926).

62   *Journal*, 5 November 1780.

63   Reproduced by George Cubitt in *Strictures on O'Connell's Letters to the Wesleyan Methodists* (London 1839), p. 66.

64   Rev. Arthur O'Leary, *Miscellaneous Tracts*, 2nd edn (Dublin 1781), p. 215.

65   In 1780 O'Leary issued *Remarks on the Rev. John Wesley's letter on the Civil Principles of Roman Catholics and his Defence of the Protestant Association.* Wesley records that when O'Leary's six letters were put into one and printed in London, the title was Mr O'Leary's remarks on the *Rev. Mr. W's Letter in Defence of the Protestant Associations in England; to which are prefixed Mr. Wesley's Letters.* The 1781 edition of O'Leary's *Miscellaneous Tracts* carried the subtitle, *In which are*

introduced, The Rev. John Wesley's Letter, and the Defence of the Protestant Association. Thus, each successive issue is a partial retraction.

66 Rev. T. R. England, *The Life of the Reverend Arthur O'Leary* (London 1822), pp. 83-4.

67 Daniel O'Connell, *Letter to the Ministers and Office-bearers of the Wesleyan Methodist Societies of Manchester* (London 6 July 1839), and *Second Letter to the . . .* (London 1 August 1839).

68 M. C. A. Mss., G. Cubitt to J. Bunting, 29 July, 30 July, 10 August, 12 August 1839, and 1 January 1840. Letters 1, 2 and 5 are printed in W. R. Ward, *Early Victorian Methodism: The Correspondence of Jabez Bunting 1830-1858* (London 1976), pp. 229-31, 237.

69 Cubitt, *Strictures*, p. 67.

70 Rev. Alexius Mills, *The History of Riots in London in the year 1780, commonly called the Gordon Riots* (London 1883), p. 54. See also Burton, vol. 2, pp. 216-18.

71 This is a representative conclusion from W. J. Amherst SJ, *The History of Catholic Emancipation 1771-1820* (London 1886), vol. 1, p. 147.

72 See the comments by Bishop Odd Hagen, Augustin Cardinal Bea, and Michael Hurley, in Hurley, *Wesley's Letter to a Roman Catholic* (Belfast 1968). Also, J. M. Todd, *John Wesley and the Catholic Church* (London 1958), p. 192; and Frederick Jeffery, *Methodism and the Irish Problem* (Belfast 1973), p. 34.

73 John Wesley, *How far is it the Duty of a Christian Minister to Preach Politics?* (London 1782). *Works*, vol. XI, pp. 154-5.

74 John Wesley, *Free Thoughts on the Present State of Public Affairs* (London 1768), *Works*, vol. XI, p. 18.

75 John Wesley, *Thoughts concerning the Origin of Power, Works*, vol. XI, pp. 46-53.

76 John Wesley, *Free Thoughts, Works*, vol. XI, pp. 26-7.

77 John Wesley, *Thoughts upon Liberty* (London 1772), *Works*, vol. XI, p. 43.

78 John Wesley, *A Seasonable Address to the more serious part of the inhabitants of Great Britain respecting the unhappy context between us and our American brethren* (London 1776), *Works*, vol. XI, p. 125.

79 See the comment by Geoffrey Holmes in John Cannon (ed.), *The Whig Ascendancy* (London 1980), p. 194.

80 John Brewer, *Party Ideology and Popular Politics at the Accession of George III* (Cambridge 1976), p. 14.

81 John Wesley, *Free Thoughts, Works*, vol. XI, p. 29.

82 ibid., p. 27.

83 Brewer, *Party Ideology and Popular Politics*, p. 190.

84   ibid., p. 21.
85   *Works*, vol. XI, pp. 34–53.
86   *Works*, vol. XI, p. 24.
87   *Letters*, vol. 6, p. 161.
88   Semmel, pp. 65–71.
89   *Works*, vol. XI, p. 103.
90   John Wesley, *A Calm Address to the Inhabitants of England* (London 1777), *Works*, vol. XI, pp. 129–40.
91   See Frank Baker (ed.), *The Works of John Wesley* (Oxford 1980), vol. 25, p. 96 note 1, for Wesley's electoral advice.
92   *Letters*, vol. 7, pp. 234–6.
93   *Letters*, vol. 4, pp. 127–8.
94   *Letters*, vol. 8, p. 265.
95   See E. G. Rupp, 'John Wesley's Toryism and our present discontents', *The Presbyter* (February 1945), pp. 3–12.
96   *Letters*, vol. 8, p. 231. For some of the ideas in this section I am indebted to Leon Orville Hynson.

3 The 1790s:
a decade of crises

The generation about which I wish to speak was, I make no doubt, the most important single generation in the modern history not merely of English religion but of the whole Christian world. For despite the holy water sprinkled by the late Dean Sykes and his pupils, there seems no doubt that the effectiveness of the Church throughout Western Europe was undermined by the same forces which were everywhere sapping the Ancien Régime, the whole institutional complex of which the religious establishments were part. The great crisis of the French Revolution altered for ever the terms on which religious establishments must work, and in so doing it intensified everywhere a long-felt need for private action in the world of religion.[1]

So began Professor Ward's presidential address to the Ecclesiastical History Society in 1972. I have no difficulty in agreeing with him that the period 1790–1820 is indeed the most crucial in the modern history of English religion for so many reasons. It was in this period that Protestant Nonconformity grew at such an extraordinary pace that it seemed as if the Church of England was on the verge of becoming a minority religious establishment. It was in this period also that enlightenment ideas were proletarianized and given a popular political and anti-clerical dimension in the writings of Paine and others. That infidel tradition which stretches down through the nineteenth century and takes in men like Carlile, Owen, Holyoake and Bradlaugh, had its origins in the last decade of the eighteenth century.[2] Moreover, this challenge from non-Anglican religion and democratic political ideas exposed weaknesses in the effectiveness of England's Church and State connection. No historian of English religion would grant such weaknesses originated in the 1790s, but a unique combination of social forces in that decade resulted in a new configuration of English religion – that is, 'the division between a conservative state church, a liberal Protestant dissent, and a radical secularism'.[3] In that respect the period 1790–1820 can be seen as one of great discontinuity in the history of English religion. Yet, on a deeper level, it is becoming more clear that popular religious culture did not change all that much from the mid seventeenth to the mid nineteenth century, particularly in rural areas.[4] It is the challenge to establishment control rather than a reorientation of entire belief systems which marks out this period as one of special importance. In that setting, Wesleyan Methodism is of major significance not only because it was the fastest growing of the evangelical communities, but also because it was both agent and victim of the ecclesiastical and political turbulence of the period.

For Methodism itself the 1790s was a critical decade. It lost its founder, experienced serious internal conflicts, was obliquely threatened with repression by political and religious establishments, suffered its first major secession, but still managed to grow more rapidly than ever before. Moreover, it was a decade overshadowed by two revolutions, one in French society and government, and the other in British industry, that irrevocably changed Western civilization, including its religion. Although the Industrial Revolution was, in the long run, to be more significant in determining the future development of Western Christianity, the revolution in France seemed to pose more immediate problems for British society in the 1790s. In politics, the revolution encouraged the growth of more radical reformist policies such as universal suffrage and annual parliaments, which had a different ideological basis (natural rights), and social constituency (urban artisans), from the reformism of the 1780s – whether that be the economical reform of the Rockingham Whigs or the redistribution of parliamentary seats advocated by the Association movement. But the growth of popular radicalism in this period should not obscure two important facts: first, this radicalism had deep-seated English roots predating Continental revolution; and, second, popular conservatism was an equally potent social force in England, at least until government repression and economic distress dampened Church-and-King enthusiasm. Both reaction and reform, therefore, fed on French revolutionary excitement, making it a bad time for moderate reformers.

The same polarizing effect is evident in religious affairs. English Dissenters, especially those of unorthodox theology and academy education, increasingly resented Anglican civic and ecclesiastical privileges. The failure to secure an enlarged toleration in 1772–3 due to royal and Anglican control in the House of Lords (though a minor concession was squeezed out of North's crumbling administration in 1779), and the fact that Anglicans occupied most of the profitable offices in the localities hardly endeared the Established Church to the Dissenters. The crisis came in 1787–90 when three attempts were made to repeal the Test and Corporation Acts. Inflamed by Pitt's desertion and Foxite support, the Dissenters voiced heady political sentiments at the meetings of the London Revolution Society in 1788 and 1789. But they overreached themselves. Overt support for French revolutionary principles and the growth of a more extreme provincial campaign against the Established Church convinced many, including Burke, that radical Dissent was subverting the whole established order in Church and State.[5] In response Anglicanism received ideological support in Burke's *Reflections*, popular support in the form of Church-and-King mobs, and parliamentary support through the defeat of Dissenting political objectives for the next forty years. All this disguised the fact that the real danger to the Established Church was not political at all, but rather its inability to adapt to new social circumstances and to control popular evangelicalism.[6] The most serious threat to the Church of England's monopoly was, therefore, not the rationalistic ideology of Price and Priestley, but competition from religious societies and itinerant preachers. Ironically, the Church of England had more to fear from its Methodist friends than from its Dissenting foes.

Not that Methodism was itself immune from the increasing social and political tension of the 1790s, though to some extent one can agree with John Walsh's conclusion that Methodism's preoccupation with evangelism and internal problems insulated it from the debates surrounding the French Revolution.[7] In any case the troubles of the French Catholic Church did not provoke much sympathy from English popular Protestants. John Pawson, President of the Conference 1793–4, wrote that

our Preacher in France has been brought before the Municipal Assembly. When they heard him speak for himself, they cried out with one voice. He is a man of God, let him go and preach where he will. Yet these are all Deists and Atheists!!! If they are, who made them so? Why those precious Priests who are so highly esteemed in England, and that wretched superstition which the Assembly has cast down to the ground. And there may it lie to the day of Eternity.[8]

Pawson also responded to English radical ideas in religious terms. He agreed with Paine's diagnosis of governmental corruption (it chimed in with his own views about the financial irregularities of Methodist preachers), but considered his remedies of 'greater liberty and more riches' for the people suitable only for a 'Nation of Saints'. Only 'more religion' could increase the happiness of Englishmen.[9] This view that Methodists were engaged in more momentous tasks than mere politics is a consistent theme running through the private papers and printed pamphlets of Methodist leaders in the period.[10]

Although Methodists viewed growing social and political tensions in France and England through religious spectacles, this does not mean that these tensions were unimportant in shaping Methodist development. Moreover, Methodism's self-image became more fragile when Wesley's guiding hand was removed after a half-century of pragmatism and unresolved problems. Large questions now had to be answered. How was Methodism to be governed? How was power to be apportioned among the major interest groups within the Methodist polity – preachers, trustees and people? What was to be the relationship between Methodism and the Church of England? As the movement entered its second phase what were to be its policies and characteristics? On what principles should these be based? How should Methodism react to new impulses from its social constituency and from the government? How was Methodism to be financed in a period of cyclical booms and slumps? In short, with whom and with what were Methodist societies in connexion now that Mr Wesley was dead?

Not surprisingly there were major internal conflicts. Even Pawson, who was not all that sorry to see the end of Wesley, reflected wistfully in 1797 that 'ever since the death of our venerable Father, our grand adversary has found us one thing or another to contend about, and it seems we have not done yet'.[11] While Pawson saw the devil and a decline in Methodist spirituality as the main problems,[12] there were others. Because Methodism was a movement in, but not of, the Church of England, and because it appealed to a lower social constituency than the other churches, it could not remain unscathed from the increase in religious conflict and social discontent. Yet the remarkable thing about Methodism in the 1790s, given the issues it had to tackle, is not the scale of internal conflict, but the fact that it developed institutional structures at the cost of only one secession. But in resolving some problems in the decade after Wesley's death, the Methodist leadership laid the foundation for new troubles in the nineteenth century, especially over the role of the preachers. In the short term, however, Methodists had more in common with each other than with the rest of the religious world. Its cohesive features were its Evangelical Arminianism, itinerant ministry, connexional structure, sense of religious community, and emotional fervour, as against political and Socinian Dissenters on the one hand and 'carnal' or Calvinistic Anglicans on the other.[13] Wesley's legacy was therefore strong in essentials if weak on peripheral matters. Consequently, when secession occurred in 1797 it was not over doctrine, and the seceders remained Methodists. Arminianism, itinerancy, connexionalism and piety made up Methodism regardless of its relationship to the Wesleyan mainstream. As a result, intricate theological disputes troubled Methodism a good deal less than the more cerebral Puritanism of the seventeenth century.[14]

Nevertheless, these cohesive factors should not detract from the importance of internal conflicts in fashioning the ecclesiastical and political character of Methodism after Wesley's death. Indeed it was through such conflicts that a new denominational self-consciousness was both reflected and created. This happened for three reasons. First, there was increasing pressure, especially from the members of new Methodist chapels in northern cities, for Wesleyanism to find its own distinctive place in English society outside the traditional, and often sterile, rivalry between Church and Dissent. Second, there were serious differences of opinion about where power and authority should reside in the Wesleyan connexion; and third, the heightened social tensions of the 1790s made it difficult for Methodism to expand its popular base *and* placate government fears about its loyalty at the same time. It is to these issues that we must now turn, because in coping with them Methodism converted Wesley's conservative tendencies into a conservative habit.

Methodism's desire to forge an identity in the period was not so much due to its own longing for fulfilment as to the practical problems occasioned by Wesley's death and the inconveniences of living within an Established Church which many Methodists thought was spiritually corrupt. John Pawson's piety often led him to exaggerate evils, but he expressed a widely held view when he wrote that Methodist prosperity ought not to depend 'upon our abiding in the dead, formal, fallen Church of England, and attending upon the ministry of carnal wicked men'.[15] The problem was what to do about it, because only a small percentage of the preachers wanted either total separation from, or integration in, the Church of England. In other words the majority of the preachers were *Wesleyans*. But Wesley's ambivalent attitude towards the Church of England could not have lasted forever, and his followers had to pick up the cheque for his renowned 'flexibility'. The issue crystallized, as one would have expected, over the administration of the sacrament. (Indeed this is a recurring problem in the history of relationships between religious societies and ecclesiastical institutions.)

That there was more at stake than the administration of the Eucharist emerges clearly from the correspondence of two of the leading protagonists, Pawson and William Thompson, an Ulsterman who was first President of the Conference after Wesley's death. Pawson believed

that our old plan is a very good one. Yet not so good that it cannot be mended. The Methodists from the beginning have followed the openings of providence, and it will certainly be the best to do so still. I am very far from thinking that the success of our labours will depend upon our abiding in the Church everywhere. Yet I do not wish for a general separation from the Church. I would not give my vote for any such thing. All that I wish for is, that in those places where we have service in the Church hours, where the people neither can nor will go to Church, and where the people in general desire the Sacrament, they should be indulged with it.[16]

Although considerably widening Wesley's own conditions for the administration of communion by Methodist preachers, Pawson, in his desire to be flexible and to follow providential openings, could claim to be in the authentic Wesleyan tradition. In addition, Pawson felt that flexibility was the best way of preserving unity, and that the Methodists who wanted the sacrament were the most lively and godly people in the connexion.[17] For Pawson, the issue was essentially one of High Church 'bigotry' versus popular piety. Thompson had a different view, alleging that the administration of the sacrament by Methodist preachers was offensive to the Church of England, a departure from Wesley's instructions, a perversion of the priestly office, a denial of ecclesiastical discipline, and certain to result in divisions.[18] To Thompson's ecclesiastical fears, Thomas Coke added political and doctrinal ones. He believed that sacramental separation from the Church of England would result in Methodism imbibing Socinian ideas and 'the political spirit of the Dissenters'.[19] As John Walsh has pointed out 'the ironical issue in the sacramental controversy' was that both parties wanted to follow in Wesley's footsteps, and to prevent Methodism from drifting into Dissent. Around this sharp shadow of Wesleyan tradition, however, was a penumbra of major differences over the nature of ecclesiastical government, the role of the people, and the political and social character of post-Wesleyan Methodism.

The dispute over the sacrament brought another conflict into sharper focus. Methodist chapel trustees, who were wealthier and socially more disposed to the Established Church than the majority of laymen and preachers, became nervous about separatist tendencies. Their nerves were set on edge by the publication of Paine's *Rights of Man* and by the riots against Dissenters in Birmingham. They tried every device from persuasion to legal action to prevent the sacraments being administered in their chapels. Preachers like Samuel Bradburn viewed the conflict between trustees and people (as represented by their preachers) in a wider political setting of people versus aristocracy. Although a bit of a windbag, Bradburn, in his letters of the winter and spring of 1791–2, conveys the flavour of social tension.

We must guard our own liberties, and our people's or an aristocratical faction will rule us with a rod of Iron . . . . I hope no man is more averse to lording it over God's heritage than I am; but I cannot give up myself and my flock to be governed by a few ignoramuses, because they have a few pounds, or hundreds more than better and wiser men.

What chiefly moved me to accept of ordination *now* was the spirit of bigoted high church-men, which seems to infect the rich *mongrel methodists* through the land. It is high time to awake out of sleep, and maintain the rights of our office . . . . This is our grand point and glory, *Piety* not modes of opinions, is the bond of our union. *Unbounded Liberty*, founded upon the *Rights of Man*, in all matters consistent with decorum and our main desire to save souls.

Vox Populi should be our motto. The *Leaders, not* Trustees, are the representatives of the people. I would sooner close the whole premises belonging to the New-Chapel than submit to be governed by that aristocratical faction.[20]

This language shows how England's social and political tensions in the years 1791–3 could be given a religious dimension through issues of church government. This is generally where the religious person gets his first experience of political conflict, albeit on a small scale.

What emerges most clearly from the correspondence of the Methodist leaders in the years 1791–3 is that those who opposed the administration of the sacrament *and* those who advocated it, were forced to construct a higher view of the ministry and of the power of Conference. The alternatives were surrender to trustee control (the effective end of itinerancy), or a dilution of ecclesiastical discipline so that the people could have what they wanted. That in turn would have resulted in the end of connexionalism. Men politically as far apart as

Thompson and Bradburn were advocating preacher unity and Conference discipline.[21] What separated them was disagreement over the policies on which preachers should unite.

In spite of, or more likely because of, widespread canvassing before the 1792 Conference in London neither party could break the deadlock and the matter was decided by lot. The sacrament was not to be celebrated in Methodist chapels for at least one more year, but, not surprisingly, the luck of the draw failed to bring peace to a troubled connexion. Reports flooded in of more militant demands to have the sacraments and the relationship between preachers and trustees deteriorated still further.[22] Professor Ward states that 'the wave of artisan radicalism in the country had its counterpart in a clamour for separation among the ordinary members and adherents of the Methodist societies which no force within the connexion could control'.[23]

In the midst of this pressure, Thompson's nerve broke. He was told that the government had been informed that 'the Methodists in general . . . are in their sentiments inimical to the British King and Constitution', and that 'they had an intention of separating from the established Church'.[24] Thompson assured Pitt of Methodist loyalty, promised him electoral support, declared allegiance to the Church of England, and solicited support for a Methodist lawsuit in the Court of Equity. Similarly, he sought Wilberforce's support by promising Methodist opposition to the slave trade.[25] Thompson gave the impression that he was representing the whole connexion by signing himself 'the first President of the Methodist Conference after Wesley's death'. Pawson cynically observed that the only thing Thompson had not promised was to raise soldiers for the war. In subsequent letters Pawson referred to Thompson as 'the first President', and privately resolved never to trust an Irishman. More seriously he and Bradburn believed that public declarations of support for king, Church and country would alienate grass-roots Methodism.

In 1793 Conference tried to paper over the widening cracks in Methodist discipline by resolving that where numbers of a society were unanimous, the sacrament could be administered by their own preachers. This was satisfactory to no one, and it was clear that a major confrontation between trustees and preachers who administered the sacrament was inevitable. It came a year later in the ancient Methodist citadel of Bristol. The bare outlines of the dispute are clear. Henry Moore, one of the preachers stationed in the Bristol circuit, administered the sacrament at Portland Street chapel in the city. In response, the pro-Church trustees of the Old Room chapel in Bristol (the oldest in the country) excluded Moore from their pulpit, thereby challenging the right of Conference to appoint preachers for the whole connexion. What is still unclear about the dispute is how far it was engineered by both sides, in a deliberate attempt to win control of the Methodist tradition.

The problem began at the inauguration service of Portland chapel in 1792. Bradburn, on the advice of the new trustees, altered the Anglican prayers and preached in gown and surplice. This infuriated the Old Room trustees, who united with the local Anglican clergy in expressing public disapproval.[26] What part Bradburn's resentment against the Old Room trustees played in 1794 is an open question, but he fervently supported Moore throughout the dispute. In fact the two leading protagonists were Bradburn and Joseph Benson, a 'High-Church' preacher who 'was appointed to the Bristol Circuit in answer to the repeated request of the friends of *old Methodism*'.[27] With the connexional system making it impossible to localize this kind of confrontation, Bristol became the centre of attention for trustees and preachers up and down the country.[28] Each side knew what was at stake and aided the general exertions in whatever way they could. Many trustees were even prepared to raise large sums of money to sustain preachers who would carry on the 'old plan of Methodism in connexion with the Church of England'.[29]

Benson's position was firmly expressed.

The Trustees as a Body, never said or thought they had 'no need of the Conference', they have respected, and do respect the Conference as much and perhaps more than Mr Moore and his party . . . the Trustees have not nor never had any 'dissenting plan or design of turning the Preaching Houses into independent Meeting Houses' – their sole aim in all that they have done being to counteract those Preachers who they verily believed had such a design.[30]

Far from being a 'trustee preacher' Benson believed he was upholding the authentic Wesleyan tradition – loyalty to the Church of England, sound financial support for chapel building and obedience to the Conference. In his view the opposition case was not so much based on popular clamour as on the shabby connexional politicking of Bradburn, Moore and others. By contrast the correspondence of Benson's leading opponents, Coke, Pawson, Bradburn and Clarke, contains a powerful mixture of class hostility, pastoral concern for the people, and the need to preserve the itinerancy at all costs. Pawson could not understand why Benson was attached to 'the rich everywhere', and Clarke considered the 'High Church Party' to be the 'vilest of Persecutors' and that 'Trusteeism', if not checked, 'would ruin Methodism'.[31] Remarkably, the conflict in Bristol did not produce a major secession. Professor Ward states that this was because 'popular backing for "Church" Methodism was being destroyed by the same complex of political and social forces as destroyed popular complaisance towards the establishment and made Church-and-King mobs impossible to raise'.[32] There is much truth in this, but it could also be argued that pro-establishment demonstrations were harder to raise because of the apparent weakness of anti-establishment forces. Political Dissent had been purged of its fiery radicalism, preferring instead to negotiate discreetly with the government,[33] and the treason trials, though unsuccessful, seriously weakened the metropolitan and provincial reform societies.[34] Moreover, the terror of the French Revolution, Jacobin dechristianization, Paine's Deism, and new problems of ecclesiastical discipline forced Methodists like Bradburn to tone down their high-flown sentiments about the Rights of Man.[35] As evangelicalism infused all denominations and as Methodists raised cash for 'decent' chapels it must have seemed to many within the connexion that they could afford to untie one of the apron strings binding them to the Mother Church without becoming disreputable. Besides, 'Church' Methodists increasingly realized that their views were incompatible with popular expansion,[36] and the other party successfully propagated the myth that separate communion did not necessarily mean separation from the Church of England. In any case the economic depression in the country, and a profound belief that any kind of connexional government was better than none at all,[37] increased the urgency of the need to make decisions at the Conference in 1795. On the whole the correspondence of the main protagonists became more moderate in the winter of 1794–5.

Even Bradburn, sensing perhaps that events were moving his way, was able to review the Bristol episode in more conciliatory language.

I think the Conference must have the sole power to place and displace Preachers. But if a majority of Trustees, Stewards and Leaders in any place, can produce a reasonable objection against any Preacher, he ought by no means to be forced upon them . . . .

Should there be any vote about leaving the Church, and becoming a separate party, I shall, to the utmost of my power, oppose our doing any such thing. All I contend for from conscience (the liberty of which is sacred) is, that where a majority of the Society who frequent any Chapel, desire the Lord's Supper from their own Preachers, they ought to have it. But that receiving it, should never be a term of communion. I declare I have no objection to your curbing the power of the Preachers; only let them not be at the mercy of a few lordly men . . . .[38]

This beguiling moderation disguises the fact that these were precisely the terms (minus episcopal government) drawn up by Bradburn, Pawson, Coke and others at the secret Lichfield meeting several months before the Bristol volcano erupted.[39]

What has not been made clear in the standard histories of Methodism is that behind the general desire for peace in 1794–5 lay vitally important principles on which neither side wished to compromise. Moreover, the resolution of these differences involved complicated negotiations about double majorities. 'Church' Methodist preachers, realizing that the popular current was against them, proposed that the sacrament should not be administered in their chapels unless a majority of *both* leaders *and* trustees decided otherwise.[40] By this means, political ideas of double majorities which were familiar to the English corporations and the French States General were imported by 'Church' Methodists to defeat populism. On the eve of the Conference Pawson expressed a different opinion.

Where a majority, or if that will not do, where two thirds of the people in any Society desire the Sacrament, let the assistant preachers desire the Trustees, Leaders and Stewards to assemble together, let them in the fear of God, take the state of that Society into consideration and if it appear to a majority of them that it would be for the glory of God for the people to be favoured with the Sacrament, then let them petition the Conference for that privilege.

Pawson then denounced the double majority idea as a recipe for future contention.[41] Although Pawson had clearly moderated his earlier views, he was still far from an agreement with the 'Church' Methodist camp.

The Plan of Pacification adopted by the Conference in 1795 was a compromise between the 'Church' and sacramentarian parties, but it was a compromise which, given the strength of popular clamour, must have given some comfort to the trustees. The plan authorized the administration of the sacrament only if 'the majority of the trustees of the chapel on the one hand, and the majority of the Stewards and Leaders (as the best qualified to give the sense of the people) on the other hand, allow it'. Although Ward interprets this decision as the 'means by which the bulk of the Methodist community could move into practical dissent, and consummated the defeat of the struggles of the lay aristocracy of the connexion in the great urban centres',[42] the radical populists viewed it as a concession to the powerful trustee lobby. Alexander Kilham, the most vocal radical within the connexion, stated that

Suppose a society consists of a 1,000 members, should 950 of them wish for the sacrament, they cannot have it, unless a majority of the stewards etc., give their consent. Their humble request has to pass through three houses, and must have a majority in each of them, before it can be granted. 1. The leaders and stewards are supposed to be the representatives of the people, and may be considered as a house of commons. 2. But should they all be unanimous for the sacrament, the trustees, who act as a house of lords, can by a simple majority, prevent their lawful claims from being granted. 3. And should both the former allow the sacrament, the conference may act as a house of popes . . . and prevent their lawful claims. This is the sum of all the liberty we have attained, after four years contention.[43]

Whatever secured the defeat of the 'lay aristocracy', therefore, it was not coercion by Conference. Indeed, John Walsh quotes numerous examples of Methodist societies which continued to take the sacrament in the local parish church until well into the nineteenth century, especially if the incumbent was an evangelical.[44] The Plan of Pacification was, therefore, more of a genuine compromise between the contending parties than has sometimes been noticed.[45] It seems that the chapel trustees assented gradually to changes that were beyond their control while searching out new ways to retain influence. Even in religious connexions, wealth and power cannot be separated for very long.

The significance of the Plan of Pacification (and the Form of Discipline, 1797) for Methodist internal polity has been satisfactorily dealt with by others,[46] but four more general points emerge from this settlement. The Methodists could no longer claim with conviction that they were merely the Church of England at prayer. Evangelical Arminianism and the itinerant system survived the social tensions of the period 1791–5 more or less intact. The preachers, despite their disagreements, were united on their own importance within the connexion, and they retained the ultimate control in Methodist policy-making.[47] Finally, a radical group within the connexion now saw it had as much to fear from the 'house of popes' as from wealthy chapel trustees.

This radical challenge to the Methodist polity dominated connexional affairs in the period 1795–7. The focal point was Alexander Kilham whose personal antipathy to the Church of England made him a zealous advocate of separate communion and a formidable opponent of anything resembling hierarchical church government within Methodism.[48] In politics he supported Grey's demands for parliamentary reform and congratulated Erskine on his defence of Hardy and Tooke in the treason trials.[49] Kilham's brashness and over-developed urge to publicize his opinions would have resulted in immediate repression, but for the support of influential preachers like Bradburn. Kilham was a nuisance, but he was relatively safe while his views reflected those of an important group within the connexional leadership. But circumstances changed in 1795 when the Whiggish and Dissenting ripples of Kilham's earlier career were transformed into radical waves that seemed to threaten everyone on board the Methodist ship. While the years 1790–1820 were the most important in the evolution of Methodist political attitudes, 1795 was particularly important, not least because of the wider instability in English society. An increasingly unpopular war and a depressed economy converted radical coteries into a mass protest movement. As a result Church-and-King mobs became as rare as wage increases. Methodism was not immune from these tensions. Pawson, for example, was worried about the fate of the preachers at the annual Conference in Manchester. He told a friend that 'between you and I if many preachers go, my opinion is, that the people will mob us. They have been ready to do it several times at Manchester, and now all sorts of provisions are so scarce and so extravagantly dear, that they will get it into their heads that we shall make them dearer still, and I believe they will fall upon us'.[50]

The attack on the King's coach and Pitt's repressive riposte were matched within Methodism by Kilham's tilt at the ministerial leadership and his expulsion from the connexion. Much has been written about Kilham in these years but no one has managed to explain him historically. Whiggish Methodist historians view him as the first great connexional liberal, the John the Baptist of Victorian Nonconformity.[51] Idealistic historians see him as the dream fulfilment of Arminian egalitarianism – the one man in eighteenth-century Methodism who was as good as his theology.[52] Traditional Methodist historians look upon him as a polemical young upstart more interested in his own opinions than in godly reformation.[53] Those more interested in the political radicalism of the 1790s see him as the popular Protestant equivalent of Tom Paine – a man essentially better than the connexion which spawned him.[54] But the best way to understand Kilham is not as an anticipator of the future but as a man moulded by the past. Like many artisans in the industrializing areas of England, Kilham, in his opposition to Catholicism, absolutism, corruption and legal manipulation, was firmly within the old-fashioned tradition of the freeborn Englishman. Of course, this tradition was given some much needed ideological stimulation by the French Revolution and Tom Paine, but it never changed its fundamentally conservative and restorative characteristics. Kilham was, therefore, not so much a Painite demolition expert as an admirer (in the style of Major Cartwright) of England's libertarian past. Although couched in Methodist vocabulary, this is what emerges from Kilham's prolific writings in the period 1795–7 to which we must now turn.

Although Kilham was ministering in Aberdeen between 1792 and 1794, he was well in touch with developments in English Methodism. As an admirer of Wesley's pragmatic providentialism, he supported the sacramentarian party against the trustees, and was delighted to accept the Dissenting logic of that opinion. Moreover, he suspected the secret discussions of the Methodist ministerial aristocracy and was outraged by the Lichfield plan. He felt this was merely a Methodist imitation of those corrupt national establishments currently under the judgement of God in England and France.[55] Kilham lobbied the 1795 Conference but emerged from it dissatisfied with the Plan of Pacification, though he was optimistic about the possibility of further reforms now that the breach had been made. He placed his faith in men like Bradburn, Crowther and Moore, and he tried to nudge them forward in his *Progress of Liberty amongst the people called Methodists* published in autumn 1795. Amid much rhetoric about the inalienable rights of Methodist societies against oppression and tyranny, what Kilham really wanted was more power for the laity in all aspects of connexional government, and less opportunity for preachers to exploit the people for financial gain. This platform of more representation and less corruption was similar to the radical critique of the British constitution.

Kilham could not have chosen a worse time to canvass such ideas. Although many preachers had deliberately used popular clamour to twist the arms of wealthy trustees, they had no intention (both for theological and social reasons) of submitting themselves to demo-

cratic control. This ministerial conservatism was given political justification when 'gentlemen of rank' made it known to Methodist leaders
in London that the government was concerned about the constitutional loyalty of provincial Methodists. Wilberforce, who was
keen to preserve both evangelicalism and conservatism, delivered
timely hints of government intentions to nervous London preachers.[56]
The effect was remarkable. Not only did Dr Coke draw up an address
to assure George III that the House of Hanover would be sustained by
a cloud of incense (Methodist prayers), but the combined pressure
from Kilham and the government was forging a reconciliation between the warring factions of Methodism which the Plan of Pacification had only partly resolved. In the words of Coke, divergent
elements within the connexion came together to deal 'a fatal blow to
Methodist Jacobinism'.[57] Even with Benson and Bradburn on the
same side, however, the address to the king was never sent, for distinctively Methodist reasons.

Two sorts of people object to the address.   1. Those who from principle wish
no distinction to be made between us and the Church. We cannot blame them,
only the Government has made that distinction, and so hath the world in
general.   2. Those who at bottom are not so affected to the Government, and
expect a Revolution to take place in a while. And you may add 3. Those who
being deeply prejudiced against the Doctor will not sign it merely because he
was the author of it.[58]

Nevertheless, such confusions and jealousies could not save
Kilham, who was both instigator and victim of a major conservative
reaction within Methodism in the autumn and winter of 1795–6. Long
before he was tried by the Conference in the summer of 1796, the
knives were out for him, even from men like Pawson and Bradburn
who had campaigned on behalf of the people against the trustees.
Bradburn's own volte-face was disturbingly complete.

1.   That the Government have cause to be alarmed, and have been so, I
     know beyond controversy. And if Alex[r] Kilham and his abetters intend
     to pursue the path which he has done of late, active measures will be
     taken by the *higher powers*! His pamphlets are a disgrace to the con-
     nexion . . . .

3.   We know, in general, we are not enemies to the King, nor have we a wish
     to alter the Government of our country. We are charged as if we were
     otherwise. We mean to clear ourselves . . . the dream of Equality among
     men so very different in age and abilities is worthy only of such

inexperienced novices as talk of it. Should a division take place among us *now*, which I greatly fear must be, it will be *essentially different* from what it would have been *last Conference*, or *any one preceding*!!! The business of the Lord's Supper is settled! The leading men on each side are agreed . . . and who is to stand against them? – Kilham and Company!!! Alas! They know not what they are about. Look at their influence and connexions! I mean to act as I have done, so far as I can; but never to give countenance to raw desparadoes, who proceed in a manner that tends to anarchy and ruin. As to the cries about the *poor*, the *war*, etc., a great deal of this is for want of information and attention. The distress of 9 in 10 of the poor is *entirely their own fault*, and unconnected with the war.[59]

'To such comments on a famine of European dimensions was the erstwhile champion of the Rights of Man reduced by the necessities of connexional politics' is Ward's appropriate judgement.[60]

Pawson's response to Kilham is even more revealing. He was dismayed by the tone of *The Progress of Liberty* and recognized straight away that separation was inevitable. In association with other London preachers, he asked for a district meeting in Newcastle to investigate Kilham's views. It was in response to this 'London Methodistical Bull' that Kilham's libertarian ideas were given full expression. The preachers' attempt to silence him he likened to the role of the attorney-general in a libel case. He attacked Methodist leadership as a 'species of popery' and his own trial was simply a contemporary version of the inquisition. Undaunted, he repeated his financial allegations, and embarrassed Pawson by quoting some of Pawson's earlier diatribes against trustee power.[61] This played straight into the hands of connexional conservatives who claimed, not without foundation, that the Kilhams of this world were brought forward by naïve preachers giving in to popular clamour for the sacraments.[62] The ground had now collapsed under the feet of moderates like Pawson. Whereas in 1793 he steadfastly opposed attempts to construct addresses of loyalty to king and country, by February 1796 he was forced to give in to conservative pressure. After receiving a letter from Kilham 'as full of sedition as it can well be', he told a friend that 'I am satisfied that the Government has received information from different quarters that we are a disaffected people, and I now believe that we are much more so than I was willing to suppose we were. I am also satisfied that it is highly necessary to prepare the Address'.[63]

There was one further twist for Pawson, because he agreed with

Kilham's financial allegations. In fact he told Atmore in confidence that Kilham knew but half of what was going on.[64] In a series of letters to Benson, Pawson complained of exorbitant travelling expenses, of the growing number of married preachers with children needing education, and of excessive wining and dining at annual Conferences. Even post chaises and servants had come into vogue among a section of the Wesleyan ministry.[65] The root of the problem was the fact that itinerant preachers were paid expenses instead of a stipend or a salary.[66] This was tremendously cost-effective, as Wesley had found, when infused by moral excellence, but it was virtually index-linked to the growing aspirations of many preachers. Consequently Pawson believed that much of Kilham's support came from young preachers jealous of the ruling élite, and from a population unwilling to foot the bill for ministerial conveniences. Thus, Kilham struck raw nerves of anti-clericalism and anti-corruption among the more politicized artisans of industrial England. He appealed also to a clique of prosperous laymen unhappy with the clerical bent of Methodist government.

Kilham was expelled from the connexion at the 1796 Conference when it became clear to him what had been explicit in private correspondence for six months – the ministerial leadership closed ranks to defeat 'Methodist Jacobinism'. In the best eighteenth-century radical tradition Kilham claimed that his trial infringed the sacred legal rights of Englishmen.[67] He was not given a list of the charges, he had no advocate, he was not tried by known laws and he was not judged by a jury of the people. (This is virtually a mirror image of claims made by the Wilkites.)[68] He expected this kind of treatment from absolute monarchs and the papal hierarchy, but not from the deliberative assembly of a Protestant religious association in the freest country in Europe.[69] Of course, Kilham's rhetorical exuberance disguised the fact that he had simply been removed from the fellowship of the connexion by his peers for a string of scandalous publications which he refused to retract. Like many radicals of the 1790s, Kilham ruined his cause by exaggerating the extent of the evils and by claiming remedies that were politically impossible to concede. Pawson was right to see him as a well-intentioned but cruel man wielding half-truths with indiscriminate ferocity. Some of these half-truths were nevertheless important. In a parting shot to the Conference, Kilham claimed that Methodism was being run by a coterie of rich preachers with a monopoly of good circuits and London connexions, so that the gap between rich and poor preachers within Wesleyanism was more pronounced than the similar distinction between rectors and curates in the Church of England. Moreover, these preachers protected themselves from criticism by controlling the flow of connexional information through their influence on the Book Committee.[70] More research is needed to determine how much truth there was in these allegations, but the Kilhamite smoke was undoubtedly caused by some kind of fire.

The Conference called Kilham a Painite and a Leveller,[71] which was more or less the same tactic employed by the English government against corresponding societies. Kilham argued with justification that it was in the Wesleyans' interest to speak thus of him, because they needed to convince both the government and their own membership of their determination to expel the radicals. As a result, Kilham, with the support of three preachers, founded the Methodist New Connexion, which immediately creamed off 5 per cent of the Wesleyan membership. It was a much smaller secession than many had feared in 1796, and some of the credit for this must go to the Wesleyan preachers themselves. Not only did they successfully brand Kilham as a revolutionary, but through the moderating counsels of Mather and Pawson some of Kilham's financial and organizational criticisms were dealt with in 1796–7.[72] Besides, by the time the New Connexion got off the ground in 1797 the high tide of popular radicalism had already passed. If external circumstances were no longer as favourable as they had been, the New Connexion soon faced internal problems similar to those of the parent body. Some members drifted back into mainstream Methodism, while others became disillusioned with the limited freedom within the new polity.[73]

The Kilhamite episode left an indelible impression on Wesleyan Methodism and on its relationship with English society. It convinced leading preachers of all shades of political opinion that they had more to fear from popular clamour than from each other's interpretation of virginal Methodism. Moreover, while Kilham's expulsion reduced government fears of Methodist disloyalty, he inadvertently gave a new vocabulary to a whole generation of political radicals who used it to attack Wesleyan conservatism in the nineteenth century. Above all, the Kilhamite secession showed that Methodism had both a remarkable inner consistency and a capacity to translate the political tensions of its environment into ecclesiastical disputes. Hence, the New Connexion was both a religious expression of political radicalism and a reinforcement of the central components of the Wesleyan legacy – Evangelical Arminianism, itinerant ministry and cell groups. Moreover, in spite of the Jacobinical scaremongering of Wesleyan conservatives, the government had little to fear from the general body of Kilhamites, although Baxter has discovered among the Kilhamites in Sheffield 'members of a new physical force radical party dedicated to revolutionary action who were active both in the Despard business of 1802 and in the attempted rising of 1817'.[74] Essentially their objective was to infuse popular religion with democratic sentiments as against the establishmentarian drift of mainstream Methodism. It is almost a Newtonian law of religious organizations that such a drift is always accompanied by, and partly created by, a more self-conscious ministry.

Perhaps the most important legacy of the Kilhamite episode was the recognition by the connexional leadership that numerical growth was not the *supreme* object of Methodist policy. Its willingness to accept numerical losses to preserve discipline was an important step in the direction of ministerial power since it devalued the laity's bargaining power. One could interpret expulsion, therefore, as a means by which preachers could withstand lay pressure. Methodism, unlike the Church of England, was a religious association of like-minded people, which did not have to embrace diverse viewpoints. This was both its strength and its weakness.

The Kilhamite secession did not end the internal difficulties of Methodism in the 1790s, but the scale of conflict in the period 1792–7 was not repeated. Nevertheless, Pawson gave hints for the future when he complained of some preachers being more concerned with chapels than with people, and of a decline in Methodist piety now that the first generation was gone. But there were optimistic signs too, especially in the growing agreement among evangelicals now that the old theological disputes between Arminians and Calvinists were in decline.[75] Yet, ironically, old sores were healed at the same time as the outbreak of a new sectarian spirit. Undenominational unions of itinerant evangelists were formed in the same year as Kilham seceded from the Wesleyan connexion.[76] None the less, some of the major questions facing Methodism in 1791 had been at least partly resolved. It had found some breathing space between the old polarities of Church and Dissent. As a result, it was to be neither a religious association within the Church of England nor a radical political challenge to it. In fact Methodism's conservative inclinations were reinforced in this decade by the fragile nature of English religious toleration, the problems of connexional discipline posed by radicals, and the influence of a more authoritarian ministry.

Table 1   *Methodist growth rates 1789–1801 (per cent)*[77]

1789	3.75
1790	2.60
1791	0.97
1792	3.61
1793	1.05
1794	13.52
1795	8.30
1796	5.62
1797	4.51
1798	2.83
1799	7.61
1800	−0.99
1801	−2.00

While the outline of Methodist internal history in the 1790s is relatively straightforward, two more difficult questions suggest themselves. Despite internal problems why was Methodism able to sustain such rapid growth (see Table 1) in this period and why did the government and the Church of England fail to take effective action against it?

Methodist growth in this period was rapid but extraordinarily uneven. In fact the years 1794–5 and 1800–1 were respectively the best and the worst for Methodism before the mid nineteenth century. Aside from these remarkable fluctuations, the underlying trend is of a movement growing more rapidly than the population itself. Explaining this expansion and its unevenness has occasioned much painstaking research and considerable historical ingenuity, but the results are still inconclusive.

Professor Hobsbawm made the first modern contribution when he stated that Methodism and radicalism grew in roughly the same places at approximately the same time for broadly similar reasons.[78] One was simply a religious, and the other a political, expression of more profound changes in English society. Edward Thompson, while not entirely rejecting that view, offered an alternative hypothesis. He suggested that Methodist revivalism took over at the point of temporal and political defeat and was, therefore, 'a component of the psychic processes of counter revolution'. Thus Methodism is portrayed as 'the chiliasm of the defeated and the hopeless'.[79] This interpretation outraged Thompson's conservative and Methodist opponents, but it has been supported by recent regional studies which have given statistical weight to otherwise more general and individualistic impressions.[80] John Baxter asserts that 'the Great Yorkshire Revival' of 1792–6 coincided with periods of political repression. Moreover, he uncovered some hard evidence for Thompson's oscillation theory in the biographical details of seven committee members of the Sheffield Society for Constitutional Information, the largest and most influential of the provincial reform societies. On his own admission, Baxter's analysis, though statistically well supported, is full of problems. The chronology of oscillation, on which the whole theory depends, is bedevilled by complicated regional time lags as the revival blazed a trail across Yorkshire. He is forced to conclude, therefore, that religious revivals have an internal psychological dynamic of their own, irrespective of the political climate in which they operate.[81] He admits that many more variables need to be taken into account – for example, the charismatic influence of revivalist preachers, and the economic and social dislocation caused by war and urbanization. Nevertheless, Baxter has done enough to suggest that there is still some value in Thompson's interpretation, regardless of its ideological slant.

An entirely different explanation is offered by Professor Ward in *Religion and Society 1790–1850*. In his view the French Revolution was not only crucial for Western political establishments, but also for religious ones. This was certainly true in England, where concepts of Church/State unity were not only theoretically formulated in Burkean language but given practical and economic expression wherever the alliance between squires and clergy had been cemented in the last quarter of the eighteenth century.[82] English society being what it was, therefore, the crisis of authority occurred in religion as well as in politics. Consequently, Ward views Methodism *and* the nationwide growth of county associations for promoting itinerant evangelism as challenges to the paternalistic Anglican establishment. From this perspective popular evangelicalism is seen as a religious expression of radicalism and not an opiate substitute for it. Thus, religious associations eroded the Established Church not by political means, but through the cottage prayer meetings and itinerant preaching of quiet humble people.

The main reason for the different approaches of Thompson and Ward is, of course, ideological. Whereas Thompson assumes that religion by its very nature is inexorably a conservative force, and a pernicious one, Ward seeks to invest popular religion with the same kind of diversity and dignity with which Thompson has already invested popular radicalism. It is also a question of perspective. Contemporary radical leaders thought of Methodism as a conservative deflection from temporal objectives, whereas Anglican Bishops denounced it as a species of ecclesiastical Jacobinism.

These debates have been placed on a firmer statistical foundation by the researches of Robert Currie, Alan Gilbert and Lee Horsley. In explaining patterns of church growth they make a useful distinction between endogenous and exogenous factors. Under the former they list many Methodist advantages such as Arminian theology, cell structure, lay participation, Sunday schools, emotional fervour, sense of community, and effective discipline. Moreover, the link between connexionalism and itinerancy proved to be a particularly successful combination of centralization and localism. Although all these things played their part in Methodist success, the main argument of the book is that 'a church's power to recruit arises from its proximity to, congruity with, and utility for those whom it recruits'.[83] In other words exogenous factors were also important, especially in the 1790s when it is difficult to account for the fluctuations in Methodist growth in any other way; though it is a weakness in their book that endogenous and exogenous factors are not explored in a dynamic relationship with each other. According to the authors the most important exogenous factor in Methodist growth was socio-economic. For example:

During the first four decades of the nineteenth century, artisans, colliers, and miners were very heavily over-represented, merchants, manufacturers and tradesmen somewhat over-represented, labourers rather (and farmers heavily) under-represented, and the aristocracy virtually unrepresented, in the ranks of Nonconformity.[84]

Thus Methodism appealed most to those skilled manual workers, including miners, who dominated the first stage of Britain's Industrial Revolution, while the Nonconformist churches in general were unable to repeat its success with the factory workers of the Victorian period. This helps to explain why the Methodist contribution to trade unionism was strongest in mining areas and weakest in areas dominated by cotton operatives. Again under exogenous factors, the authors conclude that political excitement stimulated Methodist growth, whereas economic depression limited it, because people were unwilling to add religious subscriptions to their other financial burdens in times of hardship, though interestingly Richard Carwardine

arrives at precisely the opposite conclusion in his parallel study of the
Great Awakening in America.[85]

Of course, all these explanations of Methodist growth are not
mutually exclusive, and, taken together, they represent a considerable
improvement on the interpretations offered in the older denominational
histories. Nevertheless, Ward's argument is particularly persuasive
not only because it is based on the widest range of sources and is
therefore the most comprehensive, but because it matches Carwardine's
account of the equally dramatic growth of American Methodism in
the same period. Within a generation Methodism became the largest
American denomination, due to 'the appeal of an Arminian theology
whose individualistic, democratic, and optimistic emphases found a
positive response in an expanding society where traditional patterns
of authority and deference were succumbing to egalitarian challenge'.[86]
This missionary optimism is the main reason why English Methodists
in the mass never surrendered to the millenarian speculations of the
Reformed churches, and gives the lie to Thompson's more general
chiliastic emphasis.[87]

One further reason for Methodist growth, which leads into the
second question posed earlier, is that it was not unduly restrained by
Church or State, despite the concern shown by Churchmen in the
closing years of the eighteenth century. In 1799 Pitt's old tutor and
ecclesiastical confidante, Pretyman-Tomline, Bishop of Lincoln,
commissioned a report on the state of religion in a hundred parishes of
his diocese.[88] The report told a sorry tale of Anglican weakness in the
face of the gradual secularization of rural society and competition
from predominantly Methodist itinerant preaching. Three groups of
Methodists were distinguished: those who professed membership of
the Church of England and attended sacraments within the Church;
those who had gradually moved outside the Established Church and
administered their own sacraments; and those wild men of popular
religion whose ignorance, superstition and anti-establishment rhetoric
made them thoroughly undesirable. They were the Ranters who had
their base in cottage prayer meetings, and who operated most successfully within a highly charged spiritual atmosphere. It was clear
from the report that the first group, if brought within proper discipline,
could be a pietistical asset to the Church of England. The second
group could possibly be brought back within the pale, but the Ranters
were so dangerous that proper control had to be re-established. The
most obvious way to fulfil all these objectives was to stop the
itinerancy.

In the absence of Convocation (no small disadvantage to the Church of England at this juncture), the relatively moderate Lincoln Report was buttressed by more passionate accounts of Methodist extremism in the London periodicals. The revivalistic Methodism of the West Country was a favourite theme. One clerical tourist wrote that

... the mania of Methodism has seized the West of England, and is now spreading at this instant through its remotest parts .... The feelings of the moralist revolt at the prospect; and to the politician also such a view of the Methodists as is here given must be truly alarming. To him are exhibited a vast body of people, many enthusiasts, and many infidels, all alienated from the Church-government, all looking for some great emergencies to liberate them from its restraints, and consequently all rife for rebellion.[89]

To many clergymen Methodism, enthusiasm, atheism and Jacobinism were fruit of the same tree. They were all eroding the ecclesiastical control mechanisms of eighteenth-century English society. Although their analysis was hardly sophisticated their conclusions were broadly correct.

Pressure to re-establish those control mechanisms built up in 1800. The Bishop of Rochester publicly condemned Methodism as a Jacobinical tool,[90] and the Bishop of Llandaff told Pitt that the Church of England needed urgent reform if English religion was to be saved from 'the miserable effusions of enthusiastic ignorance'.[91] The most important ecclesiastical influences on Pitt were, however, the Bishop of Lincoln and William Wilberforce, who fought a personal battle for Pitt's confidence in the spring of 1800. What exactly happened in these months is still shrouded in some mystery, but the fullest and probably most reliable account comes from Wilberforce himself.[92] It appears that the MP for Durham, Michael Angelo Taylor, as a result of a personal confrontation with an 'ignorant and forward' preacher, was determined to tighten up the law on licences for Dissenting preachers. His determination wavered a little when his election agent, who was also the leading Methodist in Durham, and his Dissenting constituents, spelt out the electoral consequences of such action. Taylor withdrew his bill, but it was taken up by the government on the advice of the Bishop of Lincoln. Wilberforce told Pitt that such a measure would create an army of Dissenting martyrs and that the safest policy was to encourage individual denominations to tighten up their internal discipline. In fact nothing was done, probably due to a combination of Wilberforce's influence, the political inconvenience of restricting English Protestant Dissent while attempting to emancipate Irish Catholics, and the pressure of more important business – the Act of Union with Ireland and European peace negotiations. Pawson, who was kept informed in April 1800, stated that the Cabinet withdrew, because the 'Bill was opposed by some Lords and Commoners to whom it was shown in confidence, as bearing too hard on the liberties of the subject'.[93]

On the whole the government was more interested in encouraging Anglican reform than in penalizing Dissenters. But Church reform came up against major problems in the shape of conservative complacency, the vested interests of lay patrons, the large number of impoverished livings and the enormous logistical difficulties of changing such an historic institution. Queen Anne's Bounty did make notable progress after 1802, but ironically its early nineteenth-century treasurer went bankrupt, leaving the Bounty financially and morally embarrassed.[94]

Although nothing was done against the itinerancy in 1800, the psychological impact of the crisis on Methodist leaders was not inconsiderable. They were worried about being bracketed with the Ranters since it was obvious that aristocratic English Cabinets could not be expected to separate the sheep from the goats of non-Anglican religion.[95] Initially Pawson and others responded angrily to the idea of a government shoring up the Anglican establishment by persecuting its competitors, but when the full seriousness of the government's intentions became known he wondered if it was not better 'to give a little than lose all'. This one-time advocate of separate communion was now prepared to abandon Methodist services in Church hours, to give up the sacrament and to reassure the Church of England of Methodist loyalty. He even asked his publishers to expurgate anti-Church sentiments from his sermons. Pawson believed that Methodism was poised to be drawn roughly into the Church, or forced into a more persecuted Dissent.[96] But, as in the 1570s, 1660s and 1680s, there was to be no wider comprehension, because neither Churchmen nor Methodists wanted it, and the state's coercive power in religious matters had been steadily eroded throughout the eighteenth century. In any case, despite the unpopularity of Pitt and the Grenvillites among some Methodist correspondents, they had no real desire to persecute Protestant Dissenters. Control not conflict was the object of their policy. In that respect timely hints of government action against

Methodism in 1793, 1795 and 1800 drew the radical sting out of the connexion, in the same way that many political radicals lost heart after the stern government measures of 1794–5.

To conclude, Methodism's inheritance of Wesley's conservatism was reinforced in the 1790s by government threats from without and radical pressures from within. Moreover, although Methodism had mounted a successful challenge to one religious establishment, it was, through its preachers, chapels, and desire for respectability, well on the way to creating another.[97]

References

1   W. R. Ward, 'The religion of the people and the problem of control, 1790–1830', *Studies in Church History*, **8** (1972), pp. 237–57.

2   See Edward Royle, *Victorian Infidels: The Origins of the British Secularist Movement 1791–1866* (Manchester 1974); and Susan Budd, *Varieties of Unbelief: Atheists and Agnostics in English Society 1850–1960* (London 1977).

3   Hugh McLeod, *Religion and the People of Western Europe 1789–1970* (Oxford 1981), p. 16.

4   See James Obelkevich, *Religion and Rural Society: South Lindsey 1825–1875* (London 1976).

5   For a recent history of the Dissenting interest in this period see Albert Goodwin, *The Friends of Liberty: The English Democratic Movement in the Age of the French Revolution* (London 1979), ch. 3.

6   V. Kiernan, 'Evangelicalism and the French Revolution', *Past and Present*, no. 1 (1952), pp. 44–56; and W. R. Ward, *Religion and Society in England 1790–1850* (London 1972), pp. 1–53.

7   John Walsh, 'Methodism at the end of the eighteenth century', in Rupert Davies and Gordon Rupp (eds.), *A History of the Methodist Church in Great Britain* (London 1965), vol. 1, p. 304.

8   M.C.A.Mss., John Pawson to Charles Atmore, 21 March 1794.

9   M.C.A.Mss., John Pawson to Charles Atmore, 22 December 1792.

10   Walsh, p. 304.

11   M.C.A.Mss., John Pawson to Joseph Benson, 25 November 1797.

12   M.C.A.Mss., John Pawson to Joseph Benson, 20 April 1796, 6 May 1796, 19 May 1796, and Pawson to Charles Atmore, 24 February 1800.

13   M.C.A.Mss., Samuel Bradburn to Richard Rodda, 7 December 1791, 19 April 1792, John Pawson to Joseph Benson, 4 July 1791, 27 June 1794, 15 December 1794.

14   Walsh, p. 287.

15   M.C.A.Mss., John Pawson to Joseph Benson, 4 July 1791.

16   M.C.A.Mss., John Pawson to Joseph Benson, 4 May 1791.

17   M.C.A.Mss., John Pawson to Joseph Benson, 12 October 1793.
18   M.C.A.Mss., William Thompson to Richard Rodda, 8 February 1792, 29 May 1792 and 31 May 1792.
19   Ward, *Religion and Society*, pp. 28–9.
20   M.C.A.Mss., Samuel Bradburn to Richard Rodda, 7 December 1791, 4 January 1792, 19 April 1792, and 23 June 1792.
21   M.C.A.Mss., ibid.; and William Thompson to Richard Rodda, 8 February 1792, 29 May 1792, 31 May 1792, and 3 August 1793.
22   M.C.A.Mss., John Pawson to Joseph Benson, 15 October 1792; Pawson to Charles Atmore, 5 November 1792, and 22 December 1792.
23   Ward, *Religion and Society*, p. 29.
24   M.C.A.Mss., all this is recorded in a letter from Pawson to Charles Atmore, 22 February 1793.
25   M.C.A.Mss., Alexander Mather sent copies of these letters to John Pawson. See Pawson to Charles Atmore 14 February 1793.
26   M.C.A.Mss., John Pawson to Charles Atmore, 5 November 1792.
27   M.C.A.Mss., Joseph Benson to Thomas Coke, 19 August 1794.
28   M.C.A.Mss., John Pawson to Joseph Benson, 20 June, 27 June, 24 September, 2 October, 9 October, 21 November, 28 November, all 1794. Pawson to Charles Atmore, 18 October 1794. Joseph Benson to Thomas Coke, 19 August 1794. The Bristol Society to Benson, 28 August, and 4 September 1794. Benson notes July 1794. James Creighton to Benson, 8 October 1794. Richard Rodda to Benson, 1 September 1794.
29   M.C.A.Mss., Thomas Coke *et al.* to Joseph Benson, 1 September 1794.
30   M.C.A.Mss., Benson's notes, July 1794, sections e and f.
31   M.C.A.Mss., Adam Clarke to George Marsden, 30 August 1794, and 8 January 1795.
32   Ward, *Religion and Society*, p. 33.
33   R. W. Davis, *Dissent in Politics 1780–1830: The Political Life of William Smith, M.P.* (London 1971), p. 88.
34   Goodwin, ch. 10.
35   M.C.A.Mss., Samuel Bradburn to Mr Reynolds, 12 April 1796. See also, Bernard Semmel, *The Methodist Revolution* (London 1974), pp. 120–4.
36   In many parts of northern England in this period communion services and Love Feasts acted as collective testimonies to the power of Methodist revivalism. See Ward, *Religion and Society*, p. 32; and John Baxter, 'The Great Yorkshire Revival 1792–6: a study of mass revival among the Methodists', in Michael Hill (ed.), *A Sociological Yearbook of Religion in Britain* (1974), vol. 7, pp. 46–76.
37   M.C.A.Mss., Adam Clarke to George Marsden, 30 August 1794, and 8 January 1795.

38   M.C.A.Mss., Samuel Bradburn to John Stonehouse, 8 November 1794.

39   M.C.A.Mss., Samuel Bradburn to Thomas Coke, 17 April 1794; and John Pawson to Charles Atmore, 8 April 1794.

40   M.C.A.Mss., John Pawson to Joseph Benson, 8 January, 5 March, 27 March and 5 April 1795.

41   M.C.A.Mss., John Pawson to Joseph Benson, 24 June 1795.

42   Ward, *Religion and Society*, p. 33.

43   Alexander Kilham, *The Progress of Liberty amongst the people called Methodists. To which is added the Out-Lines of a Constitution* (Alnwick 1795), p. 17.

44   Walsh, p. 288.

45   Aspects of this compromise are made clear by J. C. Bowmer, *Pastor and People* (London 1975), pp. 34–6.

46   ibid., pp. 19–67.

47   ibid., pp. 35, 52.

48   Kilham, *The Progress of Liberty*, pp. 1–60.

49   Walsh, p. 307.

50   M.C.A.Mss., John Pawson to Charles Atmore, 15 July 1795.

51   E. R. Taylor, *Methodism and Politics 1791–1851* (Cambridge 1935), p. 72.

52   Semmel, p. 120.

53   W. H. Daniels, *A Short History of the People called Methodists* (London 1882), p. 392.

54   E. P. Thompson, *The Making of the English Working Class* (London 1963), pp. 44–6.

55   Paul and Silas (Kilham), *An Earnest Address to the Preachers Assembled in Conference* (Manchester 1795), p. 19.

56   M.C.A.Mss., Thomas Coke to Joseph Benson, 21 December 1795.

57   M.C.A.Mss., Thomas Coke to Joseph Benson, 6 February 1796.

58   M.C.A.Mss., John Pawson to Charles Atmore, 24 February 1796.

59   M.C.A.Mss., Samuel Bradburn to Mr Reynolds, 12 April 1796.

60   Ward, *Religion and Society*, p. 35.

61   A. Kilham, *A Candid Examination of the London Methodistical Bull* (Alnwick 1796).

62   M.C.A.Mss., John Pawson to Joseph Benson, 14 March 1796.

63   M.C.A.Mss., John Pawson to Joseph Benson, 22 and 28 January 1796; and Pawson to Charles Atmore, 24 February 1796.

64   M.C.A.Mss., John Pawson to Charles Atmore, 21 October 1796.

65   M.C.A.Mss., John Pawson to Joseph Benson, 6 May, 19 May, 3 June, 9 and 14 September 1796.

66   M.C.A.Mss., John Pawson to Charles Atmore, 4 July 1797.

67   For popular attitudes to the law see John Brewer and John Styles (eds.), *An Ungovernable People: The English and their law in the seventeenth and eighteenth centuries* (London 1980).

68 John Brewer, 'The Wilkites and the law, 1763–74: a study of radical notions of governance', in Brewer and Styles (eds.), pp. 128–71.

69 A. Kilham, *An Account of the Trial of Alexander Kilham, Methodist Preacher, before the General Conference in London* (Nottingham 1796).

70 ibid., p. 51.

71 A. Mather, J. Pawson and J. Benson, *A Defence of the Conduct of the Conference in the Expulsion of Alexander Kilham. Addressed to the Methodist Societies* (n.p., n.d.).

72 M.C.A.Mss., John Pawson to Joseph Benson, 14 March, 24 March, 13 April, 1 June, and 19 October 1797. Pawson to Charles Atmore, 8 May, 25 May, and 4 July 1797. See also, Thomas Hanby, *An Explanation of Mr. Kilham's Statement of the Preacher's Allowance, intended for the perusal of all Well-Wishers to Methodism* (Nottingham 1796). It must be said, however, that Methodist leaders were better at noting Kilham's criticisms than dealing with them.

73 See J. T. Wilkinson, 'The rise of other Methodist traditions', in R. Davies, A. R. George and G. Rupp (eds.), *A History of the Methodist Church in Great Britain* (London 1978), vol. 2, pp. 280–94.

74 Baxter, p. 76.

75 M.C.A.Mss., John Pawson to Joseph Benson, 24 May 1797, and 9 April 1798.

76 Ward, *Religion and Society*, p. 49.

77 Taken from R. Currie, A. Gilbert and L. Horsley, *Churches and Churchgoers: Patterns of Church Growth in the British Isles since 1700* (Oxford 1977), p. 40.

78 E. J. Hobsbawm, *Labouring Men* (London 1964), pp. 23–33.

79 Thompson, pp. 381–2.

80 Baxter, pp. 46–76; and P. Stigant, 'Wesleyan Methodism and working-class radicalism in the North', *Northern History*, **6** (1971), pp. 98–116.

81 This is also the opinion of Richard Carwardine in *Trans-atlantic Revivalism: Popular Evangelicalism in Britain and America, 1790–1865* (Westport, Connecticut 1978), p. 56.

82 See also McCleod, p. 25.

83 Currie *et al.*, p. 90.

84 ibid., p. 56.

85 Carwardine, p. 56.

86 ibid., p. 10.

87 Thompson more or less concedes this point in the postscript to the Penguin edition of his book (1968), p. 919. See also my 'Evangelicalism and eschatology', *Journal of Ecclesiastical History*, **31** no. 2 (1980), pp. 179–94.

88 See J. H. Overton and F. Relton, *The English Church from the Accession of George 1 to the end of the Eighteenth Century* (London 1906),

pp. 262–4; and Ward, *Religion and Society*, p. 47.

89　*The Gentleman's Magazine*, **70** part 1 (1800), p. 241.

90　*The Gentleman's Magazine*, **70** part 2 (1800), p. 1077.

91　PRO, W. D. Adams Mss., The Bishop of Llandaff to William Pitt, 16 April 1800.

92　R. I. and S. Wilberforce, *The Life of Wilberforce* (London 1838), vol. 2, pp. 360–5; and John Pollock, *Wilberforce* (London 1977), p. 179.

93　M.C.A.Mss., John Pawson to Joseph Benson, 24 April 1800.

94　G. F. A. Best, *Temporal Pillars* (Cambridge 1964), pp. 224–5.

95　M.C.A.Mss., Adam Clarke to George Marsden, 8 April 1800.

96　M.C.A.Mss., John Pawson to Joseph Benson, 7 April, 15 April, and 24 April 1800.

97　M.C.A.Mss., John Pawson to Charles Atmore, 12 February 1802, and to Benson, 23 August 1802.

4 Conservatism through conflict, 1800–20

The conservative course set by Wesleyan Methodism through the upheavals of the 1790s was not altered in this period, but its pace quickened and it affected many more people both inside and outside the connexion. The reason for this is that pressure from the government (1810–12) and from the radicals (1812–20) became more serious. In addition there were two relatively new areas of conflict – the fight for control of the Sunday schools and the challenge mounted by revivalists to Methodism's internal discipline. So pervasive were the problems that it is hard to think of a single geographical area in town or country untouched by them. Indeed, many of the social tensions of a rapidly changing environment were at once absorbed, reflected and expressed in these apparently trivial but, in the localities, all-important disputes. Whereas in the 1790s, with the notable exception of the sacraments controversy, connexional disagreements were the concern of an influential minority, in this period the relationship between preachers and laymen, Conference and localities, politics and religion, and denominational control and free enterprise, became matters of general interest throughout the country. As a result non-Methodists, especially radicals with an anti-clerical bent, became more informed about the internal dynamics of the Methodist polity. But perhaps the most important consequence of this period for Methodism itself was the way in which conflict produced denominational consciousness, and threw up, in the person of Jabez Bunting, the connexion's first great ecclesiastical administrator.

Symbolically, perhaps, the period 1800–20 began with Thomas Coke acting as a self-appointed spy for the Home Office in the manufacturing districts,[1] and ended with the Manchester circuit superintendent declaring holy war against the radicals within his territory.

To all party politics the author feels himself superior; but when the contest is between a vile demagogue and his venerable king; between anarchy and social order; between modern infidelity and the creed of his fathers; he never wishes to dissemble; he covets not the ignoble slumbers of neutrality; he would blow the sacred trumpet, to call Jehovah's hosts to battle; and manfully unfurl the banners of his Country, his Sovereign, and his God.[2]

In between these extremes there were countless minor skirmishes which can be analysed under four headings: the struggle for control of the Sunday schools; problems of expansion; pressure from the government; and the response to political radicalism. For convenience these will be treated separately, but they happened contemporaneously, and interacted with one another to increase the social gap between mainstream Methodism and working-class Englishmen.

Sunday schools

The growth of Sunday schools from their paternalistic and evangelical origins in English provinces in the 1780s to their Victorian heyday is one of the most important themes not just of English educational history but of working-class culture in its widest sense. As Professor Laqueur has demonstrated, by 1851 there were over two million Sunday scholars, representing 75 per cent of working-class children between the ages of 5 and 15.[3] In economic terms at least it is not difficult to see why Sunday schools were attractive to the working classes in the period of the Industrial Revolution, because they were cheap and did not affect children's earning power during the week. In the northern manufacturing towns, therefore, Sunday schools seemed the ideal solution to the breakdown of old and inadequate educational opportunities due to population growth, migration, mass poverty, and the gradual change from domestic to factory work.[4] But Sunday education was not solely an urban phenomenon. Indeed, the surprising feature of recent work on the geographical distribution of Sunday schools is that counties like Bedfordshire, Cornwall and Dorset are as far up the league table of *per capita* enrolment as Lancashire and the West Riding of Yorkshire.[5]

The traditional picture of the northern Nonconformist Sunday school is not entirely mistaken, however, for it was in the manufacturing districts that such schools made their most distinctive contribution to working-class culture. Anniversary celebrations, street parades, Whitsun outings, tea meetings, reading books and prizes, sick and benefit societies, clothing clubs and teachers' meetings all gained a foothold in English society through the instrumentality of Sunday schools. Moreover, these activities attracted a loyal band of activists whose lives were transformed by the weekly rhythms of preparation, prayer and planning. Laqueur catches the flavour of this culture in the early Victorian period.

The five years between 1838 and 1843 saw not only the publication of the People's Charter, the Newport risings and the Plug Riots but also a parade in Bolton of 12,000 working-class children celebrating the Queen's coronation. In 1841 as Chartist agitation was growing, 1,500 children of Blackburn marched out of the town on Easter Monday for a day of pleasure . . . . The 'Age of the Chartists' witnessed scenes like that of the banker Joseph Gurney standing on the platform of Norwich waving to 5,000 Sunday school scholars as their train left the station. The children responded by singing 'The Fine Old English Gentleman' to the music of the band.[6]

In its own way the recently demolished Stockport Sunday school, a great northern cathedral which accommodated 6000 people at its peak, is as symbolic of the English Industrial Revolution as are the Manchester mills or the Crystal Palace exhibition.

The precise nature of the relationship between Sunday schools and working-class life is, as one would expect, a matter of considerable disagreement. In opposition to the prevailing orthodoxy which sees Sunday schools as evangelical and bourgeois instruments of social control, Laqueur concludes that 'predominantly working-class students were taught primarily by working-class teachers in schools largely financed, and sometimes also run, by working-class men and women'.[7] Although he has to explain away some of his own evidence to arrive at his conclusion, Laqueur boldly states that the divisions of early nineteenth-century society were not primarily between the middle and working classes, but between the idle and the industrious, the rough and the respectable, the religious and the irreligious. This attempt to see the socially divisive aspects of religious and moral values in vertical rather than horizontal terms parallels similar work on pre-industrial English communities, but it underestimates the way in which the social pressures of industrialization could divide even the respectable and the religious along the lines of class.[8] Nevertheless, Laqueur's general argument about the working-class ethos of many Sunday schools has received support from two local studies of popular education in Leeds and Spitalfields. Sunday schools in Spitalfields, one of the poorest and most populous districts of London, had, like dame schools, 'the aura of being organized by and for the people, which the charity and monitorial schools totally lacked'.[9] The people referred to, however, appear to have been the industrious sort; whether religious or radical or both, and not the destitute poor, many of whom were actively hostile to any kind of education. In Leeds the working-class community, including the teachers, united in opposition to the new controls imposed by denominational leaders;[10] though once again it seems to have been the industrious and radical sections of the working classes who got involved in the conflict with the Wesleyan preachers.

The idea that Sunday schools were indigenous to working-class culture has not met with universal favour. In a swingeing attack on Laqueur's methodology and evidence, Malcolm Dick states that 'Sunday schools were evangelical and conservative institutions, promoted and staffed by individuals from social classes which were higher than those of the scholars who attended them, and espousing an ideology which attacked the allegedly depraved behaviour and radical inclinations of the poor'. More modestly, Gail Malmgreen, in an excellent local study of Macclesfield, has shown that most teachers were drawn from a somewhat higher social level than their pupils, or were men who used education as a means of self-advancement.[11] Such disagreements may, of course, reflect genuine regional differences, and certainly do reflect the colourful diversity of the Sunday schools themselves, the incompleteness of the research, and the difficulty of using class terminology to describe a complex pattern of social relationships. It is possible, however, to arrive at some firm conclusions.

There can be no doubt that Sunday schools were begun in the 1780s by men committed to godliness and good learning as instruments of control in an environment that was becoming more alarming due to increases in population, crime, vagrancy, geographical mobility and radicalism. Unlike institutional religion, however, Sunday schools offered the working classes tangible benefits, provided they could be suitably amended to their tastes. The necessary conditions included the replacement of professional teachers by home-grown talent, the maintenance of local autonomy against denominational encroachment, the extension of the curriculum beyond pious catechisms and the integration of Sunday schools into the life of the local community. Of course these aims were not uniformly realized, especially after the 1830s when the religious denominations tightened up their discipline, but enough was achieved to make the Sunday school 'the only religious institution which the nineteenth century public in the mass had any intention of using'.[12]

Although they began as crumbs from the rich man's table, Sunday schools were numerically successful in nineteenth-century England because the working classes were able to turn the crumbs into digestible bread. The prize was literacy[13] and self-improvement, and the price was a dose of religion and paternalism. But the price was never paid in full, because 'only between 1.5 and 4 per cent of total Sunday school enrolment would at any one time belong to a church or chapel'.[14] In short, if the working classes were exploited during England's Industrial Revolution then their attitude to Sunday schools showed that they had learned something from their masters. What started off as straightforward social control ended up, for radical leaders like Bamford, Cooper, Lovett, Tillett and a host of others, as social education.[15] The fact that Sunday schools were equally opposed by ultra-evangelicals and Tories, who opposed the education of humble people beyond their station, and radicals, who thought they were establishment devices, shows that Sunday schools were social hybrids catering for those elements within the working classes that were neither acquiescent nor revolutionary.

The very success of Sunday schools was to some extent their undoing, because they were seen, from an early stage, as political and ecclesiastical prizes worth fighting for. In origin most Sunday schools were undenominational. In Manchester, for example, Anglicans, Dissenters (including Unitarians), and Roman Catholics all contributed money and prayers to the schools launched in 1784.[16] Within a decade undenominational schools were established all over the north of England – in Stockport, Macclesfield, Leek, Colne, Bacup, Burslem, Rochdale, Leeds, Bingley and so on. The seeds of future denominational conflict were, however, there from the beginning, because predictable questions had to be answered. Who should run the schools? Which liturgies should be used? Was extempore prayer admissible? Where would the children worship? These and other questions caused denominational conflict in Birmingham five years before the infamous Church-and-King riots of 1791. Interdenominational co-operation was, therefore, only skin deep from the beginning, but in comparison with what came after, the period 1780–1800 was an ecumenical golden age. By the beginning of the nineteenth century the bitter struggles for control of Sunday schools, both between and within denominations, was probably a more common feature of northern English life than the more publicized re-emergence of the radical political clubs.

The growth of a more rigid denominationalism can easily be followed through the eyes of the Methodists, who were particularly active in the early stages of the Sunday school movement and who accounted for 30 per cent of all Sunday scholars by 1851. (Anglicans had 42 per cent and other Nonconformists of all types had 28 per cent of the total.) At the end of the eighteenth century a powerful combination of Anglican exclusivity (partly for political reasons), and Methodist self-confidence (because of remarkable growth), resulted in mutual allegations of denominational imperialism and proselytism. In Manchester inter-denominational co-operation began to collapse before the end of the century, but elsewhere the pace was slower. Even by 1805 Jabez Bunting, who became the leading Wesleyan advocate of denominational Sunday schooling was able to extol the advantages of ' extensive co-operation' to the genteel subscribers of the Sunday School Union. Contrasting Scottish virtue with Irish depravity, Bunting argued that education accounted for the difference, and that the fields of England were now white unto harvest.[17] Competition for this harvest encouraged both energy and greed among the labourers. As a result denominational rivalry probably increased Sunday school provision in the shortrun,[18] but in the longrun it simply added to working-class dissatisfaction with institutional religion.

Bunting's expansive optimism gave way to a narrower sectarian temper when he spoke against undenominational schooling at a meeting of Manchester Methodists in 1826.

(1)   There was no *security*, either by *creed*, or in the *deeds* of those schools, that pure Christianity should be perpetuated in them; for the deeds in particular did not promote this.

(2)   They were unconnected with any church, perfectly independent of any, and might become Roman Catholic, Calvinistic, Socinian, or any other schools.

(3)   He objected to children of Methodists belonging to them, for they were given to the body in baptism, the subjects of Methodistical labour from the pulpit. It was proper that every chapel should have its school.[19]

The reasons for this change of approach are not hard to find. Letters coming into Bunting from preachers in the manufacturing districts show increasing dissatisfaction with undenominational Sunday schools, because they were patronized by radicals and heretics, gave too much power to the laity, were used as proselytizing instruments by other denominations and failed to recruit new members for the chapels.[20] All these disadvantages were held to be, and probably were, linked with one another. Bunting and his supporters tried to bring Sunday schools under Conference control by introducing preachers on to local management committees and by drawing up a list of detailed regulations for the operation of all the Wesleyan schools. The subsequent battle for control of the Sunday schools reflected many of the tensions in early nineteenth-century society, including class conflict, anti-clericalism, anti-centralization and sectarianism. They all crystallized over the apparently trivial issue of teaching children how to write on the sabbath.

Bunting's opposition to Sunday writing lessons after 1807 was based not so much on a desire to keep the working classes ignorant as on an evangelical preoccupation with Lord's Day Observance. This rigid sabbatarianism among a section of evangelicalism was based on the feeling that 'some quite arbitrary set of social conventions must be enforced in order to set apart the day traditionally allocated to public worship in an age when fewer and fewer of the working classes were bothering to attend church'.[21] But Bunting's sabbatarianism also had class overtones, because his alternative to secular instruction on Sundays was night school. This showed scant regard for the harsh realities of factory work which left little time for anything else. Night schools attracted only a physically and intellectually tough minority,[22] though this kind of élitism no doubt matched the Wesleyan drive for respectability in their chapels.

The length of the Wesleyan campaign against sabbath writing and the numerous resolutions against it testify to the effectiveness of local resistance to Conference policy.[23] Eventually Bunting and his supporters won control and by the 1840s most Wesleyan Sunday schools, especially in the big urban centres, no longer taught writing on Sundays. It was, however, a costly victory. Not only did the conflict reopen old sores within the connexion, as well as creating some new ones,[24] but it was well known in English localities that the Wesleyans were against secular instruction on Sundays, whereas Primitive and New Connexion Methodists, Unitarians and some others, continued the practice. The obvious inference was drawn by the English working classes.

The struggle for control of the Sunday schools showed that the Wesleyans were unable to remodel undenominational schools in their own image; they could only fracture them and brush some of the pieces into their own connexion. Moreover, the way all denominations tried to use Sunday education for recruitment purposes promised ill for any kind of state interference in week-day schooling. In that respect the infamous 'religious difficulty' in the way of national elementary education in the Victorian period had its origins in the Sunday school controversies at the end of the eighteenth century.

Problems of expansion

How Methodism should grow and where it should grow were questions that troubled the connexional leadership in the years 1800–20 almost as much as they have troubled historians ever since. The basic facts of how and when the Primitive Methodist connexion and the Methodist Missionary Society got off the ground are clear enough, but understanding these developments in a proper denominational and social context has proved rather more difficult. Professor Ward's analysis of Methodism and revivalism has stood up well to the 'new awakening' of historians' interest in this intriguing aspect of trans-Atlantic evangelical culture in the eighteenth and nineteenth centuries. Ward's argument is that up to 1820 (though rather later in Cornwall because of its distinctive mining culture) social tensions were 'sublimated in religious revival', and that the crude informality of provincial revivalists challenged the respectable ecclesiastical ambitions of a Wesleyan élite based on wealth, connexions and education. This élite responded to revivalistic enthusiasm with the attitude that 'what was needed was less revival and more denominational drill'; less expansion and more consolidation. Thus, Ranterism, which challenged Wesleyanism hard where it 'teetered between form and formalism', encouraged the very thing it was reacting against – a more rigid denominationalism.[25] This interpretation does not need much alteration, but new work on the lower echelons of English religious culture in this period suggests some modifications.

The fine line dividing acceptable mass evangelism from revivalistic excesses is one that worried Wesleyan preachers in the 1790s as much as it had, on occasions, worried Wesley himself. In fact, this has been a recurring difficulty in the history of that wing of Protestantism which has been, and still is, evangelistically aggressive. Such unease as existed, however, was tempered by the glorious figures of Methodist growth and the centrality, among Wesleyan revivalists at least, of those distinctively Methodist instruments of itinerant preaching and Love Feasts. While the source of revival could be attributed to divine power, and while the means were in the authentic Wesleyan tradition, then scruples were less important than results. But as revivalism became superimposed on revival, uneasy consciences were stirred. For example, the private accounts of the great Yorkshire revival of the mid 1790s by Joseph Entwistle, whose wisdom and simple devotion were admired by many, convey the tension of a man committed to revival but disturbed by the means.

The Lord has poured out his spirit plenteously in the Halifax circuit. They have added upwards of three hundred new members the last quarter: most of whom, so far as they can judge at present are justified. Their meetings are frequently noisy and long continued, often till midnight, frequently till morning. It is not unusual for persons to be crying out in distress in various parts of the chapel, and others praying for them. Now a number of stout fellows, kneeling around a sinner in distress, cry aloud, 'Come Lord Jesus, come quickly'. Anon, the captive being set free, they seem to shake the very house with crying, 'Glory be to God'. The noise and confusion sometimes are very great, and one could wish it otherwise; yet, as the preachers see hundreds of sinners turning from the error of their ways, they say little to put a stop to it.

Our warm friends from Woodhouse were there: they had gone beyond all bounds of decency, such screaming and bawling I never heard. Divided into small companies in different parts of the chapel, some singing, others praying, others praising, clapping of hands, etc, all was confusion and uproar. I was struck with amazement and consternation. What to do I could not tell. However, as there appeared to be no possibility of breaking up the meeting, I quietly withdrew. They continued thus until five o'clock in the morning. What shall I say to these things? I believe God is working very powerfully on the minds of many; but I think Satan, or, at least, the animal nature, has a great hand in all this.[26]

To theological doubts, were added political pressures when the government and the Church of England became more concerned about Methodist extremism. Adam Clarke, the most eminent scholar in the connexion wrote in 1800 that

. . . there is a bill about to be brought into Parliament, which from its complexion bids fair if made a law of, to annihilate our Root and our Branch. Probably you have seen the pamphlet published against us by the Bishop of Lincoln and 79 of his clergy. It appears that idle mad vagabonds called *Colliers* have been thro that district pretending to *exorcise* etc., and have subjected the genuine worth of God to much calumny and reproach.[27]

By the turn of the century Methodist preachers realized that the evangelistic energies which they had themselves unleashed were beginning to rebound on them. The problem was made worse by two additional factors, both of which were products of Methodist success. First, American Methodism which was at this time trying to introduce frontier-style revivalism into eastern cities introduced also, in the form of Lorenzo Dow, the first American revivalist to visit British shores. Second, Methodist revivalistic off-shoots in Britain showed their true Methodist colours by trying to organize themselves into some kind of connexional system.[28]

Crazy Dow, the asthmatic and epileptic son of a Connecticut farmer, cut an extraordinary figure with his 'long hair, thin face, flashing eyes, stooped shoulders, harsh voice, crude gestures and unkempt dress'.[29] With typical aplomb he made his crusading debut in Ireland in the immediate aftermath of the '98 rebellion. His mission was to take on Irish Catholicism virtually single-handed. Dow's career in Ireland was an illuminating preview of later events in England. The Irish Methodists were split between the respectable men in Dublin who wanted nothing to do with the 'Quakerised evangelist', and those in the countryside who admired his style and his success. Dow's republican politics and frequent brushes with authority, including a spell in Belfast gaol, convinced Dr Coke that he was superfluous to Irish needs. After failing to persuade him that his real calling was to missionary work in northern Canada, Coke threatened to report him to Lord Castlereagh, and eventually subscriptions were raised to send him back from whence he came.[30]

With almost impeccable timing, Dow arrived in Liverpool on Christmas Eve 1805. Bringing with him the good news of American camp meetings, which by this time had been reported in the *Wesleyan Methodist Magazine*, Dow soon made contact with an indigenous tradition of revivalistic Methodists in Lancashire, Cheshire and the Potteries. They included James Crawfoot and the Magic Methodists of Delamere Forest, Peter Phillips and the Quaker Methodists of Warrington, and Hugh Bourne and the Harriseahead colliers. Generally speaking, revivalism flourished either in very cohesive communities or among the rural immigrants to the northern industrial towns. Groups were usually led by small tradesmen with only a smattering of secular education but with a spiritually intense knowledge of the Bible. Most of the groups were beyond the control of institutions of any kind and the result was a powerful concoction of social protest laced with supernatural stimulants.[31] This quite humble religious culture threw up a kaleidoscope of spiritual experiences from camp meetings to exorcisms, and from divine interventions to celestial visions. In fact, it was on this level that Methodist splinter groups came closest to that even more bizarre subculture of popular millenarianism that was strong in the same areas and among the same social classes.[32] (Millenarian groups were, however, strong in London which was not an important centre of Methodist revivalism.)

It was when revivalist groups posed similar problems within Methodism as Methodism had itself posed for the Church of England (separate chapels, connexional system and distinctive worship) that many preachers converted unease into outright opposition. Foremost among these was Jabez Bunting who, as is well known, was linked with Manchester revivalists in his early preaching career. But the legacy of a Unitarian education, dinner-party theological discussions and bad personal experiences of revivalists in Macclesfield convinced him that Methodism was better off without the Ranters. Bunting's views on revivalism, from which he never departed, were clearly expressed in response to the visit of a local preacher to a revivalist meeting in Macclesfield.

He preached in the room occupied by the Christian Revivalists last night, to a congregation larger indeed than their own ordinary one, but not numerous in proportion either to the size of the town or to the pains which had been taken to induce the people to attend. I am told he was uncommonly flat and low spirited. They will not be able; I am pretty sure, to do much harm, if any, in Macclesfield. The people in this Town are tired of parties and divisions: and in general equally tired of the rant and extravagancies of what is called revivalism.

...Divisions *from* the church, though awful are perhaps after all less to be dreaded than divisions *in* the Church, which, I fear, would have been perpetuated, if these men had remained among us. I therefore hope that their separation will be over-ruled – for good – revivalism, as of late professed and practised was [likely if] not checked to have gradually ruined genuine Methodism. I am glad, however, that they have been the first to draw the sword. But as they have drawn it, I earnestly wish that our Preachers would take the opportunity of returning fully to the spirit and discipline of ancient Methodism and with that resolve to stand or fall. The temporary loss of numbers would probably be more than recompensed by the increase of real, scriptural piety, the restoration of good order, and the establishment of brotherly love.[33]

There are, of course, in these comments the marks of Bunting the doctrinaire interpreter of the Methodist tradition and of Bunting the ecclesiastical disciplinarian, but he was also making an informed calculation about the long-term value of revivalist methods. From other letters it is clear that what Bunting desired was a marriage between vital religion and educated opinions, because in his view revivalism was not only divisive but also silly and degrading. What has not been made clear enough is that Bunting was reflecting the views of a majority of Wesleyan preachers who were nevertheless still interested in revival, properly understood.[34] It is not hard to see how young men with some theological knowledge felt they were in danger of jumping out of the frying pan of Anglican stiffness into the fire of revivalistic excesses.

Wesleyan leaders made an error of judgement in their treatment of revivalists in the period 1803–10. In their eagerness to oppose a religious tradition that owed as much to Quaker ideas of divine illumination as it did to Wesleyan Methodism, they reacted too indiscriminately. More educated analysis, not less, would have shown them that there was a crucial difference between the temporary outbreaks of zealous individualism in some northern towns and the massive rural support for Primitive Methodism that reflected important social changes in the early nineteenth-century English countryside.[35] In short, Bunting and the preachers of his generation thought too much of revivalism as a monolithic entity rather than as something which had within it degrees of acceptability and unacceptability.

As with Kilham so with Hugh Bourne and William Clowes, the Wesleyan leadership decided that the best method of control was expulsion, but it was as much an expulsion of religious styles as it was of people. Consequently another Methodist group, the Primitive Methodists, developed outside the main connexion,[36] thereby exacerbating the very denominationalism that gave rise to them. Those leading the Wesleyans could still claim with conviction to be in the authentic Methodist tradition, but it was by 1810 considerably narrower than it had been in 1790.

The other problem of expansion facing the Wesleyans in the early nineteenth century was how to conduct their foreign missions. From Wesley's death until 1813 Methodist overseas missions came under the personal superintendency of Thomas Coke, who combined remarkable zeal with equally remarkable administrative incompetence. At the turn of the century, despite Coke's anti-Calvinism, there was a reasonable amount of co-operation with the interdenominational, but largely Calvinistic, London Missionary Society.

Geographical competition overseas and financial competition at home damaged this fragile relationship, and led to a revival of old controversies between Arminians and Calvinists. By 1813, with the ageing Coke about to sail on his last voyage, the time was ripe for Wesleyan Methodists to bring foreign missions under stricter denominational control.

The motivation behind the establishment of the first Methodist Missionary Society in Leeds in 1813 has been disputed by historians. According to Semmel, a powerful section of the Wesleyan leadership quite deliberately redirected Methodist energies overseas because it was politically unsafe and connexionally undesirable to allow uncontrolled growth at home.[37] Sidmouth's threats and undisciplined revivalism thus combined to convince preachers like Bunting and Watson that the encouragement of foreign missions was by far the safest policy. Although Semmel's interpretation fits well into the ideological framework of his book, it does not square with his own evidence, nor with the facts.

In reality, the formation of provincial Methodist missionary societies owed more to expansive optimism than to nervous insecurity. Napoleon's disasters in Russia and Wellington's triumphs in the Peninsula encouraged a formidable combination of millennialism and imperialism among English evangelicals.[38] Sensing the mood of the nation, the London Missionary Society and the Church Missionary Society cranked their local machinery into gear. So successful was the West Riding branch of the LMS in gaining subscriptions from Methodist chapels in 1813 that the local Wesleyan preachers decided to put a stop to it.[39] That Bunting was behind the formation of the new missionary society there can be no doubt, but his initiative struck a chord within a connexion that was proud of its missionary record, yet fearful lest Calvinistic Dissenters should step in and claim the glory. In essence, Bunting told the LMS in the West Riding to keep its hands off Wesleyan money. Thus, far from being a deflection from domestic expansion as Semmel suggests or a result of Bunting's ecumenism as Piggin has it,[40] the Methodist Missionary Society had its origins in the same denominational rivalry that affected all aspects of religious life in the first half of the nineteenth century.

In conclusion, the expulsion of revivalists and the formation of provincial missionary societies were not inspired by attitudes of domestic retrenchment. Rather, the young preachers of Bunting's generation were frightened by revivalistic excesses on the one hand, and of being elbowed out of the international missionary movement on the other. The result of both fears was tighter denominational discipline – not to stop growth, but to control it. Whether this policy was ill-advised or not is open to debate, but it is important to determine what the policy was.

Pressure from the government

As in the 1790s, when unspecified threats by government against itinerant preaching forced Methodists into protestations of loyalty, the more serious intentions of Lord Sidmouth in 1811 had more or less the same effect. Methodist reaction to Sidmouth's proposals against itinerant preaching is best followed through the voluminous correspondence of Thomas Allan, the London-based connexional solicitor, who was the most important layman in the connexion in the critical years between 1800 and 1820.[41] Not only was he responsible for drafting trust deeds in a prolific period of Methodist chapel building, but he was expert at interpreting the complexities of post-Restoration ecclesiastical legislation. The Methodists had established a committee for guarding their privileges in 1803, but they needed someone schooled in the thought of Locke and Blackstone to tell them what those privileges actually were. It was Allan's task to put the Wesleyan case to the politicians in this period, so his papers are a mine of information on Methodist political activities at the highest level. In fact Thomas Thompson, MP for Midhurst 1807–18 and a Methodist local preacher, suggested to Allan in 1812 that he should

write a short history of all your proceedings in obtaining the New Toleration Act that it may be known to whose exertions the Methodists and Dissenters are indebted for so great an extent of their religious privileges . . . . It might be a history of the political opinions of the Methodists at the present time and of their attachment to Government, and might operate as a powerful example to their successors.[42]

The Conference appointed Allan as general-solicitor for the connexion in 1803 and he was soon pressed into service to protect Methodist missionary rights in the West Indies. His most important contribution came seven years later and it began with a letter to Jabez Bunting asking the Conference to review four major areas of Methodist policy: the financing and administration of missions (only a third of the money given for this purpose was allocated to foreign missionaries); the selection and training of preachers; the spiritual instruction of Methodist children; and the Methodist response to certain legislative proposals.

Lord Sidmouth may possibly bring forward some motion before next conference which may have for its object the checking of the progress of itinerancy. The question then is supposing he should, what must be the line of conduct of the Methodists? How are they to oppose Lord Sidmouth? – publicly or privately? By petition and to whom? Who are to be the active agents? The Committee of Privileges or who? If the Committee, what instructions are they to have and upon what principles are they to proceed? Are the Methodists to call themselves Churchmen or Dissenters or neither? Are they to unite with other sects who may petition and how far are they to co-operate? All these are serious questions.[43]

With its first major political conflict in sight, Allan was keen to conduct Methodist opposition on principles that accurately reflected the Wesleyans' distinctive position in English society. Conflict was thus promoting denominationalism.

In the summer of 1809 Lord Sidmouth was approached by the Bishops of Gloucester and Durham to consider changing the law on the licencing of Protestant Dissenting ministers. According to them the legal requirements of the 1689 Act of Toleration were no longer adequate to deal with 'modern sectaries' who 'assembled in barns, in rooms of private houses, or in other buildings of the most improper kind, to hear the wild effusions of a mechanic or a ploughboy, perhaps not more than 15 years of age'.[44] What lurked behind the horror stories that reached Sidmouth was the feeling that the Church of England's pastoral flexibility was hampered by the legislature at a time when Dissenters were subject to few restrictions. Sidmouth and his Anglican supporters feared that the religious and political establishment would be undermined if the new Ranters were not controlled. However, they realized that little could be achieved without the support of the Dissenters themselves, particularly the Methodists whose system was based on an itinerant ministry and a plentiful supply of local preachers. In April 1811, Sidmouth opened negotiations with two leading Methodists, Thomas Coke, who always flattered those more important than himself, and Adam Clarke, who combined massive theological learning with political naïvety. Sidmouth convinced them that it was in Methodism's best interest to support a measure designed to protect the respectable by eliminating the disreputable.[45] So it was with cautious optimism that Sidmouth presented his bill to the House of Lords for the first reading on 9 May. The aim was to limit the supply of preaching certificates by insisting that every Dissenting minister be attached to a specific congregation, and by stating that each preacher needed written recommendations from several 'substantial and reputable householders belonging to the said congregation'. If these conditions were met, then Justices of the Peace were legally compelled to issue a certificate. In introducing the bill, Sidmouth stated that it was not his desire to 'cast any imputation upon the orders and classes of men', but there were persons claiming certificates 'who were coblers, tailors, pig-drovers, and chimney-sweepers'.[46] This comment brought a bemused smile to Lord Holland's face, and was seized upon by Dissenters whose congregations consisted of such 'undesirables'.

Meanwhile, there were signs that Methodist laymen were mobilizing opposition to Sidmouth's proposals. Joseph Butterworth, a founder member of the Committee of Privileges and MP for Coventry 1812–18 and for Dover 1820–6, summoned Allan to an urgent meeting with himself, Adam Clarke and Walter Griffith to discuss the bill.[47] As a result, a 'meeting of the general committee of the societies of the late Rev. John Wesley' was convened for 14 May. Although twelve resolutions were passed, there were three main reasons for the new Methodist hostility: Sidmouth's bill would destroy the preaching pattern that Wesley established; many Methodists were unwilling to apply for licences under the epithet Dissenter; and they feared they would be exposed to penalties under the Conventicle Act.[48] Armed with these resolutions, a deputation called on Sidmouth, but he refused to withdraw the bill. Adam Clarke gave meagre consolation to Sidmouth for this Wesleyan change of heart by informing him that the real opposition was coming from Methodist laymen, and by presenting him with Clarke's commentary on Genesis, which somehow illustrated 'the pure doctrines of the Church of England and the sound principles of the British constitution'.[49]

With Methodist policy more clearly defined it was left to Allan to organize an effective opposition. On 15 May Allan attended a meeting of Dissenters at the London Tavern, and, along with Butterworth and Benson, was elected to the committee responsible for whipping up Dissenting opposition. Although the Methodists co-operated with Dissenters, they cautiously preserved a separate identity and organizational structure. With the Committee of Privileges in continual session, Allan sent a copy of the Methodist resolutions to each member of the House of Lords, solicited the particular help of Lord Erskine,[50] and sent messengers into the regions armed with petitions.

By this stage the localities needed little stimulation. John Ward, a Durham Methodist solicitor who felt that the Methodists had dragged their heels over this issue, promised the support of Lord Holland and six members of the House of Commons.[51] Jabez Bunting marshalled the Wesleyans in the Manchester and Liverpool districts. By noon on Tuesday 21 May, the date of the second reading of Sidmouth's bill, Allan was able to present Lord Erskine with 250 petitions containing over 30 thousand signatures.

The debate in the House of Lords was something of an anti-climax, because the government and the Church had already deserted Sidmouth because of the intensity of opposition in the country. Still unwilling to retreat, Sidmouth's main tack was that the Dissenters opposed his bill because they did not understand it, an argument that did not impress Lord Holland, who stated that 'it was no light matter to tell that numerous class of persons, called Dissenters, that they were so stupid as not to understand acts of parliament that related to their own concerns'.[52] The bill was lost without a division, and Allan wrote appreciative letters to all the Whig peers who had spoken for the Dissenting interest.[53]

The defeat of the bill was not the end of the matter, because Allan soon discovered that Justices at Quarter Sessions were behaving as if the bill had become law. Allan compiled notes from all over the country of Quarter Sessions which refused to administer oaths in accordance with the Toleration Act.[54] Supporters of the Church in the localities were thus achieving in practice what had eluded Sidmouth in theory. Allan recognized that the character of English local government could not be changed overnight, so his main objective was to secure legislation that would give more protection. With most preachers unable to cope with the legal technicalities of the English constitution, Allan was now at the peak of his influence within the connexion. At the beginning of 1812, he scribbled down a list of priorities: see Perceval; organize petitions and collections; be temperate in all correspondence; moderate the feelings of our members; and excite their patriotism.[55]

On 15 February, Allan requested a personal interview with Perceval about the state of the law on religious toleration, pointing out to him that 'if the law were to remain as it is now construed to be, the enforcing of the penalties of the Conventicle and other antiquated acts of a similar nature would deprive thousands of His Majesty's loyal subjects of their Property and of their personal liberty'.[56] Allan prepared notes for a one-hour lecture to Perceval on the nature of

Methodism and its contribution to English society. His notes survive:

2. That Mr Wesley *never intended* to form a *distinct sect* but merely to do good among the *existing denominations* of Christians but chiefly in the Church of England. Hence members of our Society consider themselves as members of the Establishment and do not choose to rank with Dissenters . . . .

9. (On Methodism having no truck with seditious preaching.) We do not pretend to say that we could vouch for every individual but we expel the bad when found out, and our discipline is very strict . . . .

12. In times of scarcity and distress we may safely say that among colliers, miners and mechanics, Methodism has been the grand instrument of preserving subordination, and if governments were but acquainted with the happy effects of Methodism both in England and *Ireland* they would do their utmost to protect rather than discourage them . . . .

13. That we are not a political people, we simply wish to worship God and promote Christianity in the land by all means, and have been the steady friends of government . . . .

14. We conceive that the late conduct of the Magistrates is subversive of the principles of the Constitution as established at the Revolution.[57]

Allan's portrayal of Methodism as Anglican in sympathy, Protestant in character, disciplined in ecclesiastical organization, and sustainer of a stable social order, shows how persecution forced Methodism into a conservative posture in order to obtain a liberal measure. With a mixture of sympathy and caution Perceval urged the Methodists to wait for Ellenborough's judgement in a test case brought before the King's Bench. Allan asked Perceval if the government would sponsor a relief measure should Ellenborough's decision go against the Methodists. Perceval dodged the question, but he assured Allan that the government had no desire to persecute.[58]

At this stage the Methodist solicitor tried to control Wesleyan action in the provinces so that he could continue in the role of honest broker in his dealings with government. On 24 February he wrote a letter, with the Committee of Privileges' approval, to every circuit superintendent in the country, asking them to refrain from publishing or petitioning until authorized by the committee. This attempt by a metropolitan committee to establish connexional uniformity was new, and it was resented by some. In the midst of much rhetoric about the 'Jacobinical assertion of inalienable rights', John Ward told Allan that he would continue to do what he liked.[59] In April 1812 Perceval informed the Methodists that, after discussing the matter in the Cabinet, he was prepared to support 'an application to Parliament for the purpose of affording relief'.[60] The case at King's Bench was still causing delay, but after Ellenborough presented his inconclusive judgement on 6 May, Allan drafted a suitable Toleration Bill.[61] At this crucial stage in the negotiations Perceval was assassinated, and Allan transferred his attention to Lord Liverpool, with whom he communicated at weekly intervals throughout June and July.[62] The result was the passage of a new Toleration Act on 29 July 1812. The Five Mile Act and the Conventicle Act were repealed,[63] magistrates were compelled to administer the oaths to those who asked to take them, and the law protected itself against abuse by stating that exemption from military and civic duties could only be claimed by ministers without any other calling but that of schoolmaster. The act was a personal triumph for Allan, who secured all his objectives without alienating any major section of English opinion, except the High Church diehards. In the victory letter sent out by the Committee of Privileges Allan thanked Liverpool and his Cabinet, the Archbishop of Canterbury, Lord Holland and other Whig peers, Wilberforce and the Saints, the (Dissenting) Protestant Society for the Protection of Religious Liberty, and even the Quakers.[64] It seemed that the Methodists had never enjoyed such a respectable position in English society, but there was another side. The years 1811–12 saw an increase of tension between preachers and laymen, and between the metropolis and the localities. In addition, the perceptive could see that the Methodists, while posing as friends of the Church of England, had campaigned with the whole host of Protestant Dissent, and that their crusade for religious liberty was a cloak for self-interest. Representatives of radical opinion, including Cobbett, were not taken in.[65]

Four things in particular stood out from the toleration debate. First, Adam Clarke, who among Methodists had the closest relationship with Sidmouth in this period, makes it clear in his private papers that it was Anglican Bishops not government ministers who were most concerned about itinerant preaching.[66] Second, English politicians, with the exception of a few High Churchmen, recognized that a revived Dissent was now part of the English social landscape. Indeed, judging from the propaganda that Allan fed Perceval and Liverpool, the government recognized the stabilizing effect on English society of much popular religion, provided the politicians could persuade or frighten Methodist leaders into securing proper internal discipline. Thus, Sidmouth's bill was the last major attempt in English history to strike a fresh blow at religious freedom. Third, the Methodists had demonstrated to themselves, for the first time, that they had the capacity to fight their own political battles by tapping the potential of their impressive connexional machinery. Whereas in 1800 they were dependent on the good offices of Wilberforce, in 1811 they used their own personnel. Moreover, the cowering submission of Pawson in 1800 was not repeated, because the Sidmouth episode both inspired Methodist self-confidence and showed the fragility of English religious toleration. Finally, and most important of all in the context of what came after, the Methodists realized that their preaching privileges depended upon continued loyalty and good order in a period of radical ferment.

Methodism and popular radicalism[67]

As soon as the new Toleration Bill was secured the Wesleyan Conference sent out a circular to all members of Methodist societies urging them to 'Fear the Lord and the King, and meddle not with them that are given to change'.[68] It was the first of many such circulars sent out by Conference and the Committee of Privileges in the years 1812–20. The very number of them testify to their ineffectiveness, and there is now overwhelming evidence to suggest that Wesleyan discipline came under more pressure from popular radicalism in this period than at any other time in its history. Local examples are legion.

In 1812 preachers in the manufacturing districts fought a hard and sometimes dangerous campaign against Luddites. In Halifax, Bunting, among other things, refused to conduct Luddite funerals and was subsequently unable to go out at night alone. In the Sowerby Bridge circuit Methodist chapels were closed to Luddite orators, and in Holmfirth Robert Newton, a rising star in the connexion, prevented the Methodist chapel from being used as an arms store.[69] The ineffectiveness of mere institutional sanctions, as opposed to more thorough tactics, came home to Bunting in 1813 when six Luddite sons of Methodist fathers were hanged at York, an 'awful fact' that confirmed Bunting's opinion that the progress of Methodism in the West Riding had been 'more swift than solid; more extensive than deep'.[70] Throughout the Midlands and the north, Methodists faced competition from and, what was worse, were 'polluted' by, a new generation of political clubs from the Brotherhood of the Durham coal-field to the Druids of Birmingham and the Oddfellows of Burnley.

Also in 1812 a more complicated problem arose in the hosiery districts of the East Midlands when Wesleyans became involved in the anti-war petitioning of the Friends of Peace. In the midst of the worst trade crisis of the war the petitions of 1812 were directed against the Orders in Council. In the regions this campaign was led by liberal Dissenters, mostly Unitarians, but there were links with opposition Whig politicians. The Wesleyan leadership wanted to prevent the alliance forged with Dissent against Sidmouth in 1811 from spilling over into more directly anti-government activities. Despite this a Methodist circuit superintendent read out peace petitions to the crowd assembled at Nottingham Guildhall and many Methodists added their signatures.[71] The Wesleyan Conference was spared further embarrassment from this early sympathy with Whig-liberalism, based as it was on economically motivated pacifism, by the changing fortunes of war in 1813.

It was, however, the radicalism thrown up by the economic depression in the post-war period that posed the most serious problem of control for the Wesleyans. Coming under attack from two sides, from the radical press for being too reactionary and from the establishment for harbouring radicals, Wesleyan leaders, through the Committee of Privileges, transferred responsibility to preachers in the localities. Early in 1818 the committee wrote to those in the most troublesome parts, Derby, Belper, Cromford, Nottingham, Bury and Bolton, to ask for more effort against radicals and for appropriate stories of loyalty with which to appease the authorities.[72] So tight was the squeeze that in the northern manufacturing districts the well sustained growth in Wesleyan membership came to a halt in 1817 and even went into temporary decline in the years 1819–20.[73] Towns like Rochdale and Manchester suffered a 15 per cent decrease in membership between 1818 and 1820.[74] Two case studies, one from South Lancashire and the other from Tyneside, show how this happened.

In the Peterloo years, Manchester was clearly the strategic capital of the north, and Wesleyan conservatives were well served there by John Stephens, a tough circuit superintendent who expelled four hundred from the membership roll in his first year. (Expulsion was a relatively easy process within Methodism since it simply meant the non-renewal of the quarterly ticket.) Stephens's policy was equally uncomplicated.

The objects we have kept in view are 1st., to give the sound part of this society a decided ascendancy.   2. So to put down the opposition as to disable them from doing mischief.   3. To cure those of them who are worth saving.   4. To take the rest one by one, and crush them when they notoriously commit themselves. The plan is likely to succeed. . . . They are growing tired of radicalism, and as that dies religion will revive.[75]

Everything was done that could be done to save Manchester Methodism from the radicals, including the expulsion of Sunday scholars and teachers for wearing radical emblems. Stephens and his preachers were supported by leading Wesleyan businessmen, and the results of this class conflict within Methodism was class separation as the Manchester rich built their splendid chapels in the suburbs, while the poor wore their symbolic white hats in the modest Swan Street chapel.[76]

It was a similar story just north of Manchester among the depressed cotton weavers of Haslingden. For men earning seven or eight shillings a week the addresses of the Committee of Privileges passed on to them by their preachers merely added insult to injury. J. B. Holroyd, the circuit superintendent, told Bunting that

On Sunday last I had but just got out of the Chapel before I was attacked by 3 leaders, 2 Local Preachers, 1 Steward and several private members on the subjects of Lord Castlereagh's bills, and the Address from the Committee, when they told me in plain terms that the Methodist Preachers were as bad as the Church ministers in supporting government.[77]

Such anecdotes could be reported from all over the north of England. The Wesleyans weathered this storm by cementing the alliance between conservative preachers and wealthy laymen, improving the communication links between central committees and local representatives, and expelling those they could not persuade to fall into line.

The most revealing case of Methodist discipline in action took place across the Pennines in the North Shields circuit on Tyneside. Shortly after Peterloo, William H. Stephenson, a teacher at Burton Colliery school and a Methodist local preacher, spoke against the Manchester magistrates at a huge protest meeting in Newcastle. 'Most of the Travelling Preachers and respectable friends'[78] in the area were offended by Stephenson's speech, and they urged his circuit superintendent, Robert Pilter, to strike him off the local preaching plan. Unfortunately for Pilter, Stephenson refused to go quietly. He told his circuit superintendent that, since three-quarters of local Methodists were radical reformers, his expulsion would create havoc within the connexion. Pilter was sufficiently impressed by this threat to fix a district trial for Stephenson on 22 October, and in the meantime he wrote anxious letters to Jonathan Crowther, President of the Conference, and to Jabez Bunting. Crowther was unwilling to let politics become an issue of connexional conflict, especially since the Kilhamites and Ranters were prepared to welcome Wesleyan rejects. He recommended that Stephenson should be admonished, and warned about his future conduct. The subsequent trial was a model of those traditional English 'virtues' of freedom of speech, fairness, and irresolution. The discussion of abstract politics was forbidden; the issue was whether Stephenson was justified in attending and speaking at a radical meeting. The verdict went against the local preacher, and he was asked to promise that he would never attend another public meeting. Stephenson refused on the grounds that a freeborn Englishman could promise no such thing, and the meeting was adjourned until 5 November.

While the North Shields circuit agonized over their recalcitrant brother, the important decisions were being taken elsewhere, because the Stephenson case was taken directly to the Committee of Privileges in London by Jabez Bunting. Ironically the Committee met on the same day as Stephenson's first trial, and it passed two resolutions.

1. That, under all the circumstances of the case, and considering the peculiar character of the Political Assembly lately held at Newcastle, this committee are of opinion, that it was highly improper that any Member of our Body should take any part in such a meeting, and much more so, that he should officiate as a Speaker; and that we think that any person who has thus acted should be immediately suspended from all public employment among us as a Local Preacher or Class Leader, and should not even be allowed to be a Member of our Society, unless he promises to abstain from such conduct in future.

2. That it is the opinion of this committee that no persons who are enrolled as members of those dangerous Private Political Associations which are now prevalent in the Disturbed Districts of our Country, should be allowed to be Members of our Society, because, without adverting to the legal and political objections against such Associations it is, on christian grounds, obviously improper for Members of a Religious Society to expose themselves to such scenes of temptation and turbulence.[79]

Although provoked into action by the Stephenson case, the Committee of Privileges received so much information about Methodist participation in radical meetings that it decided to issue a statement to all Wesleyan congregations. The first and most important resolution reiterated Allan's stance over Sidmouth's bill.

1.   That Christian Communities, who claim at the hands of the Civil
      Government the undisturbed and legalized enjoyment of their Religious
      Liberties, are bound to evince, by their loyalty, that they deserve the
      Privileges which they *demand*; because Rights and Duties are reciprocal,
      and the Government that affords us protection is entitled to our con-
      stitutional subjection and support.[80]

Robert Pilter was armed with the October resolutions of the Committee of Privileges when Stephenson was tried for the second time.
Stephenson's colleagues relied upon his *honour* (no pledge was
extracted) 'that he would not in future act against the declared opinion
of his Brethren', and they voted seven to four against striking him off
the local preaching plan. Pilter nervously and foolishly communicated the decision to Bunting, who took it straight back to the
London committee. It was resolved 'that Mr Stephenson should be
immediately suspended from the Local Preachers' Plan, and from all
official duties in the Methodist Connexion and also, that unless he
unequivocally pledge himself to abstain from taking part in the public
and private meetings of what are denominated the Radical Reformers,
he be forthwith expelled from the Methodist Society'.[81] Stephenson
was finally dislodged, not by his preaching colleagues in North
Shields, but by a metropolitan committee in which Bunting and Allan
played leading roles. The decision had disastrous consequences for
the Wesleyans in the Newcastle area, because fourteen Independent
Methodist chapels were established within a year. But more than that,
the Stephenson case illustrated the inner tensions within Methodism
between London and the localities, between itinerant preachers and
laymen, and between conservatives and reformers. The official
Wesleyan statements of 1819 made it crystal clear to the working
classes in the manufacturing districts that they could be radicals *or*
Methodists, but not both. Not surprisingly, the serious decrease of
Methodist membership in 1820 was not surpassed until the troubled
year of 1851, and W. R. Ward has boldly stated 'that Peterloo had for
ever severed official Methodism from urban revivalism'.[82]

The relationship between Methodism and radicalism has provoked
much controversy and considerable historical ingenuity, but in the
midst of all this the important points have not been made with sufficient clarity. H. T. Dickenson, in his book *Liberty and Property,
Political Ideology in Eighteenth-Century Britain,*[83] argues that the
destruction of property in the Gordon Riots, the wave of patriotism
resulting from the War of American Independence and the popular
radicalism of the French Revolution stimulated a conservative

ideological defence of the British constitution. The basis of this defence was the belief that government was ordained by God, and that constitutional liberty, like Christian freedom, was dependent on the law. Since the law guaranteed the protection of private property, conservative theorists could fuse the twin elements of liberty and property and sanction them with God's approval.[84] In case God let them down they buttressed their arguments with prescription and pragmatism. In contrast, the radicals constructed their ideas from the platform of natural rights (not duties), thereby posing a threat as much moral and religious as it was political.

This is the point that emerges most clearly from the resolutions drafted by Thomas Allan in October 1819. Burke's footprints are everywhere.

4. It is ... the duty of the Methodist Societies to unite with their fellow-subjects of other denominations in every proper and lawful demonstration of attachment to our free Constitution, and of loyalty to our venerable Sovereign, – in upholding, by every means in their power, the authority of the Laws by which we are governed; – and in discountenancing and repressing all infidel and blasphemous publications, as well as all tumultuous, inflammatory, or seditious proceedings.

6. This committee expresses disapprobation of certain tumultuous assemblies, in which large masses of people have been irregularly collected, ... of persons not resident in the places where such meetings have been held, and calculated, both from the infidel principles, the wild and extravagant political theories, and the violent and inflammatory declamations, of those who have appeared as Leaders on such occasions, not to afford the opportunity of public deliberation, nor to effect any object of political utility, but to bring all government into contempt, and to introduce universal discontent, insubordination, and anarchy.[85]

It is not so much the political objectives of the radicals that are rejected in Allan's resolutions (in fact they are never mentioned), as their theory, theology, morality and methods. Radical ideology was completely different, which was why there could be no compromise.

But this put Methodist preachers in a difficult position. The Committee of Privileges, and their Bibles (Rom. 12:1), told them that submission to authority was a Christian duty, regardless of circumstances. Moreover, most of them believed, with some justification, that radical aims and methods – from parliamentary reform to machine breaking – would not answer their grievances. Some, like Holroyd, tried to deflect the radicals' attention from government to their economic relations with employers.[86] No doubt paternalistic ideas combined with professional aspirations caused the majority of preachers to overreact in the years 1812–20, but, as Christian ministers, what were they to do when confronted with pikes and demagogues? Choices then, as for Latin American priests now, were not easy; one could simply have wished for more anguish in the making of them.

Whatever the rightness or otherwise of the preachers' behaviour, the results of it are more straightforward. Telling men on rock-bottom wages that poverty was a Christian blessing was simply encouraging them to separate their economic from their religious life. Those who did not abandon religion altogether were forced either to join a more radical denomination or else to squeeze religion into a smaller compartment of their lives. The all-embracing holiness crusade of earlier Methodist societies was gone for good. This, as much as membership losses, was the consequence of social tension in the years 1812–20.

To the problems of control posed by Sunday schools, revivalism, government pressure and radicalism were added administrative and financial difficulties. General changes in the structure and organization of the Methodist community, such as the increases in the number of preachers (particularly married ones), and of ornate but poorly financed chapels, were cruelly exposed by the post-war economic recession.[87] More collections offered no answer to these deep-seated structural problems. The result was the decline of rural itinerancy, the virtual disappearance of the circuit horse, and financial reliance on big urban chapels with their wealthy clientele. Such chapels were competed for by the available preaching talent so that the younger preachers had different yardsticks of success from Wesley's itinerants. Thus, the growth of big preaching centres staffed by star preachers, that were so admired by nineteenth-century Nonconformists and are looked back on with such nostalgia by many twentieth-century evangelicals, were not so much a symbol of success as a witness to the death of virginal Methodism. The era also saw the end of Wesleyan Methodism as a force in working-class culture and politics.

A generalized Wesleyan conservatism was now well rooted, at least among the men of influence, but it could not be converted into a politically active Toryism until religion emerged as a major political issue in the late 1820s. The demand for Catholic Emancipation was the first stimulus.

References

1   R. F. Wearmouth, *Methodism and the Working-Class Movements of England 1800–1850* (London 1937), pp. 41–3.

2   John Stephens, *The Mutual Relations of the Rich and the Poor* (Manchester 1819), p.v., quoted by P. Stigant, 'Wesleyan Methodism and working-class radicalism in the North, 1792–1821', *Northern History*, **6** (1971), p. 98.

3   T. W. Laqueur, *Religion and Respectability: Sunday Schools and Working Class Culture 1780–1850* (New Haven and London 1976), p. 44.

4   Michael Sanderson, 'Social change and elementary education in industrial Lancashire 1780–1840', *Northern History*, **3** (1968), pp. 131–54.

5   Laqueur, p. 49.

6   ibid., pp. 239–40.

7   ibid., p. 94.

8   Martin Ingram, 'Religion, communities, and moral discipline in late sixteenth- and early seventeenth-century England: case studies', to be published in Kaspar von Greyerz (ed.), *Religion and Society in Early Modern Europe, 1500–1800* (London 1984). For some penetrating comments on Laqueur's work see Hugh McLeod, 'Recent studies in Victorian religious history', *Victorian Studies*, **21** no. 2 (1978), pp. 245–55.

9   Phillip McCann, 'Popular education, socialization and social control: Spitalfields 1812–1824', in P. McCann (ed.), *Popular Education and Socialization in the Nineteenth Century* (London 1977), pp. 1–40.

10 Simon Frith, 'Socialization and rational schooling: elementary education in Leeds before 1870', in McCann (ed.), pp. 67–92. See also W. R. Ward (ed.), *The Early Correspondence of Jabez Bunting 1820–1829* (London 1972), pp. 157, 165–6, 169, 171–2.

11 Malcolm Dick, 'The myth of the working-class Sunday school', *History of Education*, **9** no. 1 (1980), pp. 27–41. Gail Malmgreen, 'Economy and culture in an industrializing town: Macclesfield, Cheshire, 1750–1835' (unpublished PhD thesis, Indiana University 1981), pp. 313–19, 336.

12 W. R. Ward, *Religion and Society in England 1790–1850* (London 1972), p. 13.

13 See Laqueur ch. 4 for a judgement on the effectiveness of Sunday school education.

14 ibid., p. 80.

15 ibid., pp. 155–8.

16 A. P. Wadsworth, 'The first Manchester Sunday schools', *Bulletin of the John Rylands Library*, **33** (1951), pp. 299–326; and Ward, *Religion and Society*, pp. 13–16.

17 Jabez Bunting, *A Great Work described and recommended in a*

Sermon before the members of the Sunday School Union (London 1805).

18   David Wardle, *Education and Society in Nineteenth-Century Nottingham* (Cambridge 1971), p. 39.

19   Ward, *The Early Correspondence of Jabez Bunting*, pp. 228, 148–9.

20   ibid., see the indexed letters on Sunday schools.

21   Laqueur, p. 140. Also Ward, *Religion and Society*, p. 137.

22   Sanderson, pp. 145–6.

23   This is borne out by all the local studies cited earlier.

24   Ward, *Religion and Society*, pp. 172–6.

25   See W. R. Ward, 'The religion of the people and the problem of control, 1790–1830', *Studies in Church History*, **8** (1972), pp. 237–57, and *Religion and Society*, pp. 75–85.

26   T. Entwistle, *Memoir of the Reverend Joseph Entwistle* (London 1867), pp. 111–12, quoted by John Baxter, 'The Great Yorkshire Revival 1792–6: a study of mass revival among the Methodists', *A Sociological Yearbook of Religion in Britain*, vol. 7 (1974), pp. 53–5.

27   M.C.A.Mss., Adam Clarke to George Marsden, 8 April 1800.

28   W. J. Townsend, H. B. Workman and G. Eayrs (eds.), *A New History of Methodism* (London 1909), vol. 1, pp. 558–60; and Ward, 'The religion of the people', p. 244.

29   Richard Carwardine, *Trans-atlantic Revivalism: Popular Evangelicalism in Britain and America, 1790–1865* (Westport, Connecticut 1978), p. 104.

30   For Dow's career in Ireland see C. H. Crookshank, *History of Methodism in Ireland* (London 1886), vol. 2.

31   For a more detailed discussion of the social context of revivalism see John Kent, *Holding the Fort. Studies in Victorian Revivalism* (London 1978), ch. 2; and Ward, *Religion and Society*, pp. 79–80.

32   See J. F. C. Harrison, *The Second Coming: Popular Millenarianism 1780–1850* (London 1979), especially pp. 109–11; and W. H. Oliver, *Prophets and Millennialists* (Auckland 1978).

33   M.C.A.Mss., Jabez Bunting to Richard Reece, 11 June, and 15 July 1803. See also Ward, *The Early Correspondence*, pp. 8–14.

34   Stuart Piggin, 'Halévy revisited: the origins of the Wesleyan Methodist Missionary Society: an examination of Semmel's thesis', *The Journal of Imperial and Commonwealth History,* **9** no. 1 (1980), pp. 19–20.

35   For a recent analysis of Primitive Methodism in its social context see Kent, *Holding the Fort*, ch. 2.

36   J. T. Wilkinson, 'The rise of other Methodist traditions', in R. Davies, A. R. George and G. Rupp (eds.), *A History of the Methodist Church in Great Britain* (London 1978), vol. 2, pp. 304–13.

37   Bernard Semmel, *The Methodist Revolution* (London 1974), ch. 6.
38   See Semmel, pp. 152–7; and Piggin, p. 19 note 14.
39   R. H. Martin, 'Missionary competition between evangelical Dissenters and Wesleyan Methodists in the early nineteenth century: a footnote to the founding of the Methodist Missionary Society', *Proceedings of the Wesley Historical Society*, **42** part 3 (1979), pp. 81–6.
40   Piggin, pp. 22–3.
41   See my 'Thomas Allan and Methodist politics, 1800–1840', *History*, **67** no. 219 (1982), pp. 13–31.
42   M.C.A. Allan Mss., Thomas Thompson to Thomas Allan, 31 August 1812.
43   M.C.A. Allan Mss. 7. Allan to J. Bunting, 28 July 1810.
44   G. Pellew, *The Life and Correspondence of the Right Honourable Henry Addington, First Viscount Sidmouth*, 3 vols. (London 1847), vol. 3, p. 41. See also pp. 38–66.
45   See Piggin, for a comprehensive analysis of Sidmouth's negotiating tactics. Piggin is right to argue, as against Ward, that Clarke had already changed his mind before the 14 May meeting of the Committee of Privileges. Allan and Butterworth convinced him on 11 May. See Hempton, p. 15.
46   *Hansard*, 1st series, **XIX**, c.1130.
47   M.C.A.. Allan Mss., J. Butterworth to T. Allan, 11 May 1811.
48   *Monthly Repository*, **6** (1811), pp. 303–5.
49   Pellew, *Life of Sidmouth*, vol. 3, p. 54.
50   M.C.A. Allan Mss., T. Allan to T. Robinson, May 1811, Lord Erskine to T. Allan, 17 May 1811 (two letters).
51   M.C.A. Allan Mss., J. Ward to R. Middleton (care of T. Allan), 20 May 1811.
52   *Hansard*, 1st series, **XX**, c. 247.
53   M.C.A. Allan Mss., T. Allan to Marquis of Lansdowne, 23 May 1811, T. Allan to Lord Holland, 23 May 1811, and T. Allan to Lord Erskine, 23 May 1811.
54   M.C.A. Allan Mss. Private notes which have been reproduced by Ward, *Religion and Society*, pp. 60–1. Also, T. Allan to T. Robinson, 18 February 1812.
55   M.C.A. Allan Mss. Private notes.
56   M.C.A. Allan Mss., T. Allan to S. Perceval, 15 February 1812.
57   M.C.A. Allan Mss. Private notes.
58   M.C.A. Allan Mss., T. Allan to T. Robinson, 3 March 1812.
59   M.C.A. Allan Mss., J. Ward to T. Allan, 29 February 1812.
60   M.C.A. Printed copy, S. Perceval to J. Butterworth, 10 April 1812.
61   M.C.A. Printed copy, T. Allan to S. Perceval, 9 May 1812.
62   M.C.A. Allan Mss., T. Allan to Lord Liverpool, 11 June, 18 June, 27 June, 2 July, 11 July, and 29 July 1812. Also, T. Allan to T. Robinson, 7 July 1812, and T. Allan to W. Smith, 23 July 1812.

63   R. W. Davis in *Dissent in Politics 1780–1830, the Political Life of William Smith M.P.* (London 1971), states that, although the new Toleration Bill was drafted by the Methodists, the repeal of the Five Mile and Conventicle Acts was due to the Dissenting Deputies, who urged this on Liverpool on 23 June. He overlooks the fact that Allan and Butterworth were convinced that these acts had to go as early as 9 May. See the printed letters of Allan to Perceval, 9 May 1812, and J. Butterworth to ?, 25 May 1812.

64   M.C.A. Committee of Privileges' circular letter to the Circuit Superintendents, 31 July 1812.

65   *Political Register*, **XIX** no. 42, 25 May 1811, c. 1283.

66   M.C.A.Mss., Adam Clarke to George Marsden, 14 March 1810, 29 April, 6 May, 13 May 1811.

67   For helpful treatments of this theme see Stigant, pp. 98–116, and Ward, *Religion and Society*, pp. 85–94.

68   M.C.A. Address of the Preachers to the Members of the Methodist Societies, Leeds, 27 July 1812.

69   Wearmouth, pp. 43–5.

70   Ward, *Religion and Society*, p. 86.

71   J. E. Cookson, *The Friends of Peace. Anti-war liberalism in England, 1793–1815* (Cambridge 1982), ch. 10. In my view the author overestimates the degree of inter-denominational co-operation among Dissenting sects.

72   M.C.A.Mss., Committee of Privileges, 5 February 1817, and 9 January 1818.

73   Stigant, p. 105.

74   D. A. Gowland, *Methodist Secessions. The Origins of Free Methodism in three Lancashire towns: Manchester, Rochdale, Liverpool* (Manchester 1979), pp. 24–5.

75   Ward, *The Early Correspondence of Jabez Bunting*, pp. 61–2.

76   Gowland, pp. 25–7.

77   Ward, *The Early Correspondence of Jabez Bunting*, pp. 24–8.

78   ibid., pp. 21–4.

79   M.C.A. Allan Mss., Draft resolutions of the Committee of Privileges, 22 October 1819.

80   M.C.A. Printed resolutions of the Committee of Privileges, 12 November 1819.

81   M.C.A.Mss., Minutes of the Committee of Privileges, 12 November 1819.

82   Ward, *Religion and Society*, p. 93.

83   London 1977.

84   For a clear exposition of these views from the writings of Robert Southey, see Sheridan Gilley, 'Nationality and liberty, Protestant and Catholic: Robert Southey's Book of the Church', in Stuart Mews (ed.), *Religion and National Identity, Studies in Church History* (Oxford

1982), vol. 18, pp. 409–32. Southey's point was that the Church of England preserved English liberty and civilization against pagans, papists and puritans.

85 M.C.A., Committee of Privileges Resolutions, 12 November 1819.
86 Ward, *The Early Correspondence of Jabez Bunting*, p. 28.
87 For more information on this see Gowland, ch. 2, and Ward, 'The religion of the people', pp. 250–6.

5 Roman Catholic Emancipation, 1790–1830

For British anti-Catholicism, though it had obvious points of similarity with European expressions of ideological objection to Catholic beliefs and practices, was quite unique. It was peculiarly related to popularly subscribed precepts about the ends and nature of the British state; it was chauvinistic and almost general.[1]

Edward Norman's comments on the characteristics of nineteenth-century English anti-Catholicism are consistent with the conclusions of sixteenth- and seventeenth-century scholars, thereby showing the continuity of this feature of post-Reformation English society. Carol Wiener, for example, demonstrates how Elizabethan and Jacobean Englishmen expressed their anxiety, apocalyptic ideology and national identity by opposing a sinister and monolithic Catholic Church.[2] Protestantism was English; it preserved freedom; it was morally pure; and it was on the right side in the great cosmic battle between good and evil. Catholicism on the other hand, was foreign, violent, morally corrupt, doctrinally erroneous, magical, devious, and, above all, was led by a standing army of Popes, Jesuits and priests. It should, however, be stressed that although these notions pervaded seventeenth-century society, it was only at points of crisis that local community neighbourliness between Catholics and Protestants gave way to sectarian conflict.[3]

English anti-Catholicism did not disappear in the eighteenth century, but the increased security of the English state, the relative weakness of Catholicism and the lowering of religious temperatures made it a more episodic emotion. In the nineteenth century, this old prejudice was revived by new circumstances. Irish immigration reinforced the view that Catholicism was foreign and morally degrading. Once again Protestantism was imbued with ideas of national superiority, except at this time the Catholic enemy did not live on the European mainland but in major English cities. Moreover, Ireland was not just an exporter of a disreputable humanity, it was also the claimant of new political rights. These factors coincided with the heightened religious feelings of the Evangelical Revival, which also supplied an oratorical host of itinerant preachers. The match was perfect for a new generation of combat. Of course the methods, if not the emotions, had changed. The inquisition was replaced by polemical pamphlets, state persecution gave way to parliamentary debates, and the new heroes on the Protestant side were not Foxe's martyrs but platform demagogues. Only the English mob and their prejudices remained more or less the same (although it must be said that anti-Catholicism transcended English class divisions and partly restricted their development).[4]

It is difficult to overestimate the impact of this changing religious climate on Methodist political development. In the first place, Methodism as the standard bearer of the new evangelicalism was itself partly responsible for creating religious divisions. Second, Methodist hostility to Catholicism was ensured by a powerful combination of factors: its missionary campaign in Ireland; Wesley's polemical legacy; the influence of fervent evangelical theology; the fact that the Methodist system was based on a plentiful supply of half-educated itinerant preachers; and the geographical coincidence of Methodist growth and Irish settlements in northern England.

Of central importance for Methodist political development was the fact that opposition to radical politics and the Catholic claims come to precisely the same point – a shift towards popular Toryism. This was reinforced by a growing desire for respectability and a rekindled enthusiasm for the Established Church, after it had been leavened by the Evangelical Revival. Ultra-Protestant politicians and Anglo-Irish aristocrats were not slow to exploit these changes within a movement which they had earlier despised. It was, therefore, through a shared evangelicalism and anti-Catholicism that Methodist leaders first made contact with the Anglo-Irish landowning élite. Moreover, there is no evidence to suggest that such contacts had much influence on grass-roots Methodism in England, with the possible exception of the northern provincial cities. But, it is my view that liberals within the connexion woke up too late to the fact that between 1790 and 1830 the Wesleyan leadership, both lay and clerical, had become conspicuously Tory for reasons not fully appreciated by the membership. The reason for this is that only a small proportion of Wesleyan leaders had direct access to the information coming from the Irish Methodists. Unless they held high office within the connexion or had links with the metropolitan Protestant societies, there is no reason why Irish affairs should be of much interest to English Methodists.

Therefore, when Tory-conservatism and Whig-liberalism engaged each other over ecclesiastical matters in the 1830s, the politically articulate within the Methodist rank-and-file (a small but vociferous minority under the influence of provincial Dissenters), were not in sympathy with the leadership.

To sum up then, the history of Methodist opposition to Catholic claims shows how the leadership of the connexion was forced to abandon its Whiggish advocacy of religious toleration in order to defeat heresy. In an aside on Gladstone, E. R. Norman highlights this process: 'liberal principles were no bar when the adversary was believed to be essentially illiberal'.[5] If there was anything liberal in the political ideology of Methodist leaders it began to collapse under Catholic pressure, first manifested in the long campaign for political emancipation.

Political historians seeking to explain the Catholic Emancipation Act of 1829 quite rightly lay the emphasis on events in Ireland and on the reactions of politicians in London during the period 1790–1829. Similarly, the Methodist response to Catholic Emancipation can best be understood by observing the interaction between Irish Methodism and the London Wesleyan élite. The importance of the Irish branch of Methodism had already been established by Wesley's twenty-one visits. On his last visit in 1789 Methodist membership exceeded 14,000, an insubstantial figure that nevertheless represented a 500 per cent increase in the period 1770–89. A graph of Irish membership statistics would show a rapid rise from 1770–1820, a much flatter curve from 1820–44, and a dramatic fall from then until 1855. The first stage represents the period of intensive missionary efforts and the growth of Methodism in Ulster; the second shows the effect of the political and religious conflict with a more aggressive Irish Catholicism; and the third indicates the tragic effect of the Irish famine and consequent emigration. The social history of Irish Methodism has not yet been written, but it is possible to deduce its characteristics from Crookshank's distinctively Victorian three-volume history. Methodism was relatively strong in areas of long-standing English Protestant influence, including market towns, and had only moderate success among the Catholic peasantry, despite the efforts of Irish-speaking itinerant evangelists. In some respects, Irish Methodism was not so much a cohesive movement as a motley band of military personnel, Palatine settlers (in the south-east), some lapsed Presbyterians and a much larger number of enthusiastic Anglicans. There was a sprinkling of support from merchants, professionals and minor gentry, but

Methodism made little impact on those at the top and bottom of the social structure. In short, Methodism gathered up the debris of Ireland's Protestant past and built up a network of evangelical religious societies; it did not create a Protestant community *ex nihilo*. As time went on Methodism became more concentrated in Ulster due to its close links with the linen and textile industries, its attraction for urban migrants, and its ability, through Orangeism, to express Protestant economic solidarity in a more vital way than could be achieved through the Established Church alone. Irish Methodists also took a prominent part in the temperance movement (not least because Ireland's liquor trade was in Catholic hands), and contributed so effectively to education that by mid century Methodism had higher literacy rates than any other denomination.[6] However, the true significance of Irish Methodism in the first half of the nineteenth century lay not in its numbers, nor in its impact on Irish society but rather in its front-line position in the evangelical crusade against Roman Catholicism.[7] In this crusade, three events in the years 1798–1800 were particularly important: the Rebellion of the United Irishmen in 1798, the establishment of the Irish Methodist Mission in 1799, and the Act of Union in 1800.

Although the United Irishmen were in origin mostly northern Presbyterians committed to a policy of parliamentary reform, the movement changed markedly as it developed, both in personnel and ideology, until it collapsed in a bout of distinctively Irish sectarian feuding in Wexford. The rebellion of 1798 had its impact on English Wesleyanism through the colourful accounts given by Irish Methodists. George Taylor, a Methodist preacher who had been imprisoned at Gorey and Wexford, published a horrifying account of the rebellion which was subsequently serialized in the *Methodist Magazine*.[8] An equally emotive account of the rebellion from an anonymous source was sold at 'Methodist preaching-houses in Town and Country', and was later reproduced in the *Methodist Magazine*.[9] This account of what happened at Gorey no doubt made a deep impression.

At Gorey, the Popish Rebels attacked the church, and not only broke the windows, but spoiled the pews. They broke in pieces the Ten Commandments which were over the Communion-Table, and pulled the leaves out of the Bible and Prayer-Book, and strewed them in the aisles of the church. They then brought two Protestants up to the Communion-Table, and with their pikes wounded them mortally; and to conclude their horrid cruelty, they led them, while they were able to walk, back to the church door; their blood flowing in streams all the way, and staining the sacred pages of the Bible which the Papists had trodden under their feet.

These published works were supported by a substantial private correspondence in like vein between Irish and English Methodists.[10]

The rebellion of the United Irishmen rekindled old Methodist fears of the disloyalty and persecuting tendencies of Roman Catholicism. It also reinforced Methodist allegiance to 'Church and King', in contrast to the disaffection of some Catholics and Presbyterians. In this way violence deepened sectarian divisions. At times of Catholic political pressure between 1800 and 1850 Methodists were quick to quote incidents of the '98 rebellion as evidence against concessions to Catholics.[11] Above all, Ireland acted as a catalyst in the broader enmity between Methodists and Catholics.

In the same way that English Methodists supported established authorities against radicals to maintain their preaching privileges, the Irish connexion received government favours for their good behaviour in 1798. Dr Coke obtained special permission from the Lord Lieutenant for the meeting of the Irish Conference at a time when all assemblies of more than five were prohibited, and Methodist preachers were allowed to continue their travelling ministry with the help of passes from the military authorities.[12] This was important because the events of 1798 confirmed the Methodist opinion that if Ireland was to have peace then it must be converted to Protestantism. This was the motive behind the 1799 Conference decision to send out three full-time Gaelic-speaking missionaries, whose main task was to travel throughout the country preaching to Catholics. The enthusiasm of the Irish Wesleyans for this new enterprise was conveyed to the English Conference in the 1799 annual address. Many of the elements of the early nineteenth-century international missionary crusade were present. There is the existence of a 'deluded' and morally corrupt people to whom the Gospel must be taken as the only means of true enlightenment. There is a strong feeling of divine favour inasmuch as 'his gracious providence' provides the opportunity. There is the appeal of grand, heroic adventure to those who have 'entered upon one of the most arduous undertakings that have been attempted since the primitive times'.[13] In essentials the address reads like a religious counterpart to secular romanticism.

According to Crookshank the aim of this mission was nothing less than the 'subjugation of Irish Popery to the faith of Christ'. Helped by English backing, the mission to Ireland grew quickly. In 1809, there were twelve missionaries operating in six areas, and by 1816 there were twenty-one missionaries, twelve of whom preached in Irish, working on fourteen stations dotted throughout Ireland.[14] The responsibility for the financial support and administrative organization of the Irish mission was taken over by the Wesleyan Missionary Committee in London, thereby giving English Methodists a vital stake in Irish affairs. There was a remarkable volume of correspondence between the Irish missionaries, who had to report quarterly, and the committee in London. This correspondence had particular importance during periods of political tension, when missionaries assumed the roles of information gatherers and reporters.

The initial reports of the Irish missionaries were a mixture of optimism, persecution and despair.[15] After the mission had been in operation for seven years, Dr Coke prepared a more complete report for the Methodist Missionary Society. He stated that Ireland was the most important mission-field in which the Methodists were engaged, because 'three millions of the people of this land are plunged in the deepest ignorance and superstition'. He told the English Wesleyans of courageous missionaries who had to be protected by the 'magistracy and military', of the resistance of the 'Romish priests', and finally he expressed the hope that 'if the zeal of the missionaries, the support of the two conferences, and the generous assistance of the subscribers, continue, truth will prevail'.[16]

The Methodist missionary crusade in Ireland was merely the first instalment of a broader evangelical campaign in the early decades of the nineteenth century. Evangelical societies dealing specifically with the needs of Ireland proliferated: the British and Foreign Bible Society sent its publications after 1804;[17] the London Hibernian Society was formed in 1806, the Sunday School Society in 1809, the Religious Tract and Book Society in 1817, the Irish Society in 1818, and the Irish branches of the Church Missionary and Jewish Societies were established in 1814 and 1815 respectively.[18] Although a number of them were inter-denominational, the main impetus came from the Anglican evangelicals in England and Ireland. The formation of the Irish branch of the Church Missionary Society is a good example of the process at work. Although there were independent efforts within the Irish Church to found such a society, its eventual achievement owed much to the influential English evangelicals, Pratt, Wilson and Jowett. Wilson wrote on 15 June that 'without us no society would have been formed; whereas now in a few years Ireland will be covered with societies'.[19]

With these societies in full swing there was a growing traffic of gospel men passing each other on the Irish sea. Irish evangelicals came to England to plead for subscriptions, to tell tales of wonderful successes and dreadful persecutions, and some, like Hugh McNeile in Liverpool, stayed to carry the battle to Irish Catholic immigrants in English cities. Geoffrey Best catches the flavour.

By the later 'twenties the benighted Irish peasantry were a standard popular field for protestant missionary endeavour, and it was, I think, under the auspices of such Evangelical societies as the London Hibernian and the British and Irish Ladies' that the itinerant Irish orator first got his hooks into the British fleshpots. His tone at first could be simply religious, but the constitutional upheavals of 1823–33 gave him new problems and opportunities. . . . These men were a kind of religious entertainers. . . .[20]

In return English evangelicals came to Ireland to display superior English organizational and financial ability, and to have a stake in the nearest and most strategic mission-field in the Empire. In the nineteenth century, Ireland's unhappy religious and cultural divisions were deepened by two powerful imperial forces: English evangelicalism, backed by the growing self-confidence that came from industrial and military success; and an Ultramontane Catholicism that was part of a wider European Catholic revival. The former came before, and partly stimulated, the latter.

Within the broader evangelicalism the period of inter-denominational societies preceded the harder churchmanship of the 1820s, but within Methodism the Irish branch was more quickly subordinated to the organizational structures of the British connexion. After 1816, the President of the British Conference automatically presided over the next Irish one. The President was generally accompanied by a missionary deputation, and Irish circuit chairmen were delegated to attend the British Conference, which began a few days after the end of its Irish counterpart. These structural links and the temporal proximity of the two conferences ensured a continual flow of personnel and ideas from one country to the other. All influential English Wesleyans in the years 1817–50 had first-hand experience of Ireland. Bunting, for example, paid four visits to the Irish Conference in the decade after 1827.[21]

It is difficult to overestimate the impact of this combined Methodist and evangelical assault on Ireland. Desmond Bowen has shown that relations between the churches in Ireland in the period 1800–22 were surprisingly harmonious.[22] Although he overdraws the contrast before and after 1822 on the Protestant side, there can be no doubt that evangelical proselytizing either direct or through schools, prepared the way for the more radical and nationalist Catholic politics of the 1820s.[23] Castle Bishops of the old school, who were closely related to the Anglo-Irish aristocracy, gave way to more politically aggressive successors. In this process Methodists (as with Wesley in the eighteenth century) were both instigators and victims. The colourful Gaelic preaching and folk religion of early Irish missionaries like Gideon Ouseley and Charles Graham,[24] gave way to the faithful report writing of the period 1812–30, when London Wesleyans wanted ammunition for their anti-Catholic political activities. In fact, it is one of the most engaging paradoxes of Bowen's book that early Methodist and evangelical revivalists, through preaching and distributing Bibles in the Irish language, were better conservators of Gaelic culture than English-speaking Catholic priests. But, in the early nineteenth century, missionary competition, new political tensions and the monopolistic inclinations of Catholic priests, turned Methodist evangelism into Methodist sectarianism. The parallel with Wesley's own career is remarkable.

If the Rebellion of the United Irishmen in 1798 reinforced Methodist fears of Catholic violence and the establishment of the Irish Methodist mission in 1799 formalized religious competition, the Act of Union in 1800 ensured that Irish politics would be of central importance in London as well as Dublin. Irish conflicts were now guaranteed an English stage.

Orangemen against Defenders, landlords against tenants, Protestants against Catholics, nationalists against imperialists, democrats against aristocrats, Irish nationalists against English rulers – these were the conflicts which were incorporated into the British Constitution by the Union.[25]

Not surprisingly, these conflicts produced greater instability in English politics. Irish affairs caused the ministerial resignations of Pitt and Grenville in 1801 and 1807, Grey, Melbourne and Peel in the period 1834–5, and Disraeli and Gladstone in 1868 and 1873. Moreover, since the promise to consider Catholic Emancipation was part of the bait offered to effect union, failure to deliver not only weakened the Union from the outset, but meant that Irish political activity at Westminster would centre on this demand until it was conceded. In fact, 'between 1801 and 1829 the only issue that gave any measure of unity or continuity to Irish political life was that of Catholic Emancipation'.[26]

From the Methodist viewpoint the most important clause in the Act of Union was the fifth, which stated 'that the Churches of England and Ireland, as now by law established, be united into one Protestant Episcopal Church, to be called the United Church of England and Ireland'.[27] Throughout the nineteenth century the Methodists were especially committed to the support of the Irish branch of this united church, for Protestant rather than establishmentarian reasons. This is made clear in an article in the semi-official Wesleyan newspaper, the *Watchman*.

It is obvious that the important bearing of Methodism on the interests of Protestantism in Ireland is now much more clearly perceived than formerly . . . and we venture to indulge the hope that the pious and zealous ministers and members of the Church of Ireland will henceforth be seen affectionately cooperating with their Methodist brethren . . . in one grand persevering effort to resist and dissipate the papal delusion.[28]

This partly explains why the only division within early nineteenth-century Irish Methodism occurred between Primitive Methodists, who wanted to stay within the Church of Ireland, and those who wanted to follow the English model by having the sacraments administered by Methodist preachers. In Ireland it was too dangerous for Protestants to divide their strength. Indeed, this was an important reason for relative weakness of Irish Nonconformity.[29] But, as in England, Methodist loyalty to the Established Church was not reciprocated. The aristocratic wing of the Church of Ireland disliked Methodist enthusiasm, the latitudinarian wing disapproved of Methodist separatism, and the Calvinistic evangelicals frowned upon Methodist Arminianism.[30]

Reinhard Cassirer has pointed out that the political establishment in Ireland at the end of the eighteenth century (the Anglo-Irish aristocracy) saw its power threatened by four forces:

the desire for a share in the government of Ireland by the Catholics; the democratic spirit among the Protestant Dissenters, the founders of the United Irish organisation, who aimed at an understanding with the Catholics for a common struggle for national freedom and Parliamentary Reform; the struggle of the tenants, both Catholic and Protestant, against high rents and tithes; and the interference of the English government in the internal administration of Ireland.[31]

Moreover, Anglo-Irish aristocrats could exploit popular sectarianism to ensure support for the Protestant Ascendancy from the anti-

Catholic lower orders. Ironically, therefore, Irish Methodism, an enthusiastic religious minority of low social status, gave its support to an insecure Anglo-Irish aristocracy and to a Church of Ireland with strong aristocratic connections, in order to resist Catholic pressure. In addition, Roman Catholicism, which had its powerful Liberal Catholic wing on the Continent, but was a predominantly conservative force, could, in Ireland, pose as the 'friend of liberty' in its efforts to secure religious equality and political representation. Therefore, Methodists were condemned to play an illiberal role in opposition to what they considered was a violent and intolerant Catholic Church. Consequently, Methodist hostility against Irish Catholics and English radicals produced the same result – resistance to constitutional change and support for establishments in Church and State. In addition, Tory attempts to make use of the Wesleyans, and the Scottish Presbyterians for that matter, to rally the nation against Catholic claims, convinced radicals like Cobbett that Methodist anti-Catholicism was simply another facet of its anti-democratic ideology. Thus sectarian politics merely widened the gulf between Wesleyans and radicals.[32]

The Methodist response to the campaign for Catholic Emancipation is best understood in three chronological stages: first, a period of quiet opposition based on reports from Irish Methodist preachers and acted upon by a London Wesleyan élite (1800–20); second, a period of more intensive activity that had repercussions in the House of Commons, in English provincial cities and in Methodist relations with other religious groups (1821–6); and third, the dénouement of 1828–9, from the Clare election to the passage of the Catholic Emancipation Act.

The most important London recipient of Irish Methodist correspondence was Joseph Butterworth, founder of the famous law publishing firm and MP for Coventry 1812–18 and for Dover 1820–6. Butterworth was an indefatigable supporter of evangelical philanthropic societies, but his Methodist associations and his over-zealous Protestantism kept him from the Clapham inner circle.[33] His cast of mind is revealed in a series of letters to Charles Abbot, Speaker of the House of Commons from 1802–17. In 1814 he told Abbot that Ireland was being secretly infiltrated by Continental priests, one of whom 'had been an officer in the republican armies of France'. In 1817 he warned of Jesuit activities in Bavaria and Austria, and later in the year he informed Abbot about Bible Society progress in Poland and Italy. The nicest one of all came in 1824.

A very curious piece of information has very accidentally fallen into my way, by which I find that there is a Roman Catholic Association in England and Scotland. I intend to give Mr Peel a ticket of admission, which is in my possession, and which fell out of the pocket of a labourer in the factory of a friend of mine near Soho Square.[34]

The correspondence from Irish Methodist missionaries was tailor-made for such a man. In the years 1804–11, the missionaries requested Protestant evangelistic materials such as Bibles, tracts and reprints of Wesley's works on Catholicism.[35] But the tone changed in 1812–13, when Catholic claims won parliamentary majorities for the first time in the nineteenth century.

By 1812, changes in the political world, including the king's incapacity, Perceval's assassination, and Cabinet neutrality on Catholic Emancipation, favoured the Catholic cause. In June Canning's motion to take into 'consideration the state of the laws affecting his Majesty's Roman Catholic subjects in Great Britain and Ireland', was carried by a substantial majority in the Commons, while a similar motion in the Lords was defeated by just one vote. Eldon wrote that 'unless the country will express its sentiments on the Roman Catholic claims (if it has any sentiments respecting them, which I doubt), and that tolerably strongly, between Dissenters, Methodists and Papists, the Church is gone'.[36] He need not have worried about the Methodists, because Butterworth prepared for his first parliamentary session in November 1812 by issuing a printed circular to Methodist preachers and other evangelicals in Ireland. He requested information on 'the state of Ireland and the real spirit and character of the Roman Catholics to illustrate the probable affects of the measure [Catholic Emancipation] in whichever way it may be determined'.[37] Peter Roe, a Kilkenny Calvinistic evangelical, who opposed 'Popery' but feared religious controversy, wrote that 'a few of my friends are advocates for emancipation – but it appears to me that they view the question in the abstract – without taking into account the principles and Spirit of Popery, if these ceased to exist, emancipation might be granted at once'.[38] The longest and most interesting reply to Butterworth's request came from Gideon Ouseley, who subsequently published his views in the *Sligo Journal*. Ouseley advocated the abolition of tithes, state payment for all clergy – Protestant and Catholic – lower rents, and the franchise restricted to those who could read and write so that landlords would have to provide education in return for votes.[39] In short, Ouseley wanted open religious competition, and the Protestant Ascendancy to fulfil its legitimate obligations to the Catholic people of Ireland. More than any other Methodist preacher, Ouseley had a strong feeling for the destitute Irish Catholic poor, but he too became a victim of the hardening sectarianism of the 1820s and 1830s. By then he had produced a remarkable number of anti-Catholic pamphlets.[40] He had been invited by British Wesleyans to do a missionary tour of English cities.[41] He had even joined the Orange Order.[42]

The main problem confronting Butterworth and Thomas Allan in the winter of 1812 was how best to express opposition to Catholic claims. Allan wrote to the Methodist MP suggesting the possibility of recruiting Dissenting support, but

if nothing can be done I apprehend that we should have a meeting of our own brethren and let them see how our Friends in Ireland are situated and how they are likely to fare when this wicked plot contrived and supported by both wicked and infatuated men shall have been fully executed. One consequence will be an end to Methodism in Ireland. Are not the Methodists in England to take care of this *privilege* of preaching the Gospel in Ireland?[43]

The Committee of Privileges met soon afterwards and John Barber, a London preacher, wrote that

Mr Butterworth has obtained a wonderful mass of information from Ireland, relative to the conduct and views of the Catholics. It appears that they hold the very worst sentiment which their forefathers did three hundred years ago: and that if they have the power they would not leave [one] Protestant alive in the Kingdom. At the same time it is believed that if Government does not comply with their request [for emancipation] there will be another rebellion. We believe this will be the less evil of the two. We are all of the opinion that the Methodists as a body should not come forward, but do all we can to promote petitions in the Church and sign with them. This should be done in every part of the Kingdom. But if we were to come forward in a public manner, it is highly probable that most or all our friends in Ireland would be murdered.[44]

On grounds of expediency not principle, the Methodists decided against coming forward 'as a body' in 1813. With that possibility removed, and with Dissenters labouring under their own disabilities, the Methodist duo were forced back on their own initiative. As a result, 'The Protestant Union for the Defence and Support of the Protestant Religion and the British Constitution' was hatched at a meeting in Butterworth's house in early January, and it made its public appearance on 22 January.[45] Although the chairman of the

Protestant Union was Granville Sharp, a leading personality in the anti-slavery movement and first chairman of the British and Foreign Bible Society, the publicist was Thomas Allan.[46]

Allan outlined the ideological basis of his opposition to Catholic Emancipation in two pamphlets published in 1813; one was addressed to a Protestant Dissenter, and the other was a reply to the English Catholic Charles Butler's address to the Protestants of Great Britain and Ireland. Allan quoted Locke, Blackstone and Mansfield on toleration with approval, but drew a distinction between the right to have religious freedom and the right to exercise political power.[47] Throughout 1813 Allan wrote with a scholarly moderation that was admired by both friends and opponents,[48] but Butterworth was more difficult to control. William Roberts, the evangelical biographer of Hannah More, advised Butterworth against publishing his letters from Ireland.

I don't mean to question the truth of these accusations, but I cannot help thinking that the society will lay itself open to the charge of a prejudiced hostility by sending forth so much vituperative matter. . . . This would give a great handle to the *Edinburgh Review* and *Morning Chronicle* and would perhaps go near to stamp a character of prejudice upon the union and excite a suspicion of its candour which would disappoint all its purposes.[49]

Roberts put his finger on a major problem for the Protestant Constitutionists throughout the period 1800–29: how could one uphold the theory of the Protestant Constitution against Whig politicians and the liberal press without appearing to be religious bigots? For, in spite of Geoffrey Best's attempts to show the ideology of Protestant Constitutionists in its proper historical perspective,[50] the fact remains that the literature against Catholic claims was more impressive for its bulk than for the quality of its ideas.[51] With the basis of politics being widened and with the growth of a liberal intelligentsia outside aristocratic patronage, it became increasingly difficult for English and Anglo-Irish landowners, Church of England supporters and evangelical anti-Catholics to defend the Protestant Constitution with style. In that respect the Irish Protestant Ascendancy, based as it was on an upper-class minority, was simply a millstone round their necks. They were, however, afraid to jettison it, because the millstone was also the first line of defence against liberal and popular invaders.

Catholic relief proposals ran into parliamentary trouble in 1813, when Canning introduced additional securities including a government veto on the nomination of Catholic Bishops, and government censorship of correspondence with the Holy See. These securities produced a split in Catholic ranks between John Milner and the Irish Bishops on one side, and Charles Butler and the Catholic Board on the other. This split was easily exploited by Protestant politicians and the Relief Bill was abandoned after a division on Abbot's amendment to delete the clause admitting Catholics to Parliament. According to Philip Hughes 'it was the Catholic cause's dark hour':

There was division between the Catholics in Ireland and the Catholics in England, division between the English bishops, bitter controversy between the lay leaders of the English Catholics and the bishop most active in public life, no leader, no policy, everywhere suspicion and mistrust, and apparently at an end for ever the interest and goodwill of the pro-Catholic opposition, disgusted at seeing their plans wrecked by Catholics.[52]

Ironically, the kind of divisions that political pressures exposed in Catholic ranks were not dissimilar to those within Methodism fifteen or twenty years later. The political consequences of increasing sectarianism sharpened the power struggles between ministers and laymen in various denominations which had little else in common.

The years 1812–13 were particularly significant in Methodist political development for several reasons. The first and most obvious can be seen from the Allan papers. Until August 1812 Allan's correspondence is dominated by the Methodist campaign against Sidmouth's bill, and the subsequent attempts to get a new toleration act. As such there are letters to and from Whig peers committed to increased toleration and to the Society for the Protection of Religious Liberty (Dissenters). In the early months of 1813 Allan, as publicist for the Protestant Union, corresponded with a rather different constituency. In his collection there are letters from Lord Teignmouth, the Dean of Westminster, the Bishop of Durham, and assorted Archdeacons and Vicars Choral.[53] If this remarkable switch from Dissent to Church and from religious liberty to religious exclusion struck Allan as being odd, then there is no record of it.

Second, in the period before Methodist ministers were fully accepted by polite society, Methodist politics were given public expression by the London laity. When Charles Butler wanted to dissipate Methodist opposition to Catholic claims in the winter of 1812–13, he went to Butterworth.[54] When an evangelical Dissenter wanted the Methodist Committee of Privileges to resist Catholic Emancipation officially, he went to Allan.[55] Therefore, while Methodism 'as a body' had not come out against the Catholic claims (Methodists signed Anglican petitions), it was well known, in London at least, that Methodist political leaders were against any concession to the Catholics. Third, the need to protect the Methodist and evangelical missions in Ireland was making Wesleyan politics more Tory. Ironically, the expression of a traditional and popular anti-Catholicism helped to make Methodism more respectable to Tories and Anglicans.

Between 1813 and 1821, Methodists had more to fear from the upsurge in popular radicalism than from renewed attempts to achieve Catholic Emancipation, with the single exception of 1819 when Grattan's bill failed by a narrow majority. In response to this threat Allan and Butterworth simply repeated their strategy of 1812–13: Butterworth secretly sought information about Jesuits in Lancashire;[56] Allan reconvened the Protestant Union;[57] and Methodists continued to petition through Anglican parishes.[58] But the main battles came in an atmosphere of hardening sectarianism in Ireland in the 1820s. Even by the time of Grattan's bill in 1819, majority opinion in Ireland had already swung against any settlement based on rigorous securities.

Butterworth began the third decade of the nineteenth century as he had begun the second, by sending a circular to the Irish preachers requesting information about the trustworthiness of Irish Catholics should emancipation be granted. The replies were unanimous.

You desire my opinion respecting their being entrusted with political power. My dear sir I am fully persuaded it would be highly dangerous to Protestants in Ireland ... they would be driven to defend their liberties at the expense of blood.

In my judgment, political power in the hands of R.C. would greatly convulse this part of the country.

I can see no change for the better in the Roman Catholics of Ireland. I firmly believe they are as bigoted as ever they were, and therefore, that it would be as unsafe to trust them now with political power as at any former period.[59]

Henry Deery told Butterworth that he had conversed widely with friends in the Irish connexion, and he was persuaded that the opinions expressed above were 'in agreement with the judgment of our whole connexion'. Undoubtedly, the correspondence filtering into England from Irish Methodists in the 1820s was more antagonistic to Catholics than before. Missionary optimism was being replaced by a garrison mentality. Even Adam Clarke, Methodism's eminent scholar and theologian, was scaremongering in letters to Bunting from Ireland in 1823.

From the time I entered Ireland, I trod on *hostile ground*. I had got only a *few* hours out of Maghera, when it was attacked by the *Ribbonmen*, all the Protestants were driven out of it . . . the Papists were insultingly bold, and, if strong measures are not resorted to by government, I have no doubt that a general massacre of Protestants is at the door.[60]

As things hotted up in Ireland the correspondence with the London missionary committee and lay politicians was an important psychological boost for Irish Methodists who were virtually friendless in their own country. This partly explains why they did not surrender to the millennial enthusiasms of the Reformed evangelicals in Ireland, whose prophetical speculation was encouraged by the work of theologians in Trinity College Dublin, to which Methodists had no access.[61]

The first parliamentary move to secure Catholic Emancipation in the 1820s came in March 1821 when Plunket introduced two bills: the first to entitle Catholics to sit in Parliament; and the second to give the government a veto on episcopal nominations. Butterworth made his first parliamentary speech against Catholic Emancipation when he presented the petition of St Dunstans-in-the-West (drafted by Allan) against these proposals. He believed that if the bills before the House should pass, then they 'would transfer discontent from Ireland to the Protestant population of this country as well as afford great dissatisfaction to the Protestants there', and he concluded with the old evangelical paradox that he must refuse Catholic claims in the interests of civil and religious liberty.[62] This speech was significant, not because of its impact on the House of Commons, but for its implications for Methodism. Butterworth was known to be a Methodist, having earlier spoken in favour of Wesleyan missions. He was also the only Methodist MP. For those unaware of the complexities of the Wesleyan political framework, it seemed obvious that Butterworth was representing Methodist opinion. In a sense this was true, but he did not have official backing from Conference or from the Committee of Privileges.

Butterworth's next speech against concessions to Catholics came in 1823, when Lord Nugent moved that British Catholics should be admitted to the franchise privileges granted to Irish Catholics in 1793. Butterworth's strongly anti-Catholic speech was answered by Joseph Hume, the radical MP for Aberdeen. Calling the Methodists 'Protestant Jesuits', Hume stated that

the government ought to look after the Methodists, instead of the Catholics. For the last fifty years they had shown themselves most anxious in making proselytes, and most assiduous in their hostility to religious liberty; and he must say, that he believed no Roman Catholic had ever expressed such intolerant opinions as the hon. gentleman had uttered that night.

1823 was also the year in which the Catholic question assumed a new dimension, with the formation of the Catholic Association. The early progress of the association was slow and undistinguished until a one-penny, associate membership scheme was introduced early in 1824. The effect of the 'Catholic Rent' was startling. It marked the transition of the Catholic Association from a middle-class club into an impressive national movement. Not only was the scheme financially successful, but it engaged the support of the Catholic priests and great numbers of the Irish peasantry. The Catholic Association posed new problems for the Methodists, both directly and indirectly. Not only was a popular agitation more threatening, but government attempts to suppress the Catholic Association unintentionally implicated the Methodists. In Parliament Maurice Fitzgerald, MP for County Kerry, denied that the Catholic Association was a source of revolutionary danger, and argued that the 'Catholic Rent' was similar to other religious subscriptions; 'that of the Methodist Conference, for example, which was infinitely larger in amount, and which was unquestionably applied to political purposes'.[63] Although Fitzgerald's supporting facts were inaccurate, Brougham took the same tack, only in a more informed manner, in the debate on the Unlawful Societies in Ireland Bill. He stated that Methodist financial organization and pressure group tactics were not dissimilar to the Catholic Association. It was, therefore, hypocritical to legislate against one while tolerating the other. Butterworth replied by pointing out that the Committee of Privileges was not a political committee in the accepted sense, since it was convened for the specific purpose of guarding Methodist privileges.[64] Butterworth's speech was badly received by the House of Commons, and throughout the debate there was manifested a definite hostility against the Methodists. Whigs and radicals considered them to be bigots, and Protestant Constitutionists and evangelical Anglicans were mildly embarrassed by Methodist crudity. But this was nothing to the embarrassment of the Methodists, who were now compared with the Catholic Association after decades of anti-Catholic activity.

Burdett's proposals in 1825 to link Catholic Emancipation with the 'wings' (the abolition of the forty shilling freehold franchise in the Irish counties and the state payment of the Catholic clergy) had some chance of success. The government appeared to be weakening, and O'Connell displayed his middle-class propensity to ditch the Irish peasantry when the time seemed right. However, Protestant opinion outside the House was more successfully mobilized in 1825 than before by a combination of wealthy manufacturers, Anglican clergy, and proprietorial politicians. Methodist opposition also widened. G. I. T. Machin states that, although copies of an anti-Catholic petition were sent to all Dissenting ministers in Manchester, only the Methodists displayed them in their chapels to be signed. *The Times* reported a large anti-Catholic meeting in Spitalfields at which most of the speakers were Methodists.[65] However, it was in Parliament that the Catholic claims were finally demolished by stiff speeches from the Duke of York and Lord Liverpool, which convinced a surprisingly large minority.

In 1826, election year, the Methodists lost their only parliamentary representative, though not at the polls. Richard Watson preached Butterworth's funeral oration at the Great Queen Street chapel, and stated that it was a matter of 'notoriety' that Butterworth 'actively' and 'zealously' opposed political concessions to Catholics.[66] Butterworth was firmly within the early nineteenth-century evangelical ethos. He abhorred Roman Catholicism but he loved Roman Catholics. He opposed Catholic Emancipation because he supported religious toleration and liberty. Since Ireland's social and economic plight was due to the darkness of its superstition, its problems could only be solved by a national conversion to Protestantism. To that end, Butterworth advocated Protestant education, tract and Bible distribution, and missionary work. More nobly, perhaps, he opposed slavery, and he participated to the full in the abundant philanthropic societies of early nineteenth-century England.

Of more national significance was the election of 1826, in which the Catholic issue played a part. Historians are agreed about the strength of popular anti-Catholic sentiment,[67] especially in rural areas, and this is well-authenticated in the abundant and humorous anecdotes of literary figures like George Eliot and John Morley.[68] There is equal agreement that this inchoate sentiment produced only a minor change in the number of anti-Catholic MPs returned in 1826. Machin calculated that the net anti-Catholic gain was only thirteen.[69] The cause of this apparent discrepancy is to be found in the traditional and local electoral concerns of a relatively unrepresented England. Only in the larger boroughs, where electorates encompassed a wider social range beyond the control of traditional means of influence, did national issues have a significant impact. Such a borough was Leicester, where in 1826 the 'no popery' cry was raised by the corporation's Tory candidates, Sir Charles Hastings and R. O. Cave.[70] Cave also tried to bribe the framework knitters with money and a promise to support the repeal of the Corn Laws. Against the corporation candidates were William Evans and Thomas Denman, who represented the interests of Dissenters and reformers. The Catholic question was the vital issue, because it might also lead to 'nonconformist emancipation with a consequent revolution in the structure of the corporation'. Therefore, advocates of Catholic claims in Leicester in 1826 had also to be advocates of municipal reform. Consequently, the opposition to Catholic Emancipation by the Leicester corporation was simply part of a wider campaign against liberalism, radicalism, secularism and infidelity. If there was anything sophisticated about the arguments of the Protestant Constitutionists in the 1820s, it was this: the maintenance of aristocratic privileges in Church and State depended upon resistance to *any* liberal measure because the domino effect was so obvious. The corporation Tories won the expensive Leicester election, but it was a hollow victory because Cave quarrelled with the corporation over election expenses, and he became 'the principal agent of the Leicester liberals in the persistent advertisements of the corporation's sins'.

Methodist opposition to Catholic claims was, in some respects, similar to that of the Leicester corporation. It was part of a wider fear of radicalism, popular discontent and infidelity. Anti-Catholic prejudice easily fused with anti-reformist sentiments. However, the only surviving evidence of a deliberate attempt by Methodists to influence the 1826 election comes from the pen of Thomas Allan.

It remains however for you at this juncture to act and to exercise that prerogative which shall make your opinions respected. You have only to use virtuously and consistently your elective franchise and you settle that question which Statesmen pretend has puzzled them. . . . If you send Members favourable to Popery, however you may hate it, the conclusion will be that you are favourable to it, notwithstanding all the petitions you may send against. . . . Do not flatter yourselves that the struggle is over because the question was not stirred in the session of 1826.[71]

Allan was, of course, right, the 'struggle' was far from over despite the failure of Burdett's resolution in 1827. This was the first pro-Catholic motion to fail in the House of Commons since 1819 (for which there were specific political and electoral reasons), but, increasingly, circumstances in Ireland became more important than political debates in London. The events of 1828–9, from O'Connell's election for Clare to the eventual concession of Catholic Emancipation by Peel and Wellington, are well known. But historians still find it difficult to explain why the strongly conservative and anti-Catholic feeling in the country was not effectively expressed. Particularly perplexing are the divisions within the non-Catholic religious world over Catholic Emancipation – divisions within Dissent, evangelicalism and Methodism. For Halévy, the fundamental division was between the old rationalist Dissenters and the new enthusiastic evangelicals; 'from the very nature of their creed, the Evangelicals were anti-Catholic'.[72] While acknowledging that 'Revived Protestant groups were on the whole opposed to emancipation', J. H. Hexter showed that Anglican evangelicals, in Parliament at least, were less united than Halévy assumed. Instead, he argued that the cultured and sophisticated élites within evangelicalism and within Dissent (though not within Methodism, because Hexter saw *nothing* sophisticated in it) acted differently from their supporters: 'The Committee of the Three Denominations and the Church Evangelicals *in parliament* favoured Catholic relief, while the rank and file that they were supposed to lead marched in the opposite direction.'[73] This interpretation has received support from Richard Davis in his book *Dissent in Politics.*

In fact, the split in Dissent had nothing to do with creeds – there was nothing in the evangelical *creed* to distinguish it from any other trinitarian creed – and nothing to do with enthusiasm – except for anti-Catholic enthusiasm, which pre-dated religious enthusiasm by two hundred years. Only in the sense that the evangelical revival had a special appeal for those classes which were already violently anti-Catholic did it have any connexion with the question. The English lower classes . . . simply brought their bigotry with them into the revival . . . . The division in Dissent was not in the real sense a religious one, but was rather founded on class and education.[74]

Davis is wrong to underestimate the distinctive anti-Catholicism of much early nineteenth-century evangelical theology,[75] but his main distinction holds, at least within the confines of Dissent. Within Anglican evangelicalism the picture is more complicated. Ian Bradley has shown how the issue of Catholic Emancipation produced the same division in evangelical ranks as did the repeal of the Test and Corporation Acts. In Parliament, the Saints and the Whig evangelicals were generally in favour of emancipation, but the Tory evangelicals were not. The root of this division was not party loyalty, but opposing views about the effect of emancipation on Ireland. Optimistic evangelicals voted for emancipation on grounds of imperial and missionary expediency, whereas pessimistic evangelicals, who were usually those with the closest Irish connections, believed that emancipation would ruin Protestantism in Ireland.[76] The former were neither pro-Catholic nor advocates of religious pluralism; they simply believed that Ireland could not be made more Protestant by discriminatory legislation.

Similar divisions, though not at parliamentary level, appeared within the Methodist leadership in the same period. Methodism in general was more stoutly anti-Catholic than the rest of Nonconformity because of its all pervading evangelical theology, its relatively uncultivated ministry, its appeal to lower social groups, and its vested interests in Ireland. Nevertheless, there were official attempts to discourage anti-Catholic sentiment from becoming anti-Catholic political activity. The Irish Conference advised those in Methodist societies not to 'meddle with politics' and to 'sparingly enter into political conversations, but be always ready to show that you fear God and honour the King'.[77] But privately the strains were beginning to show. Matthew Tobias, chairman of the Limerick circuit and probably the only Irish Methodist leader in favour of emancipation, told Bunting that many of the Irish preachers were speaking at Brunswick clubs (ultra-Protestant societies).[78] He wanted Bunting, as Methodist President, to put a stop to this activity, but Bunting, though in favour of Catholic Emancipation with proper securities, thought it inexpedient to coerce 'the Irish preachers, who I believe are generally very hot anti-concessionists'.[79] According to Tobias, the problem went beyond the preachers.

Our county Societies are composed exclusively of Palatines, the descendants of men driven from Germany on account of their religion, they do not amalgamate with the native Irish and are all Brunswickers; and the *Brunswick Star*, a most inflammatory paper is sent by the Brunswick Clubs to every society in the circuit so that our people are kept in a perpetual political fever.[80]

Similar impressions are conveyed by other channels of communication between English and Irish Methodists. Thomas Edwards was the representative of the London missionary committee in Ireland in 1828–9. His frequent reports highlight the tensions of these years.

Reformation Societies are becoming general, the Catholic Association very active.

I suppose a higher degree of general, and intense, excitement has not prevailed at any time . . . the country generally is agitated by the rage of nasty spirit, angry political feeling, and religious controversy.

You have asked my opinion respecting the settlement of the Catholic question; but I feel a little delicacy in committing anything to paper on so momentous a subject, especially as I have been led to view the subject differently from nearly the whole of our Irish brethren. With the exception of Mr Tobias and myself, I think there is but one feeling on the subject, that is 'that concession will lead to the overthrow of Protestantism'. I have not yet been able to see that this is the necessary consequence of *some* concession.[81]

Edwards, like Bunting and Tobias, believed that a timely concession from a Tory government, combined with a strong policy on law and order, was the best hope for the successful continuation of Methodist missionary work in Ireland. Others believed, with equally convincing arguments, that Catholic Emancipation was but the first blow in the complete demolition of the Protestant Ascendancy in Ireland. According to William Stewart, Irish Catholics would follow up their success by launching an attack on the wealth of the Church of Ireland, and, if necessary, the Union itself.[82] Although in the Hexter and Davis argument this was technically a less educated and sophisticated response, it was at least realistic and, as it turned out, prophetic. After a further ten years of Catholic pressure, Bunting, who had been 'liberal' in 1829, was in alliance with the Merseyside Orangemen.

Methodists in England responded in much the same way as their Irish counterparts. R. L. Sheil's account of the huge Penendon Heath meeting in October 1828 states that 'the Protestant side had much more a clerical than an agricultural aspect', because 'not only the priests of the established religion, but many of the dissenting preachers of the Methodist school, were arrayed under the Winchelsea banner'. Sheil identified the Methodists by their 'lugubrious and dismal expression'.[83] More reliably, Eldon stated in the Lords that

having had multitudes of provincial papers transmitted to him, containing reports of the debates which had taken place at numerous meetings in the country, for the purpose of petitioning parliament against further concessions to the Catholics, he had been astonished to observe the ability and knowledge manifested by the ministers of the Wesleyan Methodists who had taken part in those debates.[84]

One such speech, which can stand for all, was made by George Cubitt at a public meeting in Sheffield town hall. Cubitt was not ashamed to declare himself a Wesleyan preacher, even though he was speaking on a political platform. His two central arguments were familiar: Roman Catholics effectively excluded themselves from the exercise of legislative power because of the 'essential intolerance' of their church; and the watertight Protestantism of the British constitution must not be violated – 'If one part of the Legislature must be Protestant, the whole ought to be Protestant. If one branch may be altered, the whole ought to partake of the alteration.' At the end of his speech, Cubitt characteristically tried to disclaim political affiliations. 'What I have said, I have not said as a party man; I belong to no political party. I gladly on all ordinary occasions, let politics alone.'[85] This was the traditional Wesleyan position when the realms of religion and politics became inseparable. Although Cubitt was not a member of a political party, that did not make his speech non-political. In fact, his arguments were those of the High Church Tories, the Eldonian constitutionalists and the Brunswickers.

Despite speeches like this in many English provincial cities, the Methodists did not organize a co-ordinated and effective opposition to Catholic claims. Wesleyans are also conspicuous by their absence from the widespread anti-Catholic petitioning of the years 1828–9.[86] This discrepancy between popular Methodist opposition and official silence has perplexed historians,[87] although new evidence from the Bunting and Allan manuscripts has clarified matters. In January and February 1829 pressure was building up on Bunting, as President of the Conference, and on Allan, as legal adviser to the Committee of Privileges, to initiate an official Methodist opposition to Catholic Emancipation. Bunting was even approached by officers of the Brunswick Constitutional Club of Ireland, who sought Methodist political muscle by eulogizing Wesleyan respectability.[88] Bunting summed up his response to these pressures in a letter to Tobias.

Private and public appeals are made to me, as the President, to originate or countenance such petitions, which of course I must refuse to do. I am sure incalculable mischief would result from it. We *as a body* never have petitioned *separately*; nor should we now, on a question so decidedly political in its aspect.[89]

Bunting's position was clear. He had spoken publicly in favour of Catholic Emancipation,[90] and he had enough political astuteness to know that it would be carried in any case. He did not want the

Methodists 'as a body' to become involved in a question 'so decidedly political'. Bunting had the full weight of the Wesleyan tradition behind him, and he was right; the Methodists never had 'as a body' taken part in political affairs. The opposition to Sidmouth's bill was different, since that was a direct attack on Methodist religious privileges. The majority of Wesleyans, however, did not see the distinction so clearly, because for them Catholic Emancipation was primarily a religious issue.

While Bunting was trying to maintain Methodist discipline from his base in Manchester, Thomas Allan was busy in London. He had already convened a meeting of the Committee of Privileges on 13 February because he feared 'that the Bill before Parliament for the Suppression of the Catholic Association might probably in some way or other [affect our] Societies in Ireland'.[91] Peel subsequently assured Allan that the Methodists were safe. Throughout February and early March Allan was in contact with the ultra-Tory peers, Eldon and Farnham, who wanted the Methodists 'to appear'.[92] With the support of Adam Clarke and others, Allan convened a meeting of the Committee of Privileges on 11 March to discuss Catholic Emancipation. Allan has left the fullest and most accurate account of the meeting.

On the 11th inst the Committee of Privileges met, but on considering the Bill it did not appear to me to affect the Methodists more than other protestants and therefore *as a Body* it would hardly be proper for them to move, especially as there might be some who would object. Indeed I have always thought that they should not act as a *Body* unless they were likely to suffer as such. We therefore unanimously resolved that 'with respect to the Bill for the Relief of His Majesty's Rom Cath subjects now before the House of Commons the Committee of Privileges do not think it their duty to take any proceedings in their collective capacity; but every member of the Methodist Societies will of course pursue such steps in his individual capacity on this occasion as he may conscientiously think right'. At our meeting I did not observe one person present in favour of the Cath claims but Dr Bunting. The letters received were without variation against them and I have no doubt that the Methodists generally throughout the country are aiding in the general exertions.[93]

Although these 'exertions' were recognized and commented upon by speakers in the House of Lords,[94] the strength of Methodist opposition to Catholic Emancipation was muted by official adherence to the 'no politics' rule. This rule came under considerable pressure in 1829, from within[95] and without, but it stood because Bunting argued forcefully for it, and old campaigners like Allan realized that this was the authentic Wesleyan position. Catholic Emancipation passed without official protest from the Wesleyans, but the bitter reaction of the vast majority of Methodist preachers in England and in Ireland showed that emancipation, far from easing religious conflict, merely ushered in a period of more intense sectarianism. In particular, the Methodists felt betrayed by Peel, the last politician of ministerial ability to resist the Catholic claims.

And here is Robert Peel – the staunch tory and anti-catholic where judgement was so unerring whose integrity was so unquestionable who knew Popery well enough to declare that Papists could give no security to a government who might be so liberal and silly as to trust them – Peel the chosen of the University of Oxford – whose very name was the rallying word for good true strong unaltering constitutional British feeling – he is convinced too that Emancipation must be granted – the apostate![96]

Ironically, this was precisely the reaction of Newman and the High Church party to Peel.[97]

In fact, Peel, as Bunting well understood, supported emancipation for conservative reasons. His aim was to maintain the peace and security of the Empire, deprive the democratic movement of one of its most powerful forces and remove an issue that had split the Tory party for many years. In short, it was politic to concede in 1829, as it had been in 1828 over the Dissenters' claims, and would be again over parliamentary reform and the repeal of the Corn Laws. The British aristocracy relinquished its eighteenth-century power by instalments. Moreover, so long as its patronage and electoral control remained more or less intact, shadows were reluctantly conceded to preserve realities. Nevertheless, one should not minimize the psychological and political impact of 1829, when a 'Tory government passed a Whig measure', a 'Protestant government broke its pledge', and 'a majority in parliament voted for an act which the majority of Englishmen opposed'.[98] Or as Norman Gash has it, 'the people of England would never have passed Catholic Emancipation in 1829; and it was as well for that cause that the country was still ruled by an oligarchy'.[99]

The relatively silent English majority remained silent for a remarkable combination of reasons. Dissenters had achieved the repeal of the Test and Corporation Acts in 1828 (with unsolicited Catholic support), and were in no position to prevent the extension of civil relief to another religious group. At the last meeting of the Dissenters'

United Committee in 1828 it was resolved that 'although the Committee had abstained in its own application from coalition with other applicants, it could not separate without expressing its desire for the abolition of all laws interfering with the rights of conscience and attaching civil disabilities to religious faith and worship'.[100] Similarly, English radical leaders supported Catholic Emancipation as a staging post on the way to a more thorough reform of Parliament. O'Connell exploited this support for tactical reasons, but he eventually sacrificed the forty-shilling freeholders in Ireland, despite strong pleas from Hunt and Cobbett.

Within evangelicalism, men like Wilberforce supported Catholic Emancipation because it seemed illogical to allow Catholics to vote, but not to sit in Parliament. Moreover, like other zealous Protestants, he believed that Ireland's religious salvation could not be achieved by political repression.[101] For thoughtful evangelicals, including the Methodist trio of Bunting, Tobias and Edwards, missionary strategy was more important than political ascendancy. The really stout opposition to emancipation came from English ultra-Tories and Irish landowners. Ironically, for social and constitutional reasons, these were the very men who found it most difficult to exploit popular anti-Catholicism. This is well illustrated in a letter from Lord Skelmersdale to Colchester, in which he stated that the establishment of Brunswick clubs in Ireland was understandable, but 'in this country they are perhaps less necessary, unless they can be carried with a *high hand*'.[102] In addition, the immigration of Catholic Irish into the big English cities had not yet reached sufficient levels to provoke a social and sectarian response from the English working classes. Perhaps most important of all was the fact that very few foresaw the full implications of Catholic Emancipation for subsequent British politics. As a result, the stoutest opposition to Catholic claims came in the early Victorian period.

Throughout the period from Wesley's death until 1829, Methodist opposition to Roman Catholic religion became more public and therefore more political. Attitudes hardened as Catholic Ireland grew more resentful of evangelical proselytizing and became more conscious of its political and social disabilities. Methodist anti-Catholicism ruined its chances of missionary progress in Ireland, but it paid unexpected returns in England. Not only did it cement Methodist respectability in the eyes of aristocratic Tories and Protestant Anglicans, but it strengthened Methodist roots in English popular culture at a time when its opposition to popular radicalism threatened

142 *Methodism and Politics in British Society 1750–1850*

its survival in industrial districts. Moreover, the transition from a primitive and flexible eighteenth-century itinerancy to appearances on public platforms in Victorian cities was facilitated as much by bigotry as by chapel building. Bunting, as usual, knew what was happening, and in the 1830s he appealed to Methodist anti-Catholic prejudice as an additional means of controlling those in the connexion who hankered after Whig-liberal and Dissenting policies.

In fact, in their opposition to radical politics and Irish Catholics, the Wesleyans set themselves against the two principal liberal crusades of the first half of the nineteenth century: religious equality and the extension of political power to new social groups. As such their strident opposition to Catholicism as an illiberal force, that would have endeared them to radicals in some other parts of Europe, condemned them in Britain to ultra-Toryism and allegations of bigotry. Until 1830, however, with its position in English society still relatively insecure, Methodism 'as a body' steered clear of political agitation. There was, nevertheless, a steady increase in political activity from Butterworth's and Allan's London associations to commendations in the House of Lords for the extent of Methodist political preaching in 1829. Finally, in the conflict between English popular Protestantism and Irish Catholicism, emancipation, far from ending sectarian politics, merely secured the right of one of the sparring partners to move from the gymnasium of Ireland to the political ring at Westminster. Future hostilities between Methodists and Catholics were bound to be more central to English political and religious life.

References

1 E. R. Norman, *Anti-Catholicism in Victorian England* (London 1968), p. 20.
2 C. Z. Wiener, 'The Beleaguered Isle: a study of Elizabethan and early Jacobean Anti-Catholicism', *Past and Present*, no. 51 (1971), pp. 27–62.
3 Robin Clifton, 'Fear of Popery', in Conrad Russell (ed.), *The Origins of the English Civil War* (London 1973), pp. 144–67.
4 See Norman, p. 16; John Foster, *Class Struggle and the Industrial Revolution* (London 1974), ch. 7; and Patrick Joyce, *Work, Society and Politics: the culture of the factory of later Victorian England* (London 1980), pp. 240–67.
5 Norman, pp. 21–2.
6 For further information on Irish Methodism see C. H. Crookshank,

History of Methodism in Ireland, 3 vols. (London 1885–8); Raymond Gillespie, *Wild as Colts Untamed* (Lurgan 1977); and Frederick Jeffrey, *Irish Methodism* (Belfast 1964).

7 See M.C.A. typescript, Adam Clarke to the Methodist Preachers in Great Britain, 21 October 1822; and The Answer of the British Conference to the Annual Address of the Irish Conference, 1839, in *Irish Conference Minutes* (1840).

8 George Taylor, *A History of the Rise, Progress, and Suppression of the Rebellion in the County of Wexford in the year 1798* (Dublin 1800). Serialized in the *Methodist Magazine* (1804).

9 Anon., *An extract of a letter from a Gentleman in Ireland to Mr William Thompson* (London 1798). *Methodist Magazine* (1799).

10 See, for example, I.W.H.S.A. Mss., Adam Averell to Joseph Benson 7 June 1798.

11 W. West, *Observations and Reflections on what is styled Catholic Emancipation* (Liverpool 1812). Henry Fish, *The Workings of Popery ... in which the question is briefly viewed in relation to the Maynooth Grant* (London 1845).

12 Crookshank, vol. 2, pp. 144–8.

13 An Address from the Irish to the British Conference (Dublin, 13 July 1799), in *Irish Conference Minutes*.

14 See the map produced by J. R. Binns in 'A history of Methodism in Ireland from Wesley's death in 1791 to the re-union of Primitives and Wesleyans in 1878' (unpublished MA thesis, Queen's University Belfast 1960).

15 M.M.S.Mss., Charles Graham to Dr Coke, 11 September and 23 November 1802.

16 M.M.S.Mss., Dr Coke's draft on Irish Missions for the report of 1806.

17 See M.M.S.Mss., Graham, Hamilton and Peacock to Coke, 24 March 1806.

18 Most of these societies are listed by F. K. Brown, *Fathers of the Victorians* (Cambridge 1961), pp. 329–40; and A. R. Acheson, 'The Evangelicals in the Church of Ireland 1784–1859' (unpublished PhD thesis, Queen's University Belfast 1967), pp. 70–95.

19 Brown, p. 281.

20 G. F. A. Best, 'Popular Protestantism in Victorian Britain', in R. Robson (ed.), *Ideas and Institutions of Victorian Britain, essays in honour of G. Kitson Clarke* (London 1967), pp. 115–42.

21 He came as Secretary of the English Conference in 1827, as President in 1829, as a Missions Secretary in 1833, and again as President in 1837.

22 Desmond Bowen, *The Protestant Crusade in Ireland 1800–70* (Dublin 1978).

23 See Nicholas Canny, 'Why the Reformation failed in Ireland: une question mal posée', *Journal of Ecclesiastical History*, **30** no. 4 (1979), pp. 423–50.

24 Bowen, pp. 34–7.

25 Reinhard Cassirer, 'The Irish influence on the Liberal movement in England 1798–1832, with special reference to the period 1815–32' (unpublished PhD thesis, University of London 1940), p. 60.

26 J. C. Beckett, *The Making of Modern Ireland 1603–1923* (London 1966), p. 295.

27 Statutes at Large XLII, 648f., 40 George III, c. 67.

28 *Watchman*, 13 July 1836.

29 See Bowen, p. 62.

30 Acheson, p. 137. See also, Henry Abelove, 'George Berkeley's attitude to John Wesley: the evidence of a lost letter', *Harvard Theological Review*, **70** (1977), pp. 175–6.

31 Cassirer, p. 36.

32 S. Maccoby, *English Radicalism 1786–1832* (London 1955), pp. 454–5.

33 Brown, pp. 351–2, 505.

34 *The Diary and Correspondence of Charles Abbot, Lord Colchester*, ed. by his son Charles, Lord Colchester, 3 vols. (London 1861), vol. 2, p. 468, and vol. 3, pp. 9, 22, 358.

35 M.C.A.Mss., Gideon Ouseley to Joseph Butterworth, 29 May, and 3 August 1804; Charles Graham to Joseph Butterworth 13 March 1805. Butterworth also had first hand experience of Ireland. See *An Account of the Religious and Literary Life of Adam Clarke*, by a member of his family, 3 vols., (London 1833), vol. 2, pp. 255–76.

36 Lord Eldon to Dr Swire, 22 September 1812 in Horace Twiss, *The Public and Private Life of Lord Chancellor Eldon*, 3 vols. (London 1844), vol. 2, p. 255.

37 M.C.A. Printed Circular, Joseph Butterworth to Methodist preachers and others in Ireland, 4 November 1812.

38 M.C.A.Mss., Peter Roe to Joseph Butterworth, 24 December 1812.

39 M.C.A.Mss., Gideon Ouseley to Joseph Butterworth, 25 November 1812; and *Sligo Journal*, 21 May 1823.

40 Gideon Ouseley, *Letters to Dr. Doyle on the Doctrines of his Church with an easy and effectual plan to obtain Immediate Emancipation* (Dublin 1824), *Error Unmasked* (Dublin 1828), *Letters in Defence of the Roman Catholics of Ireland in which is opened the real source of their many injuries, and of Ireland's Sorrows: Addressed to Daniel O'Connell* (London 1829), *A Review of a sermon preached. . . at the opening of the R. Catholic Chapel in Bradford, Yorkshire* (Dublin 1829). Ouseley maintained his output in the 1830s.

41 William Arthur, *The Life of Gideon Ouseley* (London 1886), pp. 240–1.

42 His charter can be found in the I.W.H.S.A.

43 M.C.A.Allan Mss., Thomas Allan to Joseph Butterworth, 3 December 1812.

44 M.C.A.Mss., John Barber to George Marsden, 18 January 1813.

45 M.C.A.Allan Mss., a one page minute of the meeting in Butterworth's house, 13 January 1813. See the printed resolutions of the first meeting of the Protestant Union, held at the Crown and Anchor Tavern, London, 22 January 1813.

46 M.C.A.Allan Mss., first drafts of Protestant Union publicity are to be found in Allan's hand.

47 Thomas Allan, *Letters to a Protestant Dissenter relative to the Claims of the Roman Catholics* (London 1813).

48 M.C.A.Allan Mss., Lord Teignmouth to Thomas Allan 5 August 1813. See also, Charles Butler, *Reminiscences* (London 1822), p. 250.

49 M.C.A.Allan Mss., William Roberts to Joseph Butterworth, 8 February 1813.

50 G. F. A. Best, 'The Protestant Constitution and its supporters', *Transactions of the Royal Historical Society*, 5th series, **8** (1958), pp. 105–27.

51 See Cassirer, p. 169.

52 Philip Hughes, *The Catholic Question 1688–1829, a Study in Political History* (London 1929), p. 271.

53 Many of these letters were not addressed to Allan but to the officers of the Protestant Union. They did, however, end up in his hands. See M.C.A.Allan Mss., William Coxe, Archdeacon of Wiltshire, to John Hickin, 4 February; Rev. George Strong, Vicar Choral of St Asaph, to Granville Sharp, 15 February; Bishop of Durham to John King, 19 April; Granville Sharp to Dr Vincent, 26 January; Bishop of St David's to Thomas Allan, 30 August; and Lord Teignmouth to Thomas Allan, 5 August, all 1813.

54 M.C.A.Mss., Charles Butler to Joseph Butterworth, 3 February 1813.

55 M.C.A.Allan Mss., A Dissenter to Thomas Allan, 8 March 1813.

56 M.C.A.Mss., Joseph Butterworth to James Bogie, 20 May 1819.

57 M.C.A., see the printed resolutions of the Protestant Union (London 17 April 1819), the drafts for which are in the Allan manuscripts.

58 Allan, Butterworth and other London Methodists petitioned with the parishioners of St Dunstan's-in-the-West. See the printed introduction to a petition in the Allan Mss., 2 June 1819.

59 M.C.A.Allan Mss., William Stewart, Henry Deery, Andrew Hamilton and John Stuart to Joseph Butterworth, 12, 13, 19 and 29 May 1820.

60 M.C.A.Mss., Adam Clarke to Jabez Bunting, 27 June, and 4 July 1823. The first letter is reprinted by W. R. Ward in *The Early*

Correspondence of Jabez Bunting 1820–1829, Camden 4th series, vol. 11 (London 1972), pp. 89–91.

61   See Bowen, pp. 64–7, and my 'Evangelicalism and eschatology', *Journal of Ecclesiastical History*, **31** no. 2 (1980), pp. 179–94.
62   *Hansard*, NS, **IV**, c. 1184–6.
63   *Hansard*, NS, **XII**, c. 149.
64   *Hansard*, NS, **XII**, c. 511–20.
65   See G. I. T. Machin, *The Catholic Question in English Politics 1820 to 1830* (Oxford 1964), pp. 54–5.
66   Richard Watson, *A Sermon on the death of Joseph Butterworth, Esq.* (London 1826).
67   See Best, 'Popular Protestantism'; and J. H. Hexter, 'The Protestant revival and the Catholic question in England, 1778–1829', *Journal of Modern History*, **8** no. 3 (1936), pp. 297–319.
68   George Eliot, 'The Sad fortunes of the Rev. Amos Barton', in *Scenes of Clerical Life* (1858); and John Morley, *The Life of William Ewart Gladstone*, 2 vols. (London 1905), vol. 1, pp. 53–4.
69   Machin, p. 195; and Hexter, pp. 309–11.
70   See R. W. Greaves, 'Roman Catholic relief and the Leicester election of 1826', *TRHS*, 4th series, **22** (1940), pp. 199–223; and Peter Jupp, *British and Irish Elections 1784–1831* (Newton Abbot 1973), pp. 129–35.
71   M.C.A.Allan Mss., notes on Catholic Emancipation (perhaps for a Protestant Union circular, or for use as an election speech).
72   Élie Halévy, *A History of the English People 1815–1830* (London 1926) p. 216.
73   Hexter, pp. 297–319.
74   R. W. Davis, *Dissent in Politics 1780–1830: the Political Life of William Smith, M.P.* (London 1971), p. 230.
75   See Sheridan Gilley, 'Protestant London, No-Popery and the Irish poor, 1830–60', *Recusant History*, **10** no. 4 (1970), pp. 210–30.
76   See Cassirer, pp. 167–225, and Ian Bradley, 'The politics of godliness: Evangelicals in parliament, 1784–1832' (unpublished D Phil. thesis, University of Oxford 1974), pp. 178–89, 299–301. Bradley's analysis is sound, but his voting lists are based on an unsatisfactory definition of what constitutes an evangelical. Hexter's article is even more unreliable in that respect. For a broader interpretation of evangelical divisions in this period, see Ian Rennie, 'Evangelicalism and English public life, 1823–1850' (unpublished PhD thesis, University of Toronto 1962); and the works cited in my 'Evangelicalism and eschatology', pp. 179–94.
77   The Annual Address of the Conference to the Members of the Wesleyan Societies in Ireland, July 1828 and 1829 in *Irish Conference Minutes*.

78 I.W.H.S. Mss., Matthew Tobias to Jabez Bunting, 28 November 1828.
79 Jabez Bunting to Matthew Tobias, 23 February 1829, in Ward, pp. 202–3.
80 I.W.H.S. Mss., Matthew Tobias to Jabez Bunting, 17 March 1829.
81 M.M.S. Mss., Thomas Edwards to the Mission Secretaries, 7 and 13 January 1828, and Edwards to George Morley, 24 February 1829. See also, William Cornwall to George Morley, 3 February 1829.
82 I.W.H.S. Mss., William Stewart to Joseph Entwistle, 24 March 1829.
83 M. W. Savage (ed.), *Sketches, Legal and Political, by the late Right Honourable Richard Lalor Sheil* (London 1855), vol. 2, pp. 202–3. Sheil's antipathy to Methodists dates back to earlier conflicts with Butterworth. See Thomas MacNevin (ed.), *The Speeches of Richard Lalor Sheil* (Dublin n.d.), pp. 353–6.
84 *Hansard*, NS, **XX**, c. 1313.
85 George Cubitt, *A Speech delivered in the Town Hall, Sheffield, February 18, 1829* (Bristol 1829).
86 In 1828 there was a petition from Methodists in Brixham, and in 1829 there were petitions from Methodists in Derryanville, Portadown, Armagh, Buckingham, Maidstone, Marlborough and Wellingborough. *Journals of the House of Commons*, LXXXXIII and LXXXIV (1828–9). Methodists signed petitions of the Established Church and other Protestant groups.
87 I review this historiography in 'Thomas Allan and Methodist politics 1800–1840', *History*, **67** no. 219 (February 1982), pp. 13–31.
88 M.C.A., a two-page printed circular to the Ministers of the Wesleyan connexion signed by T. P. Magee, Charles Boyton and Hugh Eccles, postmarked 8 March 1829.
89 Jabez Bunting to Matthew Tobias, 23 February 1829, in Ward, pp. 202–3. See also John Aikenhead to Bunting, postmarked 21 February 1829, ibid., pp. 201–2.
90 T. P. Bunting, *The Life of Jabez Bunting*, 2 vols. (London 1859 and 1887), vol. 2, p. 215.
91 M.C.A.Mss., John Mason to Jabez Bunting, 14 February 1829.
92 M.C.A.Allan Mss., Thomas Allan to his son Thomas, 9 March 1829.
93 M.C.A.Allan Mss., Thomas Allan to his son Thomas, 19 March 1829. See also Journal of Joseph Entwistle, 14 March 1829. Thomas Jackson, in *Recollections of my own Life and Times* (London 1873), p. 407, alleges a more dramatic intervention by Bunting.
94 *Hansard*, NS, **XX**, c. 1307–13.
95 See William Vevers to Jabez Bunting, 16 March 1829, in Ward, pp. 204–6.

96 M.C.A.Mss., Richard Treffry jnr to George Osborne, 11 February 1829. For a similar reaction from Ireland see Robert Huston, *The Life and Labours of the Rev. Fossey Tackaberry* (London 1853), pp. 171–3.

97 David Newsome, *The Parting of Friends* (London 1966), pp. 94–5.

98 See Cassirer, p. 235.

99 Norman Gash, *Aristocracy and People: Britain 1815–1865* (London 1979), p. 140.

100 B. L. Manning, *The Protestant Dissenting Deputies* (Cambridge 1952), p. 252.

101 Robin Furneaux, *William Wilberforce* (London 1974), pp. 319–22.

102 Lord Skelmersdale to Lord Colchester, 3 December 1828, in *The Diary and Correspondence of Lord Colchester*, vol. 3, pp. 589–90.

6 Educational politics, 1820–50

The fortunes of the national education system in England were caught between the general determination that it should be religious, and the difficulties of deciding on what grounds of common acceptance that could be achieved. These difficulties were not unusual or in any way inexplicable or necessarily, as is sometimes suggested, deplorable. They were bound to happen in a society which prized its religion highly, and which was politically freer than any other in Europe. The difficulties arose because conscientious compromise was impossible on matters which meant life or death to the State as well as heaven and hell to the individual.[1]

Between the political and ecclesiastical absolutism of the *ancien régime* and the pluralism of the twentieth century came 'Europe's age of religious polarization'.[2] The distinctive cultural characteristics of this polarization varied from country to country, but in England, and in Ireland for that matter, it was most marked in the sphere of education, because, more than any other issue, education encouraged denominational rivalry, and brought religion into conflict with the state's interventionist social policies. That no simple solutions could be found to such conflicts is clear from the denominational heat generated by educational debates, at least up to the First World War in England, and apparently forever in Ireland. The reasons for this are to be found in the peculiar political, religious and social circumstances in both countries. According to Professor Best, no satisfactory system of national education could be established in nineteenth-century Europe except where one religion was utterly dominant, or where a government was strong enough to override sectional dissatisfaction, or where there was a powerful tradition of inter-denominational co-operation.[3] One might add that a national educational system could have been achieved either through the back door of bureaucratic encroachment (Utilitarian radicals and many politicians, including Russell and Peel, favoured this strategy), or where a religious consensus emerged through fear of the possible alternatives. This almost happened in Ireland in the 1830s when the Catholic Church so distrusted Protestant proselytism that it temporarily accepted a solution which it later repudiated, and might have happened in England if the secularist challenge had been more serious.

The reality was that religious denominations of all kinds, from Anglicans to Dissenters, and from Wesleyans to Catholics, had expended enormous energy in building schools from 1790 to 1850, and were fearful lest the state's superior financial resources should rob them of their glory. If working-class adults had shown themselves indifferent to institutional religion, then perhaps their children could be won back through institutional education. As with Sunday schools in the first quarter of the nineteenth century, so with day schools in the second quarter,[4] education was a prize worth fighting for. But the same problem that denominations faced over Sunday schools resurfaced, because the working classes generally preferred to pay more for an inferior education in dame schools than to accept the religious paternalism of voluntary schools.[5]

The Methodists, whose major contribution to Sunday schools disguised their comparatively insignificant contribution to daily education, entered the elementary education contest surprisingly late (after 1835), but their principles had already been formed through the disputes over the control of Sunday schools and Irish national education. In putting these principles into political action in the period 1837–47, Wesleyan Methodism emerged as an important extra-parliamentary pressure group. Moreover, its special relationship with the Church of England and with Peelite Conservatism, was seriously damaged because, by 1845, the one had become theologically, and the other politically, unsafe for evangelical Protestants.

The earliest hint of a distinctively Wesleyan educational policy came in response to Henry Brougham's proposals in 1820. Brougham's plan, which had to be dropped, was designed to supplement the work already being done by the inter-denominational British and Foreign School Society and the Anglican National Society. He wanted to establish schools under Anglican control in any parish where 'there was no school within the district, or none in the adjoining districts sufficiently near to be available to the inhabitants of that district, or that there was only one school where two were necessary'.[6] The Anglican bias of Brougham's proposals was, in T. P. Bunting's words, a source of 'considerable alarm' to provincial Methodists.[7] Jabez Bunting's correspondence shows this to be true, but in almost every case Methodist opposition was the result of Dissenting pressure.[8] The Committee of Privileges met but decided to take no con-nexional action against Brougham's scheme,[9] and Bunting explained why in a letter to the Carlisle circuit superintendent.

Party interests and petty considerations should not hinder so great an object. Particular clauses it is desirable to have omitted or modified; and to this the Committee will attend in due time. But as to opposing the *Bill in toto* and *limine*, this would *on our part* be unbecoming and improper. Dissenters are opposed to all *Religious Establishments* and of course to every form of National Instruction connected at all with an Establishment. But the Methodists as a Body have not adopted such views. What we ultimately may do must be done by ourselves and not in common with them.[10]

The Methodists did not object to the basic principles of Brougham's bill, a more national system of daily education incorporating the teaching of the Scriptures; they simply disliked, though not as intensely as the Dissenters, the privileged status given to the Church of England. Such an independent stance taken up by the largest non-Anglican religious community in the country was clearly going to create special problems for politicians who found it difficult enough to manage the old divisions between Church and Dissent. On the other hand, it did at least leave more room for political manoeuvre. The next attempt to introduce a national system of daily education took place not in England but in Ireland, and Wesleyan educational policy was profoundly affected by it.

Irish national education[11]

Because of the peculiarities of Irish history, the English government was obliged to tackle the problem of elementary education in Ireland before it had to do so in England. There were several reasons for this. First, eighteenth- and early nineteenth-century educational policy, which was based on the need to maintain the Protestant Ascendancy, had by the 1820s become unacceptable to the Church of the vast majority of Irishmen. Moreover, the opposition of the Catholic Church mattered more then than it had done earlier because of the new political and religious aspirations created by the campaign for Catholic Emancipation and the new aggressiveness of Protestant proselytism. Second, because of Ireland's semi-colonial status there was a much stronger tradition of legislative interference in Irish society than was true in England. Finally, there was a growing con-sensus among churchmen, administrators and politicians about the kind of educational system that might be acceptable to the majority of Irishmen.

The historical circumstances leading to the Irish educational experiment, the nature of that experiment, and the way it subsequently developed are not only of central importance to Irish social history, but are also a kind of dress rehearsal for similar debates over English national education a decade later. Indeed, educational developments in Ireland both parallel and contrast with the English pattern; England started off with a denominational system that evolved into a national and more secular one, whereas Ireland started off with a national and religiously neutral system that evolved into a denominational one. In both countries, the years 1830–50 were of special importance.

Until the beginning of the nineteenth century, the chief educational provision for Ireland came in the form of government endowed schools, whether of the parish, diocesan, royal or charter variety. This tradition of state interference supported by penal laws against Catholic education was designed primarily to bolster up the Protestant Ascendancy. Catholics were consequently forced to set up a network of 'hedge schools' to which they clung with the same kind of tenacity as the English working classes did to their dame schools. In the wake of the Evangelical Revival in the period 1790–1820, Irish education was transformed by the establishment of Protestant educational societies designed to convert illiterate Catholics while educating them. These included the Association for Discountenancing Vice and Promoting the Knowledge and Practice of the Christian Religion (1792), the London Hibernian Society (1806),[12] the Baptist Society for Promoting the Gospel in Ireland (1814), and the Irish Society for Promoting the Education of the Native Irish through their own Language (1818). It is difficult to get accurate figures for the number of children in these schools, but by 1825 the number would not have been much below 100,000 pupils, to which must be added the 150,000 children claimed by the Sunday School Society for Ireland.[13] (No doubt there was an overlapping membership.) The educational achievements of the predominantly English evangelicals in Ireland were therefore far from negligible, but the most important footholds were gained between 1805 and 1820, because after that the Catholic Church fought back with the only effective instruments at its disposal, boycott and protest.

The one society which enjoyed a measure of Catholic support was the originally undenominational Kildare Place Society, which, with the help of parliamentary grants, had established 1634 schools for

132,530 pupils by 1830.[14] This society fell victim to Ireland's growing religious and political tensions, and it became unacceptable to Catholic churchmen when its managers allocated grants to the Protestant societies. O'Connell's resignation from the society, and condemnation of it from Catholic Church leaders as far apart as the liberal Doyle and the conservative MacHale, meant that from 1820 the Kildare Place Society as an undenominational institution was living on borrowed time. A powerful combination of evangelical proselytism and Catholic self-consciousness rendered absolete the old pattern of educational provision in pre-Catholic Emancipation Ireland.

A royal commission was set up in 1824 to investigate alternatives, and through the maze of prolific report writing it became clear that any future national system must be based on two principles neatly summed up by Peel in the House of Commons: 'first to unite as far as possible . . . the children of protestants and catholics under one common system of education; and secondly, in so doing, studiously and honestly to discard all idea of making proselytes'.[15] The obvious way of achieving these objectives was through a system of combined literary and separate religious instruction for Protestant and Catholic children. This seemed logical in the abstract, but nineteenth-century churchmen did not see such a sharp distinction between the secular and the sacred.

The royal commission was disbanded in 1827 having made nine reports, but its work, though valuable, was unfinished. It was left to a subsequent parliamentary committee chaired by Thomas Spring-Rice to construct the proposals that in time formed the basis of Lord Stanley's famous instructions to the Duke of Leinster in November 1831. These instructions were virtually the written constitution of Ireland's new system of national education. Stanley stated that the Kildare Place Society was inadequate to meet the educational needs of Ireland because 'its determination to enforce in all their schools the reading of the holy scriptures without note or comment' was obnoxious to the Roman Catholic Church. The main aim of the proposed system was to unite the children of different creeds in a common school, and to that end a board of education drawn from several denominations was to have complete supervisory power over schools, finance, and all books, literary or religious. The schools were to open four or five days a week for combined literary and moral instruction, leaving the other few days for separate religious instruction by the clergy.

The single most important fact about the new Irish education system is that it failed to achieve its main objective, the creation of undenominational schools with no possibility of proselytism. There were, of course, demographic and administrative reasons for this failure, but the basic problem was that the so-called consensus was only skin deep from the beginning, and depended for its survival on an older generation of liberal churchmen. By mid century the three vested interests of Catholics, Anglicans and Presbyterians had made the Irish education system thoroughly denominational, in fact if not in theory.[16] Paradoxically, the attempt to forge an undenominational system not only heightened inter-denominational rivalries, but also increased tensions within denominations as pro- and anti-national education factions fought the issues out in Presbyterian synods, in Anglican magazines, and within the Catholic episcopate. No measure could have rebounded more completely. In short, the very thing that made the old system unacceptable – increased religious competition – also made the new proposals unworkable. Perhaps the remarkable thing in retrospect is not that undenominational schooling failed, but that anyone thought it might succeed.

Although the Methodists played little part in the development of national education in Ireland, Irish national education played a considerable part in moulding Methodist educational opinion. The Wesleyan contribution to education in Ireland, as in England, was initially through Sunday schools, which by 1824 had almost 10,000 pupils in 138 schools.[17] But in 1822, social unrest in Ireland caused the same kind of numerical decline in Irish Methodism as that which affected the English connexion after Peterloo. The following year, in a complete review of its missionary strategy in Ireland, the committee in London asked the Irish preachers for their views.[18] They unanimously called for 'schools, Bibles and more missionaries who can speak in the native tongue'.[19] The missionary society in London then sent Valentine Ward, one of its agents, to investigate the possibility of establishing day schools in Ireland, and his extensive report was completed by December 1823. Ward was pleasantly surprised by the scale of the education already provided by the Protestant societies, but he recommended that Methodist schools should follow the religious policies of the Kildare Place Society. Detecting the hostility of priests to any kind of proselytism, Ward proposed that Catholic children should use their own version of the Bible and that catechisms ought not to be used at all.[20] The Irish preachers were appalled by Ward's liberalism,[21] but they saw the point when

Catholic priests withdrew their children from the new Methodist schools at the slightest hint of proselytism. As Ward's successor, Thomas Bewley, pointed out, by 1825 the Methodists had to make an unwelcome choice between accommodating the curriculum to the satisfaction of the Catholic clergy or having no Catholic children in their schools. But the chief problem was that the Methodists could not have chosen a worse time to launch missionary day schools than in the religious climate of the mid 1820s. The other Protestant societies had enjoyed success in more tranquil times, but by 1824 it was too late. Ironically, the schools of the Hibernian Society, which were supported in Parliament by Butterworth, made it more difficult for the Methodists to succeed with their own efforts. Such problems did not prevent the Wesleyans from expanding their day schools, but the uneasy relationship with the Catholic clergy merely confirmed their prejudices about Catholic intolerance.

Just before Stanley's proposals were made public, the subject of Irish education was brought to the forefront of the English Methodist Conference when Adam Clarke was censured by Bunting for failing to transfer control of six privately endowed day schools to the Methodist Missionary Society.[22] The oldest ex-president in the connexion was eventually pressurized into signing over the schools just before he died, but the fact that Bunting and others were beginning to take the whole business of Irish education more seriously boded ill for the reception of Stanley's proposals six months later.

The first Methodist response to Stanley's instructions came in a series of articles by Richard Watson in the *Wesleyan Methodist Magazine*. He gave the scheme a cautious welcome, since if Roman Catholics would not send their children to 'schools taught in the Protestant mode', then the crux of the question was 'whether it is better to leave the Catholic peasantry wholly without education, or grant it to them in this way'.[23] Watson clearly preferred the latter, and although he moderated his enthusiasm in subsequent articles his views were still poles apart from Bunting, who described the proposals as 'well-intentioned perhaps, but bad in principle . . . and in its practical bearings both on strict Catholics, on Protestants, and on the half-enlightened and inquiring class of nominal Papists, who now send their children in large numbers to Bible Schools, inconceivably mischievous . . .'.[24]

Bunting, not being the sort of man to let his opposition remain private, chose a meeting of the book committee to launch an attack on Thomas Jackson, editor of the magazine, for allowing Watson's articles to be published. Jackson refused to give in and the complaint was formulated in a resolution to be discussed at Conference. Simultaneously in Ireland, according to the private despatches of Elijah Hoole as agent of the missionary committee for Irish schools, the Irish preachers were incensed by Stanley's plan and wanted the English Conference to take some action.[25] The scene was set for a confrontation over Irish education at the Wesleyan Conference in Liverpool (1832), with Bunting and the Irish preachers on one side and Jackson, Watson and James on the other. On the surface Bunting was not in a very strong position, because it was he who first introduced political comment into the *Methodist Magazine* when he was editor in 1821. In addition, it was put to him in the course of debate that his advocacy of Catholic Emancipation and his opposition to Irish national education were inconsistent.[26]

Notwithstanding such embarrassments, Bunting delivered an impressive speech. He refused to accept that his opposition to Irish national education was politically motivated, since it was no more dabbling in politics to oppose that measure than it had been for Methodists to speak out against Lord Sidmouth's bill in 1811, and the Luddite disturbances soon after. Were issues like these not the main reason for maintaining the Committee of Privileges? He explained his opposition to the government plan.

I object because *as a Dissenter* I am not allowed to have a school, unless certified, and if certified to have an inquisitorial examination of books. I take up this subject religiously; I declare my faith that the Roman Catholics cannot be benefited, but by being turned over to Protestantism, and this cannot be done by imperial Parliament. Protestant children are turned over to Socinianism and Calvinism, and Roman Catholic children are delivered to ignorance and superstition.[27]

No clearer statement of evangelical principles could have been delivered, and it marks a departure from Bunting's attitude to Brougham's proposals twelve years earlier. Then, Bunting supported national education in principle, but objected to some of the clauses (Watson's ground in 1832), whereas the Irish scheme was totally unacceptable for two major reasons. In Brougham's plan, the whole Bible was central in the curriculum but in Stanley's scheme, Bible-reading during the four or five days of combined education was replaced by a series of biblical extracts with moral comments, which, taken together, owed more to ethical humanism than to Christian dogma.[28] Second, the denomination that stood to gain most from Brougham was the Church of England, whereas in Stanley's proposals the main beneficiary would be the Roman Catholic Church. Bunting and the Irish missionaries could not tolerate government money going to the support of religious heresy. What they wanted was an extension of pre-1831 principles; more money for the Kildare Place Society and the Protestant voluntary groups. Catholic demands were making the Methodists more conservative.

There were two further consequences of Bunting's stance in 1832. After his apparent liberalism in 1829, Bunting was now much closer to the Irish preachers because of their common opposition to Catholicism, and this 'alliance' was to last through the next two decades. Second, Bunting could no longer countenance any system of integrated national education unless three conditions could be met: the centrality of the whole Protestant Bible in the curriculum; the absolute minimum of bureaucratic control over schools; and the assurance that religious error would not be state-aided. Moreover, Bunting's views mattered more after 1832, because within a year his two most forceful opponents over Irish education, Watson and James, were dead, and Bunting was in control of the connexion's chief press organ, the *Watchman* newspaper, which appeared in 1835.

As the Irish educational system became more denominational, and therefore undeniably more Catholic, the *Watchman* pressed home Bunting's views in the late 1830s.[29] What particularly galled the Wesleyans by this stage was that a conservative wing within the Catholic Church led by MacHale objected to the Irish system of education because it was not Catholic enough. James Dixon, a Bunting supporter and an ultra-Protestant, delivered a lecture at Sheffield, York, Manchester, Birmingham, Barnsley and Bradford stating that

any one at all conversant with this system would imagine it to be sufficiently Popish . . . and yet this is not sufficient to satisfy the cravings of the Popish Church. . . . This is not all . . . it is understood that Dr MacHale has appealed to the Pope from the authority of the State; so that his Holiness is brought in to decide whether the Three Estates of this realm have the right to establish, and, to a very limited extent indeed, direct even a pro-Popish system of education in this country.[30]

The emergence of education as a major aspect of state social policy, coming on top of three decades of hardening denominationalism, produced a more intense era of religious conflict. It also played into the hands of conservative churchmen of all denominations from Henry Cooke, the Ulster Presbyterian, to John MacHale, the Catholic

Archbishop, and from Hugh McNeile, the Liverpool Anglican, to Jabez Bunting, the Methodist 'pope'. A bumpy ride was in store for any English politician trying to construct an integrated educational policy, but the effort had to be made to remedy the socially unacceptable and politically dangerous illiteracy rates in the northern industrial areas.

The Whig proposals of 1839

The controversy surrounding Irish education was soon given an English dimension when the liberal municipal corporation in Liverpool tried to meet the rising tide of Irish immigration by employing the 'Irish system' in its two corporation schools.[31] The opposition to the Liverpool experiment included Anglicans, Wesleyans and conservative councillors, but it was led by Hugh McNeile, an Ulster-born Anglican evangelical who held the dubious distinction of being the foremost anti-Catholic orator in Victorian England. The importance of the Liverpool corporation's schools outweighed their size, for both supporters and opponents saw them as the thin edge of a potentially very thick English wedge. As McNeile put it, 'this is no local matter. It begins in Liverpool it is true. It must have a local commencement. But it cannot end where it begins. It is a feeler of the national pulse'.[32]

With the Whigs about to tackle education after meeting with defeat in other aspects of their ecclesiastical policy, 'the national pulse', as far as the Wesleyans were concerned, was far from healthy. While no consensus over education had emerged within the Whig and radical camps, the various strands of opinion from Slaney and Brougham to Wyse's Central Society of Education (1838) were not congenial to conservative churchmen of all denominations. In their view the Whigs, the Radicals, the Utilitarians and the Irish, though in fact divided among themselves, were forming an unholy alliance to deprive the nation's children of their religion. In response to Wyse's motion for the creation of a board of education in 1838, which in some respects represented the high water-line of radical pressure, the *Watchman* newspaper asked, 'will Christian England look quietly on and see an Irish Romanist, supported by such men as Mr Hume, defraud us of our religion under the pretext of teaching us arithmetic?'[33]

In such an unsuitable climate for a 'truly religious education' Bunting, for one, hoped that nothing at all would be done by the Whigs. Instead, he hoped for the continuation of the existing system of state grants for the two big educational societies. Yet neither society was fully acceptable to the Wesleyans; the National Society because of its Anglican formularies, and the British and Foreign Schools Society because it would not allow Methodist catechisms in its schools. In education, as in other matters, the Wesleyans were caught in the middle of England's traditional ecclesiastical division. Bunting was, therefore, quite happy with the state's educational policy as it stood, except that the Wesleyans were not getting any money, and he knew that unaided the Methodists had not the financial resources to build up an effective network of elementary schools. The obvious deduction was that the present system needed to be extended to 'other recognized bodies',[34] but not too far, lest Roman Catholics and infidels should be helped as well. In short, he wanted part of the cake that Anglicans and Dissenters were already eating, but he had no wish to share it out any further. Bunting knew he would not get these terms from the Whigs, especially with Wyse and O'Connell supporting them, so he preferred to wait. What is striking about Bunting's educational policy is not the obvious sectarian logic of it, but that he held such an optimistic view of Methodism's importance, that sooner or later an English government (and he thought it would have to be a Conservative one), would endow Wesleyan schools.

The shock of what had happened in Ireland, and the realization that the government would soon do something in England, led the Wesleyans to develop connexional machinery with specific responsibility for education. A small subcommittee was appointed by Conference in 1836, and it reported a year later. At this stage the Wesleyans had 3339 Sunday schools with 341,447 scholars, nine daily infant schools and twenty-two week-day schools. The report called for more effort but advised only a small financial commitment until government policy was made clear. What the committee wanted was 'not merely schools, but Church schools, which, being systematically visited by the Preachers, may prove doors of entrance into the Church of God'.[35] As with Sunday schools, the Wesleyans wanted to bind their week-day educational activities to the broader ministry of the Church, an ecclesiastical ambition which could not easily be harmonized with any government measure. On the eve of the 1839 Whig proposals a permanent Wesleyan Committee of Education was established by Conference. With Bunting, Thomas Jackson, John Scott, George Cubitt and Edmund Grindrod as the major figures on the committee, it was clear that Bunting's men and Bunting's policies were in the Methodist educational vanguard from 1838 onwards.

They soon knew what they had to face because Russell gave the bones of his scheme to the Commons in February 1839, and the flesh was added in April by a minute of the Privy Council's committee on education.[36] Russell wanted to place the supervision of education and the distribution of grants under a Committee of the Privy Council from which clerics were deliberately excluded. The government proposed to increase its contribution from £20,000 to £30,000 a year, to be paid according to local need rather than the size of voluntary contributions raised by British and National societies. The existing principle of proportionality had heavily favoured the Anglican National Society, which obtained 70 per cent of government money in the years 1833–8. Government grants would also be paid to 'reputable' schools outside the two societies, including Catholic schools, provided they accepted state inspection. Finally, a normal school for teacher training and two model schools were to be established on a nonconfessional basis. In these schools 'general' religious instruction was to be Bible-based (Roman Catholics could use their own versions), and 'special' denominational teaching was to be given by the resident Anglican chaplain or by visiting Dissenting ministers. Russell's aim was, therefore, to circumvent the 'religious difficulty' by increasing state control, reducing the influence of partisan churchmen, redressing the balance between Church and Dissent, and elbowing denominational instruction into a 'special' category. It was also a formal rejection of the Church of England's right to supervise the education of the nation.

Russell won cautious support from Dissenters, although voluntaryists were concerned about the extent of central control; but Anglicans of all shades of opinion were opposed to the Whig plan. Evangelical Anglicans thought it was too popish, conservative Anglicans saw it as another attack on their educational dominance, and High Churchmen disliked its erastianism and anti-clericalism. This combined opposition was all the more intense because the Church of England had made valiant efforts to extend its own educational contribution by creating twenty-four diocesan and sub-diocesan boards of education in 1838–9. As W. F. Hook put it, 'we may fairly assert that we have the education of the people in our hands; and why should it be taken away from us?'.[37]

Wesleyan opposition to Russell's plan was based on quite different principles, though what exactly they were was a shade unclear at the time. The first *Watchman* editorial after Russell's speech in the Commons stated unequivocally that it is far safer for our institutions, and a policy far more magnanimous and worthy of a Protestant people, that the voluntary principle shall alone be confided in, and every denomination of Christians be left at liberty to educate their own youth in their own principles. Who amongst us would not cheerfully forego Government grants in aid of education, if thereby Roman Catholic ambition, left to its own unassisted resources, shall be baulked of its contemplated prey?[38]

This opinion, that if Wesleyans wished to stop grants to Roman Catholics then they would have to sacrifice their own grant, was put to Bunting by Thomas Allan, who was keen for the Methodists to employ a clear-sighted and principled policy.[39] Allan's own anti-Catholicism and fear of government inspired secularization forced him to use a Nonconformist argument, voluntaryism, to solidify Wesleyan opposition to a liberal measure. This same argument was pressed on Bunting by Edward Baines jnr, editor of the *Leeds Mercury*, who later became a doctrinaire advocate of voluntaryism in education. He told Bunting's son that

the Wesleyans, inasmuch as they 'pay' to the support of the School Societies assisted by Government, have as much right as the Church to have their catechism used in those Schools. Now we turned this position against your father – as an argumentum *ad hominem* – by showing that it was just as cogent for the Roman Catholics as for the Wesleyans; and yet he maintained that the former ought to receive no 'public aid' whatever. Here is an inconsistency, as it seems to me; and I do not see how it can be explained away.[40]

In opposing the Whig proposals of 1839, the connexion entered into its most active political campaign since the opposition to Sidmouth in 1811. In May, a joint meeting of the Education Committee, the London preachers and the Committee of Privileges passed eight resolutions expressing the grounds of Methodist opposition. It was resolved that the Whig scheme was in violation of the Protestant Constitution, 'inasmuch as it contemplates the training and employment *by the State* of Romish (among other) teachers, and particularly recognises the corrupted Romish translations of the Holy Scriptures'.[41] Methodism now took on all the characteristics of an advanced extra-parliamentary pressure group: a standardized petition embodying the United Committees' resolutions was sent to all Wesleyan congregations (Bunting claimed 126,595 signatures); a small subcommittee was formed to co-ordinate the campaign; news coverage was given by the *Watchman* newspaper;[42] speeches were made and pamphlets produced;[43] and MPs were contacted.[44]

The intensity of opposition from Anglicans, Methodists and Tories forced Russell to abandon the normal and model schools idea in early June. His amended plan was a partial reversion to the previous system of supporting the two educational societies, but supervision by a secular board remained, as did the possibility of other groups making application for government aid. Bunting came out against the amended plan in an important speech on 10 June, just two days before the United Committees drew up their final resolutions on the Whig proposals. Bunting rejected state intervention (apart from money), either by the Committee of the Privy Council or by a system of school inspection, and he was afraid that indiscriminate government grants could go to 'schools in which the errors, the superstitions, and the idolatries of Popery will be inculcated'.[45] There was clearly no further room for negotiation, and the Wesleyans duly drew up a series of resolutions that closely reflected Bunting's speech. This final statement of Wesleyan educational policy in 1839 was not an endorsement of voluntaryism, however, because Bunting's more sectarian position had triumphed. The Methodists welcomed the idea of government aid going to other religious denominations, so long as the Authorized Version of the Bible was the basis of the curriculum.[46]

In 1839 a crumbling Whig administration had engaged a more self-confident Anglican Church, the most numerous non-Anglican denomination, and the Tories. As a result its educational policy was almost in tatters, except for the important retention of the educational Committee of the Privy Council. As Whig-liberal social policies failed, the Wesleyans were jubilant over the success of their opposition, but it was an opposition that had three major consequences for the connexion.

First, the strength of Wesleyan resistance was tailor-made for opposition politicians who were uneasy about opposing the Whig measures merely on the grounds of Church exclusiveness. Stanley, Egerton, Acland, Teignmouth and Gladstone all used Methodism for political purposes; and Gladstone was so pleased with the Wesleyans that he even advocated their reunion with the Church of England.[47] Peel himself made great play of the fact that the Wesleyans, who stood to gain most from the Whig proposals, still opposed them.

The Wesleyan Methodists have been treated like children. When they came forward in support of the anti-slavery question, and so strongly advocated the abolition of the slave-trade, then credit was given them for the highest discretion and for the purest motives; but now that they came forward to oppose the Government scheme of education, although it is impossible that they can be influenced by any but the purest motives, they are designated as the victims of credulity and misapprehension.[48]

That Tory politicians used Wesleyan opposition in their own political interest, rather than treating the Methodist case seriously, can be seen from the fact that only Ashley, among parliamentarians, wanted the Wesleyans to be given the status of a third state-aided educational society.[49]

Bunting knew very well that his views on education, which he argued were strictly based on religious principles, were of political benefit to the Tory party. This caused connexional disharmony, when Wesleyan petitions were sent to Thomas Galland, the Whiggish circuit superintendent in Leeds, asking him to distribute them to Methodist congregations. Caught between the Scylla of Conference discipline and the Charybdis of his local Whig associations, Galland refused to sign the petitions himself but distributed them to the Methodist societies. Galland felt he had to defend this ambivalent position in a letter to the *Leeds Mercury*, in which he protested about the use of connexional agitation for political purposes 'whether it was so designed or not'.[50] Predictably Galland and his supporters were cudgelled by the Buntingite Tories at the next annual Conference.[51] The most revealing speech was made by Dixon, who stated that the Wesleyan Education Committee was not guilty of political bias since both Whigs and Tories sat on it, but 'if the Government retire from the Protestantism of this country, may we not interfere?'. The ace in the conservative pack was a common Methodist Protestantism among Whigs and Tories alike, and this is the card that Bunting and Dixon played to Galland's obvious discomfort. But Bunting was not just contending for the conservative side in Conference; he wanted, at best, complete unanimity, or, at worst, silent acquiescence for the 'official' Methodist policy. Whig-liberals like Galland were not just to be fought, they had also to be silenced.

A second consequence of Methodism's opposition to the 1839 Whig proposals was a much closer relationship with the Protestant Association, a fanatically Orange organization that flourished in northern towns with large Irish populations. Although the *Watchman* had been rather cool in its comments about the Association in the mid 1830s,[52] by the end of the decade Methodist participation in it had grown dramatically. No doubt stung by O'Connell's hostile comments in Parliament during the education debates,[53] Wesleyans were to be found on Protestant Association platforms in Liverpool, Manchester, Warrington, Wigan, Northwich, Sheffield and Macclesfield.[54] Not only were Wesleyan preachers keeping company with 'no popery' polemicists like McNeile, Hugh Stowell, Henry Cooke and the Earl of Roden, but some preached ultra-Protestant sermons from their own pulpits, much to the annoyance of some within the congregations. Jonathan Ledger spoke for many when he 'wished that those clergymen and Methodist preachers who figure in "No Popery" lectures and at meetings of the "Protestant Association" would permit their zeal to flow in streams of Christian benevolence'.[55]

A third consequence of Methodist opposition to Russell's proposals lay in the realm of education itself. The cold logic of the *Watchman*, Thomas Allan and Edward Baines triumphed in fact, if not in theory, over the optimistic hopes of Bunting and Ashley. The Wesleyans not only had to make do without government aid, but they were also under pressure to instigate something fairly impressive themselves if they were not to merit the tag of 'foes of education'. Although hindered by lack of money due to the business recession, the Wesleyans had, by 1842, expanded the nine infant and twenty-two week-day schools of 1837 to twenty-eight infant and 234 week-day schools.[56] The Methodist educational achievement, on limited resources, leaves one to wonder what might have been achieved had they accepted government aid and left the Roman Catholic Church to its own devices.

By welcoming the principle but rejecting the methods of state aid in 1839, Bunting, unlike the voluntaryists, had not given up hope for the future; instead he was pinning his faith on a Tory administration. But would the Peel who spoke so warmly of the Wesleyans in 1839 deliver the goods when in power?

The educational clauses of Graham's factory bill (1843)

The Wesleyan reaction to Graham's factory bill cannot be understood without taking into account the theological developments of the previous decade. Ironically, the very pressures that forced Wesleyan preachers into a more conservative position in the 1830s – the weakness of the Tories, the constitutional revolution of 1828–32, Whig ecclesiastical policy in Ireland, democratic ideas and popular infidelity, worldliness in the churches, and an intellectual spirit of rationalism and radicalism – provoked also a High Church reaction within the Church of England.[57] As many historical theologians have pointed out, Methodists and Tractarians shared common ground in their emphases on a pure ministry, world-denying holiness, and suspicion of state interference in religious affairs. Such common ground as existed, however, was not recognized by contemporaries, who thought the two sides were naturally opposed. The result was a protracted theological controversy which began in 1836 and raged with increasing bitterness until it peaked in 1842.

With a fervour not seen since eighteenth-century Anglican attacks on Wesley's 'enthusiasm', High Churchmen carried the fight to the Wesleyans, initially in pamphlets,[58] but then through the columns of the *British Critic*.[59] It was in a book review for the *Critic* that Newman made the statement, which was later taken up by Pusey and others, that 'the history of Methodism is, we do not scruple to say, the history of a heresy; being nothing short of a formal heresy, good could not come from it, nor will good come of it'.[60] Such language left no room for accommodation, and when Newman produced the notorious *Tract 90* in 1841, an exasperated Bunting told Conference that 'unless the Church of England will protest against Puseyism in some intelligible form, it will be the duty of the Methodists to protest against the Church of England'.[61] The Wesleyans looked for comfort from the evangelical Anglicans they had met through Bible Societies and 'no popery' crusades, only to find that, though bitterly opposed to Puseyites, they were not as 'low' church as many Anglican church historians would have them.[62]

The controversy between Wesleyans and Tractarians reached its peak in 1842 when Pusey wrote to the Archbishop of Canterbury alleging that Wesleyanism was 'degenerating into a developed heresy', because it taught 'justification by feelings', which in turn produced antinomianism and an inadequate theology of the sacraments.[63] At times Pusey seemed to be attacking a species of Methodist revivalism which the connexion had itself long since repudiated. Whether Pusey exaggerated for polemical effect or whether he was ignorant of Methodist ecclesiastical developments in the early nineteenth century is an open question. In any case the Methodist counter-attack was in full swing through articles in the *Magazine* and the *Watchman*, and the publication of ten Wesleyan *Tracts for the Times*.[64] The central theological issues were the nature of justification, the role of the sacraments, the weight to be given to scripture and tradition, the validity of the Wesleyan ministry, and the doctrine of the Church. It is no accident that the main protagonists in this controversy were E. B. Pusey, the Regius Professor of Hebrew at Christ

Church, Oxford, and Thomas Jackson, the son of a Yorkshire farm labourer, because the dispute was as much about the different religious styles to be taken to the unchurched masses, as about Christian dogma. High-Church doctrine and Oxbridge aesthetics confronted evangelical fervour and northern grit. Consequently, Jackson turned the charge of antinomianism back on the High Churchmen 'who can only admire religion when it is adorned with gold lace and ostrich feathers'.[65] In the same vein the author of *Lyra Apostolica, an Impious Misnomer* asked 'will the manly sense and healthy religious feeling of this great Protestant country brook the insult offered to the ashes of our Reformers by a few gowned recluses at Oxford?'[66] Indeed, not since the campaign against Sidmouth's bill had so many Wesleyan preachers boasted of their influence among the tough manual workers of darkest England.[67]

There were even deeper emotions than these running through Methodist writings. The very Church that they had looked upon as 'the great breakwater against the swelling tide of Popery' now seemed full of popish holes. A mixture of betrayal, fear and incomprehension led some to see it as a conspiracy 'to exasperate the Wesleyan societies against the Church of England, and thus weaken the Protestant interest; . . . so the Church of Rome may regain her lost ascendancy'.[68] As with all cries of this sort, the Jesuits were held responsible.[69]

All these theological and cultural disagreements had important social and political consequences, because tract warfare was translated into real religious battles in English parishes where High-Church incumbents used their remaining social patronage to discriminate against Wesleyans.[70] Thus, both in theory and in practice, relations between Anglicans and Wesleyans reached their lowest point in 1842. Political confirmation came a year later.

While Methodists and Tractarians were abusing each other, Sir James Graham, Home Secretary in Peel's ministry, was considering the government's educational policy. In response to Brougham's suggestion that the government should introduce 'a general parish plan' of rate-aided schools, Graham confessed that he was not optimistic about the success of *any* national education system. He wrote that

Religion cannot be separated from the system, and amidst the conflict of contending sects the State, if it makes a choice, must prefer the established creed; and this preference is the signal for an attack on the measure, and for resistance to the rate or tax which dissenters must pay, . . . religion, the keystone of education, is, in this country the bar to its progress.[71]

Peel saw a minefield ahead and advised Graham to extend the power and financial resources of the Committee of the Privy Council rather than attempt any kind of direct legislation. Graham finally settled on a compromise between Brougham's comprehensiveness and Peel's caution by trying to lay the foundation of a national system of education through factory schools. This had the advantage of tackling the problem where it was most urgent, especially after the disturbances of 1842, and, if successful, it could be easily extended. After comprehensive discussions with Blomfield (Bishop of London), Kay-Shuttleworth (secretary of the Committee on Education), Horner and Saunders (factory inspectors), Graham was ready to show his proposals to the Cabinet and to the Bishops of Chester and Ripon, in whose dioceses lay most of the factories. It is still not entirely clear why Graham's original ideas were pushed in a more Anglican direction, but Saunders and Blomfield between them bear most of the responsibility.[72] The root of the problem was, however, that Graham did not seek out Dissenting views before introducing his bill. The Wesleyans claimed that they were never consulted. Only when opposition was in full swing, did Graham try to negotiate a compromise with Dissenters, but by then it was too late.

On 28 February 1843, Ashley moved an Address to the queen requesting her consideration for 'the best means of diffusing the benefits and blessings of a moral and religious education among the working classes of the people'. Graham made this the occasion for bringing his own proposals before the House. Children between the ages of 8 and 13 were not to work more than six and a half hours in any day, thereby allowing three hours for education. This was to be provided by a system of schools managed by trusts and financed by local rates, small fees and, if necessary, exchequer subventions. The trusts were to be composed of seven people (the local Anglican priest as chairman, two churchwardens, two mill owners, and two ratepayers selected annually by JPs), and would have the power to appoint a master 'subject to the approval of the Bishop of the Diocese as to his competency to give religious instruction to members of the Established Church'. Only the Authorized Version of the Scriptures was to be used, and, to guard against proselytism, the children of Dissenters would not have to attend Anglican religious instruction.

The bill was given a lukewarm reception by most Anglicans who were afraid of too much state interference on the one hand, and of too many concessions to Dissenters on the other. The warmest response came from men like Ashley and Hook whose intense commitment to working-class education outweighed their ecclesiastical scruples. Graham's difficulty was that what was marginally acceptable to Anglicans was totally unacceptable to Dissenters. Predictably they objected to the Anglican bias in the composition of trusts and in the choice of masters. Moreover, why should Dissenters pay rates for the support of schools whose management and religious ethos treated their children like second-class citizens? The ability to 'contract out' of Anglican religious instruction, which was so admired by the bill's supporters for its liberality, was, to the Dissenters, a reinforcement of their social and religious inferiority. With anti-Puseyite emotions not far from the surface, the Dissenters labelled the scheme as 'a sort of Church of England Junior', and Miall's *Nonconformist* hailed it as a scheme in which 'the State schoolmaster was to do the work which the State priest was unable to effect'.[73]

The Wesleyan reaction was as usual more complicated than that of either Anglicans or Dissenters. The first crop of letters from the provinces that flooded into Bunting and the Committee of Privileges was wholly opposed to Graham's plan.[74] Abraham Farrar, the Liverpool North circuit superintendent, told Bunting that

everything good is to be discarded which cannot be brought within the pale of the Establishment, and that all our efforts put forth during nearly a century in raising congregations and societies, building expensive places of worship and collecting thousands of children in Sunday schools, deserve only to share the fate of the Socialism and Chartism of the day – and ought to be swept aside to make an open platform for the full operation of the Oxford Tractarians![75]

Such rhetoric was commonplace and in some areas it was translated into a full-blown attack on the establishment principle with a corresponding shift towards voluntaryism in education.[76]

Bunting was now in a difficult position. He had supported the Church and the Tories in the 1830s as bulwarks against Whigs, Radicals, Dissenters and Catholics. But it seemed in the early 1840s that a 'Puseyite' Church was about to be endowed by a Tory administration under the pretext of education. Bunting disliked Graham's proposals as much as anyone, but he knew that voluntaryism was no answer. He explained his strategy to a meeting of the united committees of education and privileges in April.

I think it [Graham's Bill] is unmendable. There are two propositions: (1) To oppose it in a sort of knockdown way, and thus join the Dissenters. This I think not the best. (2) To try to get the objectionable parts altered. I fear there is no prospect of doing this, but we shall be in a better state by having made the attempt. . . . We must not talk gossip, but I believe that the history of the Bill is this: The Radicals are at the bottom of it. The measure the Whigs brought in being thrown out, the Government consulted the High Church party. They ought to have consulted the Wesleyans and Dissenters.[77]

At such a crucial time in the evolution of Wesleyan political opinions Bunting could not afford to take a back seat. The minutes of the Committee of Privileges made it clear that he, in close association with John Scott, was the principal figure on the specially appointed sub-committee that negotiated with Graham and drew up the official Wesleyan resolutions of 6 April.[78] Although they approved of separate religious instruction and the use of the Authorized Version in schools, the Methodists objected to the composition of the trusts, and the fact that rate-supported schools would place their own daily and Sunday schools at a serious financial disadvantage. Aside from a technical point-by-point rebuttal of Graham's proposals, the Wesleyan resolutions were underpinned by vigorous opposition to Tractarianism and a request for state financial help to develop Methodist schools.[79]

Graham was surprised by the strength of Wesleyan opposition. He told Peel that 'it is quite clear that the Pusey tendencies of the Established Church have operated powerfully on the Wesleyans, and are converting them rapidly into enemies'.[80] This was largely true, but it should not obscure two other important facts. First, Graham ought to have been aware of the Dissenting hostility to Tractarianism before he introduced his bill; and second, the Wesleyans would not have supported his proposals in any case. The Methodists supported the Church of England not for what it might achieve if properly endowed, but for its key role in the maintenance of England's Protestant Constitution. Thus, Wesleyans backed the Church of England more as a constitutional safeguard than as a competitive rival. It would have taken a man with much more religious sophistication than Graham to have found a way through England's sectarian maze in the early Victorian era.

Although Graham knew at an early stage that his education scheme was unlikely to succeed, he negotiated with the two groups whose opposition was not based on militant anti-establishment feeling – the

Wesleyans and the Roman Catholics. Ironically, the person who most forcefully put the Wesleyan case (more state money for denominational education and minimal state interference), was Nicholas Wiseman, the Catholic President of Oscott College.[81] A common enthusiasm for church-controlled education united Wesleyans and Catholics in theory, even if they despised each other in practice. Graham paid particular attention to Wesleyan and Catholic objections when he outlined modifications to his bill in the House of Commons on 1 May.[82] These concessions merely weakened Anglican support without mitigating Dissenting opposition. Graham finally withdrew the educational clauses of the factory bill in a moving speech to the Commons: 'I looked for peace, and I have encountered the most angry opposition, therefore I withdraw the educational clauses, although I take that step with deep regret, and with melancholy forebodings with regard to the progress of education.'[83] Privately he told Stanley that since the Dissenters refused to co-operate then the only alternative was to rely more on the Church.[84] Bunting was therefore right to argue that voluntaryism played straight into the hands of the Church of England. Even Baines was forced to admit as much twenty years later.[85]

The Dissenting 'victory' of 1843 was achieved by extra-parliamentary pressure, because except on a motion by Roebuck, the House never divided on the question. In the four months from March to June 1843, 25,205 petitions with 3,988,633 signatures were presented against Graham's bill, of which 8945 petitions and 910,000 signatures were from the Wesleyan Methodists alone.[86] The scale of the opposition ensured that no system of 'combined education' could be considered for the foreseeable future. But the consequences were even more profound. As Professor Gash has it:

The lesson of the crisis was clear. Defence of the Church was one thing; enlargement of the Church another and quite different one. For all its revival since 1832, the Church of England, as a State establishment, could no longer in practice call upon the State either for wider pastoral privileges or even for peculiar financial assistance. This in itself marked a fundamental change in Church–State relationships which no amount of Anglican activity or confidence could undo.[87]

If the defeat of Sidmouth's bill in 1811 meant that the Established Church could no longer expect legislation to ruin its competitors, the defeat of Graham's bill in 1843 meant that the government could no longer sponsor legislation for Church extension funded by public money. Instead, the state continued to pay large sums to the Anglican National Society. This policy was less controversial, but just as effective in maintaining Anglican superiority over Dissent in the provision of elementary education.

Graham's defeat in 1843 nevertheless increased Dissenting self-confidence, symbolized by the formation of the British Anti-State Church Association a year later; but it was a self-confidence which the Wesleyans had no desire to encourage. Shortly after Graham withdrew his bill, Hull Terrell, the Dissenting Deputies' secretary, invited the Wesleyans to a victory meeting at which future plans could be discussed. Although the Wesleyans were ready to oppose an increasingly 'heretical' Church, they were not yet ready to join Dissent. The Committee of Privileges tactfully declined the invitation on the grounds that such a meeting 'would scarcely be restrained from exciting feelings of resentment towards parties associated with the late measure'.[88] The Wesleyans had helped defeat the educational clauses, but they still wanted government money; it would not do to celebrate victory too heartily. As in 1811–12, when the Wesleyan leadership tried to prevent a brief alliance with Dissent from spilling over into the Friends of Peace movement, so in 1843–4 it resisted cooperation with anti-establishment societies. Wesleyans were conspicuous by their absence from the British Anti-State Church Association.

As in 1839, the Wesleyan victory of 1843 was, in educational terms, a pyrrhic one. By 1843 the Methodists had only 290 day schools with 20,804 scholars, and Bunting knew that the current provision, in relation to the need, was hopelessly inadequate: 'Let us make no farce about day school education; we must have more money if it is to be done. In the estimation of public men Sunday schools are not national education. I am of that opinion. Why not admit this to ourselves? Let us establish day schools. . . . Let us go body, soul, and spirit into it.'[89] In October 1843 John Scott carried a motion committing the Wesleyans to 700 schools in seven years. The progress over the next few years was commendable but painfully slow.

    1844   332 daily schools with 25,463 scholars
    1845   331 daily schools with 30,686 scholars
    1846   370 daily schools with 34,287 scholars
    1847   395 daily schools with 37,341 scholars[90]

It was clear that by voluntary effort alone, the Wesleyans could not meet their own objectives, quite apart from the enormous need. With the Wesleyan Education Committee chronically short of funds, the bait of state money was a constant attraction. The bait was finally taken in 1847 when, largely through Ashley's mediation, they negotiated a compromise with the Committee of Council which agreed to give grants to schools superintended by the Wesleyan Education Committee subject to mutually acceptable inspection.[91] The deadlock was broken because the Whigs decided to make separate settlements with the Wesleyans and the Roman Catholics. The latter were dealt with a year later, and this gave a relieved Methodist leadership time to sell the idea to the connexion. The Wesleyans left the rest of Dissent high and dry, but they had done so for a price. Edward Baines had mistakenly hoped for Wesleyan help to defeat the Whig minutes of 1847, which he described as an 'Educational Dictatorship' and as an 'irretrievable step . . . towards the State endowment of all religions in this country'.[92] Baines was disappointed, because within the Wesleyan connexion denominational conservatives triumphed over Dissenting voluntaryists. Ironically, this was facilitated by the mediation of an evangelical and Tory Anglican with Whig politicians.

The Wesleyans had been on the Church's side in 1839 and then with the Dissenters in 1843, and showed in 1847 what their intentions had been all along; to achieve the best possible terms for themselves regardless of parties. In negotiating these terms the basic principle was to obtain state aid for Wesleyan connexional schools, or schools not antithetic to Methodist doctrines, while excluding Roman Catholics and Tractarians from similar benefits. The narrowness of this can be easily criticized now, but at the time the Wesleyans were convinced that they stood for the preservation of truth against the whole spectrum of heresy. The Wesleyans were religiously and politically midway between Church and Dissent, and could be heroes or anti-heroes to either depending on circumstance. Peel and Gladstone spoke in their favour in 1839 and the Dissenting Deputies in 1843. Not surprisingly, the politics of the Wesleyan leadership were not always understood by the connexion as a whole and tensions inevitably arose. In 1843 official policy came under attack from pro-Church *and* pro-Dissent wings,[93] and in the 1848 Conference several preachers attacked the connexion's educational policy, because the Wesleyans were receiving government money in common with Roman Catholics. The answer came, of course, from Bunting, but it was not the answer he would have given in 1832.

The state of the case is this: Ultra Dissenters say that all state-aided education should be secular; the country says: 'We cannot recognise any system
as education of which the Christian religion does not form an essential part;
we have not an absolute right to say that Roman Catholics shall use our
authorised version, or to say that Roman Catholic schools are too bad to be
dealt with like others. We have gained a national recognition of the principle
that the Scriptures and the doctrines of our religion shall be an essential part
of British education, and, that no Popish priest can be a master in these
schools!'[94]

Moreover, the heated educational debates in Conference between
1832 and 1848 exacerbated other tensions within the connexion, and
form an important background to the major rupture in the mid
nineteenth century.[95]

In the first quarter of the nineteenth century, the problem of control
manifested itself within Methodism over issues like Sunday schools,
revivalism and radicalism, but in the second quarter the most pressing
matter was the daily education of working-class children. How should
children be taught about the Christian faith, and who should teach
them? What were the respective responsibilities of the state, the
Established Church, and other religious denominations in the education of the nation? How much should working people be taught
about merely secular matters? These were the questions that had to be
faced as the appalling facts of illiteracy in the industrial areas became
more urgent. As the traditional forces of Church and Dissent prepared themselves for the inevitable battle, the Wesleyans were a third
and confusing element. They could not let the Established Church
dominate national education after 1840, because it was theologically
unsound. On the other hand, the Wesleyans could not give unequivo-
cal support to Dissent for the same reason. Why should the ratepayer
have to pay for the support of heresy? More important, how could the
British Isles and then the world be converted to evangelical Protestantism if the British state was bolstering up its enemies?

What was logical to the Wesleyans was tortuous and bigoted to
their enemies, and Methodist educational policy was the subject of
attack from every conceivable religious and political group. However,
the numerical strength and superb political organization of the
Wesleyans meant that their support was much sought after. Yet in
their strength was also to be found their weakness, for though no
denomination showed more concern for education through Sunday

schools in the early part of the century, its intensely sectarian position after 1832 hindered the development of a national system of daily education. On the other hand its careful monitoring of state policy and Church ambitions ensured that English education, in the nineteenth century at least, would neither be under the control of a secular bureaucracy, nor tied too closely to the Church of England.

References

1   G. F. A. Best, 'The religious difficulties of national education in England, 1800–70', *Cambridge Historical Journal*, **12** (1956), p. 173.

2   Hugh McLeod, *Religion and the People of Western Europe 1789–1970* (Oxford 1981), p. 15.

3   Best, pp. 158–9.

4   See David Wardle, *Education and Society in Nineteenth-Century Nottingham* (Cambridge 1971), pp. 55–6. He states that in Nottingham the chronological boundary between the establishment of Sunday schools and voluntary provision of day schools was about 1830.

5   P. McCann (ed.), *Popular Education and Socialization in the Nineteenth Century* (London 1977), pp. 29–30, 87.

6   *Hansard*, NS, **II**, c. 68.

7   T. P. Bunting, *The Life of Jabez Bunting*, 2 vols. (London 1859 and 1887), vol. 2, p. 185.

8   W. R. Ward (ed.), *The Early Correspondence of Jabez Bunting 1820–1829* (London 1972), pp. 69–71.

9   M.C.A.Mss., Minutes of the Committee of Privileges for 1820.

10   Ward, *The Early Correspondence*, p. 70.

11   Much of the general background for this section is based on D. H. Akenson's book, *The Irish Education Experiment* (London 1970).

12   Allan and Butterworth were enthusiastic supporters of this society. Its annual reports, published in London, are a mine of information on evangelical attitudes towards Ireland in the crucial period 1806–29.

13   These figures are based on the claims made by the various societies. They may therefore be inflated.

14   See the tables in Akenson, pp. 86–7.

15   *Hansard*, NS, **X**, c. 843.

16   For the extent of this denominationalism, and of its clerical basis, see Akenson's tables, pp. 214–24.

17   C. H. Crookshank, *History of Methodism in Ireland* (London 1888), vol. 3, p. 68.

18   M.M.H., Printed circular dated 29 March 1823.

19   M.M.H. Mss., the replies of the missionaries were collected and sent off

in the form of a report. Gideon Ouseley published his own opinions in a
letter to the *Sligo Journal*, dated 16 May 1823.

20   M.M.H. Mss., Report of Mr Ward's visit to the Irish Missionaries in the
     Autumn of 1823 (22 pages). It was received on 8 December 1823.

21   M.M.H. Mss., William Stewart to Messrs. Taylor and Watson, 29
     November 1823.

22   Benjamin Gregory, *Side-Lights on the Conflicts of Methodism* (London
     1898), pp. 102–4.

23   *Wesleyan Methodist Magazine* (1832), pp. 68, 304, 383.

24   W. R. Ward, *Early Victorian Methodism: The Correspondence of
     Jabez Bunting 1830–58* (London 1976), p. 16.

25   M.M.H. Mss., Elijah Hoole to John James, 18 January, 9, 12 July, and
     29 October 1832.

26   Gregory, p. 119.

27   ibid., p. 120.

28   Akenson, p. 159.

29   *Watchman*, 16 September, 4 November 1835, 23 March, 5 October
     1836, 1, 15 February, 20 December 1837, and 30 June 1838.

30   James Dixon, *The Present Position and Aspects of Popery and the
     Duty of Exposing the Errors of Papal Rome*. A lecture first delivered in
     Sheffield, 12 December 1839 (London 1840), pp. 12–13.

31   See James Murphy, *The Religious Problem in English Education, The
     Crucial Experiment* (Liverpool 1959).

32   ibid., opposite p. 1.

33   *Watchman*, 20 June 1838.

34   Bunting gave a clear synopsis of his views in a letter to Thomas Binney
     dated 5 April 1838. Ward, *Early Victorian Methodism*, pp. 202–3.

35   *Wesleyan Education Reports* (1837).

36   The most useful accounts of the Whig proposals of 1839 are D. G. Paz,
     The Politics of Working-Class Education in Britain 1830–50
     (Manchester 1980), ch. 6; N. Gash, *Reaction and Reconstruction in
     English Politics 1832–1852* (London 1965), pp. 76–80; and G. I. T.
     Machin, *Politics and the Churches in Great Britain 1832–1868*
     (Oxford 1977), pp. 65–8.

37   Quoted by Machin, p. 66.

38   *Watchman*, 20 February 1839.

39   M.C.A. Allan Mss., Thomas Allan to Jabez Bunting, 11 June 1839,
     reproduced by Ward, *Early Victorian Methodism*, pp. 220–1.

40   ibid., p. 221.

41   M.C.A., Printed Resolutions adopted by a Meeting of the United Com-
     mittees in London on 21 May 1839.

42   *Watchman*, 22 and 29 May 1839.

43   See, for example, George Osborn, *No Popery in Schools Supported by
     the State* (London 1839).

44   The Manchester Methodists wrote to their MPs through the columns of

the *Morning Chronicle* (2 June 1839).

45   *Speech of the Rev. Dr. Bunting delivered in London, on Monday June 10th 1839, in reference to the Government Scheme of National Education recently abandoned and to the Government New Scheme just proposed* (Manchester 1839), p. 9.

46   This is made clear in Resolution three part one adopted by the United Committee on 12 June 1839. The resolutions were published at the end of Bunting's speech.

47   *Hansard*, 3rd series, **XLVIII**, c. 294, 563, 625, and 753.

48   *Hansard*, 3rd series, **XLVIII**, c. 679.

49   ibid., c. 283. See also Lord Ashley to Jabez Bunting, 7 June 1839, in Ward, *Early Victorian Methodism*, p. 219.

50   W. R. Ward, *Religion and Society in England 1790–1850* (London 1972), pp. 246–7.

51   Gregory, pp. 268–79.

52   *Watchman*, 18 May 1836.

53   *Hansard*, 3rd series, **XLVIII**, c. 618–20. See also Daniel O'Connell, *To the Ministers and Office-Bearers of the Wesleyan Methodist Societies of Manchester* (London 6 July and 1 August 1839). Both letters were published in pamphlet form in Manchester (1839).

54   These meetings were reported in a book of press cuttings preserved in the Methodist Church Archives. See also Ward, *Religion and Society*, pp. 212–14.

55   *Pulpit Politics, The Correspondence of the Rev. W. M. Bunting, 'an old Wesleyan Preacher', Mr. Holland Hoole, and Mr. T. H. Williams, with additions* (London 1840), p. 27.

56   *Wesleyan Education Reports* (1843).

57   Owen Chadwick, *The Mind of the Oxford Movement* (London 1960), pp. 11–14; J. C. Bowmer, *Pastor and People* (London 1975), pp. 229–48; and W. R. Ward, 'Church and society in the first half of the nineteenth century', in R. Davies, A. R. George and G. Rupp (eds.), *A History of the Methodist Church in Great Britain* (London 1978), vol. 2, pp. 87–92.

58   See, for example, Epaphras, *The Church of England compared with Wesleyan Methodism* (Bristol 1836); Thomas Jackson's reply, *The Wesleyans Vindicated* (London 1837); and *The Cause of the Wesleyans weakened or a Review of two pamphlets reprinted from the Church of England Quarterly Review* (London 1837).

59   *British Critic*, xix (1836), pp. 12–73, and xxi (1837), pp. 167–85.

60   A Review of *The Life and Times of Selina, Countess of Huntingdon* in the *British Critic*, xxviii (1840), pp. 263–95.

61   Gregory, p. 317.

62   For example, McNeile claimed that the Church of England had the right to exclusive control of any revenue voted by Parliament for education. See W. Vevers, *The Claims of the Clergy: A Letter to the Rev.*

Hugh McNeile, Being a Reply to his Speech in the Amphitheatre, Liverpool, April 27 1843, Addressed to the Wesleyan Methodists (Derby 1843); and the *Watchman* (26 April 1843).

63 E. B. Pusey, *A Letter to His Grace the Archbishop of Canterbury, on Some Circumstances Connected with the Present Crisis in the English Church* (Oxford 1842).

64 The Tracts were published anonymously, but Dr Bowmer has discovered the authors from the Minutes of the Book Committee. The full list of titles and authors is as follows. George Osborn, *'Why don't you come to Church?'*. Dr Hannah, *Wesleyan Methodism not a Schism*. W. L. Thornton, *Apostolical Succession – A Summary of Objections to the Present Claim*. George Turner, *Wesleyan Ministers True Ministers of Christ*. George Osborn, *Modern Methodism, Wesleyan Methodism*. George Cubitt, *Justification by Faith an Essential Doctrine of Christianity*, Humphrey Sandwith, *Lyra Apostolica, an Impious Misnomer*. F. A. West, *Baptism not Regeneration*. Alfred Barrett, *Wesleyans have the true Christian Sacraments*. John McOwan, *A Letter to 'A Country Curate'*.

65 Thomas Jackson, *A Letter to the Rev. Edward B. Pusey, D.D.* (London 1842), p. 99.

66 *Lyra Apostolica, an Impious Misnomer* (London 1842), p. 16.

67 See, for example, *Wesleyan Methodism not a Schism*, p. 13; and Jackson, pp. 107–8.

68 Jackson, p. 109.

69 Henry Fish AM, *Jesuitism traced in the Movements of the Oxford Tractarians* (London 1842).

70 The full extent of this is not yet clear but see *Lyra Apostolica, an Impious Misnomer*, p. 1; Jackson, p. 109; Bowmer, pp. 234–5; and James Obelkevich, *Religion and Rural Society: South Lindsey 1825–1875* (Oxford 1976), pp. 161–2.

71 C. S. Parker, *Life and Letters of Sir James Graham 1792–1861* (London 1907), vol. 1, pp. 338–9.

72 Paz, pp. 114–25.

73 Quoted by Gash, p. 87.

74 M.C.A. Mss., Minutes of the Committee of Privileges, 23 and 29 March 1843.

75 M.C.A. Mss., Abraham Farrar to Jabez Bunting 31 March 1843, reproduced by Ward, *Early Victorian Methodism*, pp. 283–4.

76 ibid., pp. 284–6.

77 Gregory, pp. 512–13.

78 M.C.A. Mss., Minutes of the Committee of Privileges, 4 and 6 April 1843.

79 M.C.A., Printed Resolutions adopted by meetings on 6 April, 10 May, and 20 June 1843.

80 Parker, p. 345.

81   For more information on Roman Catholic attitudes see J. T. Ward and J. H. Treble, 'Religion and education in 1843: Reaction to the "Factory Education Bill" ', *Journal of Ecclesiastical History*, **20** no. 1 (1969), pp. 79–110.

82   *Hansard*, 3rd series, **LXVIII**, c. 1104.

83   *Hansard*, 3rd series, **IXIX**, c. 1569.

84   Parker, p. 344.

85   See Clyde Binfield, *So Down to Prayers: Studies in English Nonconformity 1780–1920* (London 1977), pp. 80–91; and Ian Sellers, *Nineteenth-Century Nonconformity* (London 1977), p. 79.

86   Figures taken from the *Wesleyan Education Reports* (1843), p. 18. For more information on Dissenting opposition see B. L. Manning, *The Protestant Dissenting Deputies* (Cambridge 1952), pp. 340–6; and R. G. Cowherd, *The Politics of English Dissent* (London 1959), pp. 125–9.

87   Gash, p. 89.

88   M.C.A. Mss., Minutes of the Committee of Privileges, 27 June 1843.

89   Gregory, p. 352.

90   *Wesleyan Education Reports* (1844–7).

91   The intricate details of these negotiations are set out in the *Wesleyan Education Report* for 1847, pp. 47–78. See also Ward, *Early Victorian Methodism*, p. 353; and Paz, pp. 134–6.

92   Ward, *Early Victorian Methodism*, p. 351.

93   For a pro-Anglican view from a Wesleyan see Anon., *The Education Bill and the Wesleyans, being reasons for having declined to sign the Wesleyan Petition against that Measure, stated in a letter to a friend* (London 1843). Pro-Dissent views within Methodism were especially strong in Leeds – e.g., Ward, *Early Victorian Methodism*, pp. 286–7.

94   Gregory, pp. 428–9.

95   John Kent, 'The Wesleyan Methodists to 1849', in Davies, George and Rupp (eds.), vol. 2, pp. 243–5.

7 Partisanship and protest, 1830–50

Although the conservative habit of the connexional leadership had been established in opposition to popular radicalism in England and Roman Catholicism in Ireland, it was, until 1830, still possible to claim that this was not motivated by political partisanship. Rather, it was part of one's Christian duty to resist anarchy on the one hand and heresy on the other. But after 1830, the Whig commitment to reform extended both to English and Irish Churches, thereby making religion a major party issue for the first time since Anne's reign. The ecclesiastical question which now entered political calculations was on what basis should established churches exist within the state, after they had lost either the numerical support, or the passive acceptance, of the majority of the population. The Irish Church never had the former and the English Church was on the brink of losing the latter. In the climate produced by the constitutional revolution of 1828–32 prophets of ecclesiastical doom poured forth their fears. After leafing through Owenite newspapers in July 1832, Arnold felt that old slogans like our 'pure and apostolic church' and 'our glorious constitution' had had their day. 'The Church, as it now stands, no human power can save; my fear is, that, if we do not mind, we shall come to the American fashion, and have no provision made for the teaching of Christianity at all.'[1] Arnold's pessimism was shared by Whately, Archbishop of Dublin, who believed that the Reform Bill was the beginning of the end for established churches in the British Isles.[2]

Pessimistic comments like these from churchmen were founded on hard social realities. O'Connell's signal demonstration of power in 1829 spoke for a more militant Catholic Ireland, and English Nonconformists emerged from the repeal of the Test and Corporation Acts with more provincial bravado than at any time since the late 1780s. The established churches were now under attack from a bewildering range of opponents, from Swing rioters in rural England to tithe agitators in rural Ireland, and from the doctrinaire voluntaryism of Scottish immigrants to the anti-church rate demonstrators in English towns.[3] The Church of England, therefore, not only had to meet its English Nonconformist critics but also the transferred hatreds of vociferous Celtic immigrants. The fact that it also acquired a host of Irish-born evangelical defenders, many of whom became major clerical figures in Lancashire,[4] was cold comfort for those with a more sedate view of the Anglican mission.

The character of religious conflict, as well as the complexity of the issues, can be appreciated only by examining three different but interlocking areas: parliamentary politics; extra-parliamentary politics; and tensions within and between the denominations. At the parliamentary level, Whigs and Tories were as united on the need to preserve the Established Church as they were divided on tactics and policies. Although both Whigs and Tories were more willing to reform the Church than to remedy the grievances of Dissenters, the Whigs were looked on by friend and foe alike as being the party most likely to make concessions to popular forces, whether Dissenting, Catholic or radical. Nevertheless, the general mood of dissatisfaction with Whig achievements in the 1830s from all these groups, illustrates the danger of overdrawing the distinctions between Whig and Tory ecclesiastical policy. If any issue seemed to crystallize party differences, it was the appropriation of Irish Church revenue, yet that issue split the Whig Cabinet as decidedly as it occasioned Tory opposition.[5]

Outside Parliament, religious politics infused municipal corporation elections,[6] and gave rise to massive extra-parliamentary protests in the golden age of 'pressure from without'.[7] Dissenting grievances in the 1830s (including church rates, exclusion from the universities, and marriage and burial rights), opposition to state educational policy in the period 1839–43, protests against the state endowment of Maynooth College, and the campaign to disestablish the Church of England all gave rise to impressive extra-parliamentary crusades. They also contributed much to the distinctive temper of early Victorian England. The age of Chartism and of the Anti-Corn Law League was also the age of the May meetings in Exeter Hall (the financial capital of evangelical philanthropy) and of Miall's *Nonconformist*. The Arnolds, father and son, saw in this enthusiastic religious culture the characteristic flaws of the English mind – 'narrowness of view and a want of learning'[8] – which, of course, made it all the more powerful. But as well as 'jealousy of the Establishment, disputes, tea-meetings, openings of chapels [and] sermons',[9] there was a commendable interest in all aspects of social policy and a vigorous provincial press. This was a culture that threw up its fair share of idiosyncratic characters from Elijah Dixon, a Peterloo veteran who celebrated his conversion by total immersion in the Rochdale canal, to Henry King Spark, the proprietor of the *Darlington and Stockton Times*, leader of the Darlington incorporation movement and a denominational traveller from Wesleyanism to Anglicanism via Unitarianism.[10]

The complex interaction of religious forces in the 1830s which perplexed politicians of all persuasions, created its own tensions within the denominations. In such a climate governmental attempts to promote religious peace by legislation rebounded in an extraordinary way. Tractarianism, voluntaryism, Orangeism and Ultramontanism all surfaced in opposition to Whig policies, even if they owed their origins to deeper religious and social currents. That well-established denominations experienced internal problems boded ill for the Wesleyans who were neither Churchmen nor Dissenters, and whose ecclesiastical polity was still a bone of contention within the connexion. With English society in a ferment of class and sectarian conflict, on which were superimposed new problems from the Celtic fringes, it would have needed an extraordinary amount of wisdom and luck for Wesleyan Methodism to have emerged unscathed from the period 1830–50. The fact that the connexion suffered numerous secessions in these years is, therefore, as much a comment on the state of English society as it is on the connexional leadership.

Perhaps the best way of investigating the relationship between Methodism and politics in this period is to work from the top to the bottom of the movement, and from within to without. This method produces four main topics: the politics of the Wesleyan leadership in the 1830s and their virtual collapse in the 1840s; the growth of connexional opposition resulting in various secessions; the electoral behaviour of Methodists as a rough guide to their social and political aspirations; and the relationship between Methodism and popular politics.

The politics of the connexional leadership

It is true, that in the spirit of our Founder we have felt it our duty to stem, as far as in us lay, the tide of revolutionary fury, as urged onwards by the Roman Catholics of Ireland and the Dissenters of England, with a view to sweep away our ecclesiastical institutions.[11]

According to the most recent estimate, the number of English periodicals published in the years 1824 to 1900 exceeded 50,000, a high proportion of which were religious. There is no more complete literary record of any civilization than there is of Victorian England, from the most provincial of outposts to the most obscure of denominations. 'Periodical literature was a fad', and subscription to a religious journal 'served Victorians as a kind of self-identification'.[12] Methodists of all shades expressed their distinctiveness through denominational magazines, but the bestseller by far was the *Wesleyan Methodist Magazine*. It entered about 24,000 homes each month by the 1840s, substantially more than the more renowned periodicals of the liberal intelligentsia. It was a typical denominational organ, in that the proportion of 'timeless' religious articles to news was high. Its constituent elements were biographies, sermons, missionary notices, book reviews, small articles on general knowledge, obituaries and some rather undistinguished poetry. Whatever the value of Matthew Arnold's attack on Nonconformist culture as a whole, he was right to seize on a Nonconformist periodical as its most characteristic means of transmission.

Until 1821, when Bunting introduced the section 'Retrospect of Public Affairs', the Methodist magazine was purely religious, but in 1835 it heralded the beginning of a new Wesleyan publication, a weekly newspaper called the *Watchman*. This venture was justified by reference to the recent measure of parliamentary reform which conferred the vote on many Methodists, and by the 'passion' for change that was so 'extensively prevalent'. The new publication was to be 'free from party violence'; its function was merely to bring before its readership the most important passing events, 'with such suggestions as would lead to a just conception of their character and public bearing'.[13] Even such careful language showed that the paper was to be opinionative as well as informative, political if not party-political. In fact, the paper was hatched by a group of wealthy Tory laymen in Manchester and Liverpool including James Wood, first President of the Manchester Chamber of Commerce, Thomas Sands, a Liverpool merchant, and James Heald, a cotton-spinner and banker who became Tory MP for Stockport in 1847. Bunting was in on the plan from the beginning, exercised considerable editorial control, but decided not to seek official Conference backing for it.[14] He knew well that the 'no politics' rule could not be bent any further after electioneering on behalf of a Tory candidate at precisely the same time as Rayner Stephens was suspended for anti-State Church activities.[15]

The real value of the *Watchman* lies in its week-by-week unfolding of Wesleyan Tory attitudes in response to Whig-Liberal policies in Church and State. In fact, Wesleyan Toryism has been subjected to so much abuse by contemporaries and historians that it is worthwhile pausing to find out exactly what it was. The *Watchman's* columns and Bunting's correspondence reveal four main elements. The first was the idea that Christians should support the existing order, because to do otherwise was to doubt God's providential goodness. Wesleyan Tories disliked political strife and party conflict, because they saw 'politics in the one-sided terms of a Tory establishment which, by virtue of its peculiarly native and time-honoured qualities, rendered unnecessary an alternative form of government'.[16] Thus, in spite of its obvious Tory bias, the first *Watchman* editorial declared the paper's aim was to moderate 'the effervescence of party feeling on both sides'.[17] This was quickly followed, without conscious incongruity, with a spirited attack on the Whigs' Irish policy. How much this misunderstanding of the nature of politics was due to a blinkered religious perception and how much was due to dissimulation is not entirely clear, but Bunting, even more than the Lancastrian laymen, knew the political consequences of his actions. Nevertheless, even he was reluctant to admit that Methodism, as a corporate body, favoured any particular party. When forced to acknowledge that the Methodist campaign against the Whig educational proposals of 1839 had party significance, Bunting stated that Wesleyan actions were motivated by religious principles: 'if any political party in the country choose to place themselves between our fire and the object at which it is really directed, that is their affair – not ours'.[18] It was this kind of argument on the part of Wesleyan Tories that so nettled connexional Liberals. They did not mind the fact that individual Methodists had Tory opinions but they protested about the operation of a 'no politics' rule that had virtually become a 'no Whig-Liberal politics' rule. In a Conference debate about Joseph Rayner Stephens's contribution to the Church Separation Society, Thomas Galland stated that 'there are two kinds of neutrality: (1) a total abstention from the subject, or (2) fair play by allowing advocacy on both sides'.[19] With their predetermined views on the kind of politics a respectable Christian should be involved in, Wesleyan Tories were not prepared to meet either of Galland's criteria.

A second element in the Wesleyan Tory creed was anti-Catholicism, which took on party significance initially because of Whig ecclesiastical policy in Ireland and then because of the Lichfield House compact of Whigs, Radicals and Irish Repealers.

Although in retrospect it can be seen that the 'Lichfield House Conspiracy' (as the *Watchman* called it) brought 'the progressive emasculation of both the Radical and O'Connell's parliamentary parties',[20] it seemed to Wesleyan Tories at the time that a formidable phalanx of Liberals, Radicals, Catholics and Dissenters was about to deal the fatal blow to Britain's shaky Protestant Constitution. The fact that the leader of this parliamentary 'alliance', Lord John Russell, had already described Methodism as 'a powerful drug' of illusory and transitory worth, scarcely endeared Whig-Liberalism to Wesleyan leaders.[21]

Into this political climate the *Watchman* brought three fundamental principles. The first was the desire to see Protestantism progress at the expense of Catholicism in Ireland: 'It is in Ireland that the battle has, both religiously and politically, to be fought.'[22] Second, in the great crusade against popery the obvious tactic was to support the Established Church both in England and in Ireland. It had the triple advantage of being at the centre of the political doctrine of the Protestant Constitution, the church of the Methodists' founder, and the most wealthy Protestant denomination in Ireland. Third, Peel's rearguard opposition to the appropriation of Church revenue and to extreme Dissenting demands led Wesleyan Tories to think more highly of his style of conservatism than a candid examination of his post-Tamworth principles would have allowed.[23] The seeds of future disillusionment were thus sown in the extravagant flattery of Peel's conduct in 1835.[24] Wesleyan Toryism, in its party-political aspect at least, was based on an unsophisticated and partly mythological perception of the actual state of English politics in the 1830s. Rather like many of Peel's own supporters, Wesleyan Tories were better at diagnosing ills than in offering a cure.

From 1835 to 1837 the *Watchman* opposed every aspect of the government's Irish policy, from its church and tithe bill to its proposals for municipal reform. The crux of the matter was this.

Lord John is a man of circumstances. . . . He will maintain the Protestant religion in Ireland, if Irish notions and prejudices will permit; at present he will concede Corporation Reform; if that is not enough he will concede more: perhaps the Church and Protestantism may, with some modifications, be maintained; if not they must be conceded! The Protestants of Ireland may now read their doom should the present ministers remain in office. . . . But, Protestants of England! you under God are to determine whether this counsel shall stand – whether this policy shall be pursued, to the destruction of all that your Protestant fellow-subjects in Ireland hold sacred. Will you see their religion, their connection with Britain, their liberty, their property, their lives, immolated on the altar of Popery?

[On Municipal Corporation reform] This measure . . . will greatly increase the democratic power in Ireland, and that power will be wielded exclusively by the Papists.[25]

With truth being higher than democracy, no concessions could be made to Irish Catholics beyond what had been given in 1829 and in 1833.

There was a further twist in Wesleyan anti-Catholicism, because the Tory leadership appealed to this emotion within its membership to defeat Whig-Liberal concessions to Dissenters in England. For example, a narrow Commons majority in favour of the government's Church Rate Bill in 1837 was gained, according to the *Watchman*, by the votes of Catholic MPs: 'We earnestly appeal to the consciences of such of our readers as may approve of the present measure, and ask them, whether they are satisfied to receive it from the hands of a Roman Catholic majority?'[26]

A third element in Wesleyan Toryism was a genuine commitment to the *principle* of religious establishments as a declaration of state support for Christian values. This commitment was, of course, put to the ultimate test in the 1840s by the Disruption in Scotland and by Tractarianism in England, but in the 1830s the principle of establishment seemed to offer the best protection against the 'wide-spreading Atheism, Socialism, and Libertinism of the age'.[27] Thus, the same complex of political, social and intellectual forces, that provoked a range of responses in the churches from Tractarianism and voluntaryism, and from pre-millennialism to ultra-Protestantism, nudged Wesleyan leaders towards Church and Tory politics. They resisted militant voluntaryism, whether in education or in other areas, because they believed it to be the midwife of secularism. A similar argument was employed by Thomas Chalmers, whose writings made such a profound impact on Bunting and other conservative Wesleyans,[28] in an important series of metropolitan lectures on the value of religious establishments.[29] Describing disestablishment reformers as ecclesiastical Luddites, Chalmers stated that the religious free trade idea, upon which most voluntaryist arguments were based, took no account of human sinfulness. How could the laws of supply and demand operate when men, because of the Fall, had no religious demand? Chalmers struck deep chords within the breasts of his Wesleyan hearers when he expounded on the twin evils of Roman Catholicism and bureaucratic Utilitarianism. As with Methodist educational policy, Chalmers wanted state money for the support of the Protestant religion with no strings attached. Although apparently taking the fight to the opposition there was an unmistakable grain of pessimism in Chalmers's lectures, stemming from his experience of the Glasgow slums. He believed that religion in urban Britain was a spent force, unless dedicated clergy, with the state apparatus behind them, devoted themselves to the reclamation of God's poor. Such an appeal to the pastoral office was not lost on the Wesleyan leaders.

Bunting himself had always defended the establishment principle in Conference by referring to Wesley's example and to the Methodist constitution,[30] but his correspondence and the *Watchman*'s columns show that Wesleyan Tories increasingly appreciated the wider significance of religious establishments.[31] Not that they were against all Dissenting claims; they merely opposed those that constituted a direct attack on the establishment's ability to carry out its proper functions of Christianizing the nation. Church rates fell into this category, opening up the universities did not.

A fourth aspect of Wesleyan Toryism, its social aspirations, is more difficult to pinpoint. A letter from Bunting's son to his mother in the mid 1830s conveys the flavour of official Wesleyanism's social setting.[32] His descriptions of chapel inaugurations, rounds of sermon tasting, after-service dinners financed by lay worthies, and of 'attentive and respectable' congregations are illustrative of a contented conservatism. Though still unwelcome in polite society, Wesleyan Tories had found a social niche which was neither self-confident enough to serve as a basis for Dissenting militancy nor insecure enough to fuel an aggrieved radicalism. In short it was the Toryism of aspiring respectability, somehow perfectly summed up in Jabez Bunting's acquisition of an American doctorate. Within Methodism this classical façade of a chapel culture appealed neither to those whose Puritan industry had virtually won control of a town (as in Rochdale) nor to those whose gains from the Industrial Revolution had never been consolidated (as in Manchester). By contrast, Wesleyan Toryism was a mixture of pride in Methodist achievement, and the fear that liberals, Catholics and radicals would snatch it away from them.

Against a general atmosphere of weakness and decline in the administration, the Whigs posed fewer problems for Wesleyan Tories after 1837, with the notable exception of Russell's educational proposals. Nevertheless, Whig concessions to Irish Catholics and

English Dissenters had moved the religious conservatism of the Wesleyan leadership firmly into the party-political arena. The *Watchman*, taken by many for its Methodist news, provoked complaints from all over the country against its Tory bias.[33] This was particularly resented because of the failure of its liberal Methodist competitors, and because extra-Wesleyan sources, including *The Times*, assumed that the *Watchman* was the connexion's official political organ.[34] The fact that the Archbishop of Canterbury, England's leading newspaper, and Tory politicians now saw the political usefulness of the Wesleyans only rubbed salt into the wounds of connexional liberals.[35] Whatever would they have made of Disraeli's *Coningsby*, if their religious and political convictions had allowed them to read it?

'I am told these Wesleyans are really a very respectable body' said Lord Fitzbooby, 'I believe there is no very material difference between their tenets and those of the Establishment. I never heard of them much till lately. We have too long confounded them with the mass of the Dissenters.'[36]

The Conservative election victory of 1841 was, according to the Wesleyan leadership, divine confirmation of their courageous stand against the Whigs in the 1830s. Interpreting the result in terms of a 'combined Protestant and Conservative reaction', the *Watchman* stated that it was the most important historical event since Waterloo, and that 'a path of political usefulness more splendid than was ever opened to man' now lay before Peel.[37] Yet only four years later Wesleyan Tories were disconsolate, and Bunting's policies had collapsed around him. Peel, the conquering hero of 1841, had by then become the greatest betrayer of religious principles ever to hold the office of Prime Minister. Such disenchantment was partly attributable to Graham's factory education proposals, but the main reasons are to be found at the Celtic fringe, in Scotland and in Ireland.

The Disruption crisis in the Church of Scotland over the respective rights of lay patrons and local congregations in the appointment of ministers was of special concern to the Wesleyans, because it seemed to them that the evangelical party in Scotland performed the same role as did Methodism in England.[38] Thus, as Puseyites and voluntaryists battered away at the Wesleyan ministry, it is not surprising that Bunting sought evangelical relief at the hands of Chalmers and his Scottish supporters. Both wanted a spiritually pure established church maintained, but not corrupted, by the state. In retrospect that was the weakest point of Chalmers's argument in his London lectures on established churches. 'Such may be the line of demarcation between the civil and the ecclesiastical', he stated, 'that while the State maintains the teachers of religion, it meddles not with the things that are taught.'[39] To support his point Chalmers chose the unfortunate illustration of a West Indian planter paying for missionary labour on his estate. Whatever the impact of such an appeal on metropolitan evangelicals with a hunger for mission, it cut no ice with politicians. With reasoning typical of the man, Peel could not understand how established churchmen, whose entire ecclesiastical edifice depended on the law, could be so churlish when the law worked against their theological interests. 'It is a perfect anomaly and absurdity', he told the House of Commons, 'that a church should have all the privileges of an establishment . . . and yet claim an exemption from those obligations which . . . must exist on its side with reference to the supreme tribunals of the country.'[40]

Although the crisis in the Scottish Church was not so acute for Wesleyans as for Scots evangelicals, it did make a considerable impression on the Wesleyan leadership in two respects. First, although Bunting and the Methodist Conference supported Chalmers throughout the crisis, it was made clear in Conference debates that Wesleyans should be careful lest in opposing lay patronage in the Scottish Church they were seen to be supporting principles of ecclesiastical democracy that were unacceptable to their own connexion. James Dixon, for example, spoke against the inclusion of any reference to the Scottish problem in the annual address to the Methodist societies in case 'our people should want to abolish the itinerancy by keeping a minister they take to without regard to the rights and interests of the rest of the Connexion'.[41] Only a few years earlier a semi-official Conference publication on *The Constitution and Discipline of Wesleyan Methodism* expounded a high view of the Wesleyan pastoral office against the democratic participation common to both Independent and Presbyterian Churches.[42] Nevertheless, Dixon's warning went unheeded and the disputed reference to the Scottish Church was retained in the annual address.

We do unhesitatingly declare our adherence to what we consider to be by far the most important principle involved in the recent discussions – the one great principle, namely, that it is the right of every church to claim, in matters which are plainly and in their very nature spiritual and ecclesiastical, and especially in relation to the sacred functions belonging to the admission, ordination, appointment, suspension, and deposition of ministers, an unfettered freedom of action.[43]

Although the evidence is too slight to be conclusive, Bunting's own position in 1843 was probably more complicated than the editors of his correspondence have allowed.[44] There is no doubt that Bunting was a firm admirer of Chalmers, and believed with him that the evangelical cause in Scotland was in the hands of the Non-Intrusionists. In addition, Bunting must have been flattered by the attention paid to him by Scots evangelicals after a decade of abuse from English Dissenters and Methodist seceders.[45] On the other hand he must have sympathized with Peel's view that to make ministers 'dependent upon the popular voice would be to degrade the office of the minister and to deprive him of all chance of being useful in his sacred calling'.[46] Caught between the Scylla of state thraldom and the Charybdis of ecclesiastical democracy, Bunting's correspondence is ominously silent on Scottish affairs in 1842–3, and his Conference contributions were a good deal more tentative than has been suggested. In fact Bunting, far from pressing a strongly worded pastoral address on an unwilling Conference, seems to have acquiesced in it out of a sense of evangelical solidarity with Chalmers and his friends.[47] Apart from ill-health, the reason for Bunting's uncertainty was that the Scottish Disruption brought him face to face with the inadequacy of his earlier policies. The rub was this. How could one support church establishments *and* evangelicalism, when Tractarianism in England and state interference in Scotland made it impossible to embrace both ideals? 'I once hoped that such a thing was possible as an Established Church without state interference', Bunting told Conference, 'but now I see it to be impossible. I wish two thousand clergymen would leave the English Church in the same way.'[48] What is remarkable is not that Bunting's policies ran into difficulties in the 1840s, but that the religious triumphalism of Exeter Hall had raised such unrealistic expectations among evangelicals in the 1830s. Whereas the Wilberforce generation combined religious earnestness with a political realism appropriate to their social status, Bunting's generation allowed their religious success to cloud their political judgement.

If the Disruption in Scotland exposed raw nerves within the Methodist polity, it led also to an important change in Wesleyan political and ecclesiastical opinions. Whatever the complexities of discussion behind the 1843 pastoral address, there can be no doubt that it 'implied a more critical attitude towards the English Church than any official act of Conference for over half a century'.[49] The *Watchman* carried an epitaph for an era when it stated that 'there is no Established Church in existence on behalf of which, as it now stands, we could conscientiously contend'.[50] But Wesleyanism was still not contemplating an alliance with militant Dissent on a voluntaryist platform. Rather its leaders were heading inescapably in the direction of Evangelical Alliance, in which denominational distinctiveness could disappear below the surface of anti-Catholicism and anti-liberalism.

The chief religio-political issues of 1843, Graham's factory education proposals and the Scottish Disruption, scarcely endeared Peel's administration to the Wesleyan leadership, but neither had much damage been done. Peel, after all, had tried to strengthen established churches, not weaken them. The problem for the Wesleyans in 1843, therefore, lay not so much with Peelite Conservatism, as with the very theological and spiritual essence of established churches in Britain. As a result the Wesleyan leadership was forced into the absurd position of supporting religious establishments in principle but not in practice. Such political and ideological impotence not only kept Wesleyans out of the Anti-State Church Association (1844), but left them vulnerable to Peel's ecclesiastical liberalism in 1844–5, which surprisingly took them by surprise. It was, therefore, Peel's attitude to Unitarians and, more important, to Irish Catholics, that finally exposed the futility of Wesleyan Toryism.

The Dissenters' Chapels Bill of 1844 assuring Unitarians of their right to retain old Presbyterian chapels subject to certain conditions was a bitter blow to the Wesleyans. The *Watchman* called it the 'Unitarian Fraud Legalization Bill' and the 'Trinitarian Spoliation Bill', but the rub was as much material as it was theological, because the unamended bill left the door open for Methodist seceders to claim against the parent connexion.[51] Bunting successfully petitioned the Attorney-General for a technical change in the bill as it passed through committee, but the damage had already been done. The fact that Peel had entered the division lists with Lord John Russell, Sharman Crawford and Richard Lalor Sheil was neither forgiven nor forgotten.[52]

In a review of Conservative legislation in 1844 the *Watchman* confessed to being fairly content, with the exception of one class of measures.

We of course refer to those measures which have an immediate bearing on the interests of scriptural truth and evangelical religion. The principal of these were the Bills for repealing the remaining penal enactments against Roman Catholics, and for promoting bequests and endowments for the perpetuation of Popery in Ireland, and the Bill for quieting Socinians and Arians in the possession of property entrusted in former years for the promulgation of orthodox truth. ... It is to be remembered that these concessions are avowedly but the precursors of others. ... We need a new party in the Legislature whose great principle shall be that the Word of God is the safest guide for nations as well as for individuals.[53]

The Wesleyans had travelled some distance in half a century from nervous petitions to the government for the protection of their religious liberties against Anglican opposition, to the call for a new political party to govern the nation on evangelical principles. Being hitched to the Exeter Hall bandwagon no doubt increased the self-importance of metropolitan Methodists, but it did little else.

If Wesleyan Tories were dissatisfied with Peel's record in 1844, the following year brought greater horrors, and once again Ireland was the cause. The root of the problem was that Peel's attempt to woo moderate Catholics away from O'Connell's Repeal agitation with timely concessions was anathema to those employing religious standards of truth and error. Well-substantiated rumours about the further endowment of Maynooth College angered Wesleyans who were now bewildered by the apparently insatiable demands of Irish Catholics, and the inability of successive governments to remain firm.[54] According to the *Watchman*, each concession was a prelude to a fresh demand. Concessions were not received with thanks but grasped as rights, with complaints about the extent of the favour. The crux of the matter was that the Irish Catholic leadership demanded rights commensurate with the population under its control, and evangelical Protestants refused to admit that their mission to Ireland had failed. The Wesleyans were faithful to their Protestant principles throughout the nineteenth century – what had changed was the character of Irish Catholicism and therefore what was politically feasible. The theory of the Protestant Constitution was fast disappearing in the light of practical problems of government.

Peel introduced the Maynooth Bill in February 1845, and by March the Committee of Privileges had committed the Wesleyans to a massive extra-parliamentary pressure campaign in which all Methodist congregations were requested to petition Parliament,[55] despite some unease about the increasing frequency of denominational agitations.[56] Meanwhile, the Committee of Privileges' secretaries, Prest[57] and Stamp, kept their fingers on the pulse of the wider anti-Maynooth campaign through the meetings of the organizing committee at the London coffee house. Bunting, by a remarkable coincidence, was President of the Conference for the year 1844–5 as he had been in 1828–9, and he was kept informed by regular letters from Prest.[58] It was Bunting who chaired the aggregate meeting of London Wesleyans at the City Road chapel in April. Claiming that the Maynooth issue was religious and not political, Bunting stated that Maynooth had become the centre of the great world battle between truth and superstition. Maynooth-trained priests not only interrupted missionary efforts in Ireland, but also in the colonies. Bunting defended his earlier support for Catholic Emancipation by drawing a distinction between civil rights for Catholics and state funding of Catholic religion. 'Let them have a college if they like', he said, 'but let them pay for it.' Bunting even permitted himself a jibe at O'Connell, that all Methodists must become 'repalers [sic]: What we will endeavour to repeal, if unfortunately it should pass into law . . . is the bill for extending and perpetuating the grant to Maynooth'.[59] Bunting followed this up several months later by offering O'Connell a £500 subscription 'to the Repeal Association, which shall be paid as soon as the Act of Union is repealed'.[60]

A. S. Thelwall, the recorder of the anti-Maynooth campaign, described the Wesleyan meeting as the most enthusiastic of all.[61] Five days later it was a different story when 1039 delegates assembled for the anti-Maynooth conference in London. It proved impossible to contain anti-Catholic Anglicans and militant voluntaryists within the same body. Thus the anti-Maynooth agitation, at the crucial time, fragmented into two parts symbolized by the two conferences: the anti-Maynooth conference comprising Anglicans, Congregationalists, led by John Blackburn, and Wesleyan Methodists, and the Crosby Hall conference comprising Independents, Congregationalists of Miall's stamp, and Methodist secession groups.[62] Thereafter the respective protagonists spent as much time attacking each other as they did opposing the measure itself. Supporters of the bill were, of course, delighted.

While non-Wesleyan Methodists took the line that it was bad for the government to endow any denomination, but worse that it should endow Roman Catholicism,[63] Wesleyans contrived to argue that establishment *or* voluntaryist principles were subordinate to the main point at issue.[64] As such they played an important part in the anti-Maynooth conference, in which Wesleyan delegates took it in turn to express the unanimity of their congregations; John James for Liverpool, George Osborn for Manchester, Robert Newstead for Leeds, Ralph Wilson for Newcastle-upon-Tyne, Edward Walker for Birmingham, Jacob Stanley for Bristol, William Vevers for Derby, John McClean for Scotland, and many others besides.[65] Prest could boast that 'one thousand petitions have been presented, up to this time, to the House of Lords, from the Wesleyans. I am in a position to astonish that House, on any night that I may please to do so'.[66] Dixon was presumptuous, but probably accurate, when he told the conference that 'I am a Methodist preacher; and if you will permit me, I will try to represent the opinions of something like a million and a half of Her Majesty's subjects.'[67] In response to such unanimity, politicians could only wonder why the 'petitions from the Wesleyans were all verbatim the same', or why country petitions were sent to Parliament from London.[68] Whether these facts were attributable to connexional efficiency or to metropolitan stage management is a question that was never fully investigated. It did not matter in any case, because mass petitioning did nothing to interrupt the bill's progress, an observation that led Bunting into some interesting comparisons of English politics in the first and second quarters of the nineteenth century.[69] As Parliament became more representative, petitioning assumed less importance.

Despite the Conservatives dividing 149–148 against the third reading, the Maynooth Bill passed the Commons with a comfortable majority. At the end of May the action moved from the Commons to the Lords and, outside Parliament, from England to Ireland. Prest set off for Ireland on the 26th, and when he arrived in Dublin he told Bunting that he would try 'to do something to arouse the Wesleyans here which, of course, I shall endeavour to do, in concert with Mr Waugh, if I can move him and the Dublin ministers'.[70] Who would have thought in 1829 when Bunting and Tobias were trying to control the Irish preachers, that sixteen years later the secretary of the Committee of Privileges, with Bunting's approval, would be in Dublin trying to persuade the Irish preachers to oppose a government concession to Roman Catholicism? The Protestant character of Irish Methodism had not changed, however, and no exterior urging was necessary. Irish Wesleyans were prominent in anti-Maynooth demonstrations in Ireland throughout May and June, and seven sat on the Irish anti-Maynooth committee.[71]

Wesleyan opposition was in vain, and the Maynooth Bill received its third reading in the Lords on 16 June. As Chadwick has aptly put it, 'extraordinary though it then appeared, and extraordinary though it still appears, Peel passed an act of parliament to give money to the Roman Catholic church in Ireland. Scottish churchmen asked the government for money and were refused. English bishops asked the government for money and were refused. Catholic bishops from Ireland asked for money and extracted it from a Tory government'.[72] Peel's resolution, and the support he received from other leading statesmen, enabled the government to carry the Maynooth Bill against enormous extra-parliamentary pressure. The Wesleyans were left disillusioned with politics and with politicians. Bunting, now a man in his late 60s, gave eloquent testimony to his disappointment with Peel:

It is a strange thing to have lived long enough to hear a minister of the crown of Great Britain lay down as a maxim, an oracle, an axiom which was to regulate his own and the proceedings of both parties in the state; that, when any question is brought before parliament bearing on religion, it is to be decided not at all on religious grounds, but exclusively on political grounds. A shocking sentiment – and I greatly regret that it should have proceeded from a man, of whom, in the main, I have always been inclined to think more respectfully, than some others have.[73]

Bunting was not just exorcizing the ghost of his own Wesleyan Toryism, but was also pointing out the real significance of the Maynooth Act. Edward Norman is right to see it as a major constitutional landmark in the transition from the confessional state of the early nineteenth century to the liberal state of the early twentieth, and it was opposed by men who knew what they were doing. Men like Bunting believed in 'the religious office of the state', and fought hard in 1845 'to prevent its ruin'.[74] The irony from the Methodists' point of view is that between 1790 and 1830, they did much to erode the confessional basis of the state in practice, only to find themselves committed to it in theory by the early Victorian period.

The years between the Great Reform Act and the repeal of the Corn Laws had been unexpectedly tough for evangelical churchmen with a commitment to the establishment principle. Powerful forces of reaction and reform had so eroded their ecclesiastical and political platform that, by the time of Maynooth, they had little left to cling to except each other. The problem was, of course, less acute for Anglican evangelicals, who could still take up cudgels against rival theological traditions within their own religious corporation, than for Dissenting, but anti-voluntaryist, evangelicals like the Wesleyan Methodists. Caught between radical Dissent and the theologically unacceptable Established Church, Bunting and his connexional supporters had used Peel as a crutch until it too collapsed from under them. The attractions of the Evangelical Alliance were obvious. The idea of an Alliance had been floated by Thomas Chalmers in the early 1830s, and was taken up by the *Watchman* when the Oxford Movement began to show its Anglo-Catholic colours.[75] Bunting was an enthusiastic advocate for 'a close and affectionate Union of all Protestant Christians' even before the political disappointments of Peel's administration.[76] A genuine desire for evangelical unity had been forged at the anniversary meetings of the missionary societies in Exeter Hall, when it seemed that a heathen world would fall to evangelical Protestantism, if only Roman Catholicism, Puseyism and liberalism could be held in check. Wesleyan preachers, with Bunting especially prominent, took part in Christian union meetings in 1843, and by 1845 Prest's diary shows how the anti-Maynooth agitation was followed almost immediately by Evangelical Alliance committees in which many of the same names reappear.[77]

A preliminary conference for promoting Christian union was held in Liverpool in October 1845. Its resolutions show a combination of genuine desire for Christian union and a sense of the need for greater solidarity against Catholicism and infidelity.[78] Some of its more pious supporters were nervous of the Alliance's anti-Catholic pedigree, and tried to nudge it along more positive pathways. For example, Alfred Barrett, an eminent Methodist theologian, told Bunting that if the Alliance were to be

formally and specially an Anti-Popish confederation, I fear it would be difficult to keep it free from the distraction and excitement of merely secular politics. . . . I would not give up the Anti-, the *aggressive*, character of the movement but I would have it move against more evils than one. Let us secure the adhesion of the established-clergy and we protect their fidelity and deprive Tractarianism of its harvests; let us gain the nonconformist ministry and their minds will be no longer embittered by exclusivism; let us gain the Christian laity and we deepen their interest in the ordinances and ministry of the gospel; let us call forth an enthusiastic loyalty to the throne of Christ our Lord, and Popery will be more dismayed than even by an adverse bill in Parliament.[79]

This plea did not soften Bunting's anti-Catholic zeal when he, along with 160 other Wesleyans took part in the first Evangelical Alliance conference in London from 19 August to 2 September 1846.[80] A survey of the Wesleyan participants is revealing. About 30 per cent had also attended the anti-Maynooth conference and around 50 per cent came from London, South Lancashire and Ireland.[81] For such Wesleyans, the Evangelical Alliance was a way of testifying to their anti-Catholicism, their political pessimism, their missionary zeal, *and* their evangelical inclusiveness, which after all had been one of the most noble aspects of the Methodist tradition. For Bunting personally, his earnest commitment to the Alliance was a welcome respite from the ecclesiastical conflicts that had dominated his life for about two decades.[82]

This sketch of the Wesleyan leadership's politics in the 1830s and 1840s needs to be accompanied by several warnings. The first is that the preoccupations of the leadership did not percolate very far into the connexion, as subsequent sections on electoral and popular politics will show. Second, Bunting, although clearly an influential figure, was not without considerable support from Wesleyan preachers who looked upon him as the most reliable interpreter of the authentic Wesleyan tradition. Third, it would be a mistake to analyse Methodist politics solely in terms of its own peculiar history. Thus, a comparison with Irish Presbyterianism in the same period shows how external circumstances could affect churches of quite different theological traditions in much the same way. Both were at their most radical in the 1790s yet by 1840 their two most eminent ecclesiastical statesmen, Henry Cooke and Jabez Bunting, were Peelite conservatives.[83] Their shared evangelical hatred of Catholicism and Liberalism not only eroded the dissidence of their Dissent, but forced them into tight corners within their own denominations.

Indeed, the political similarities between Cooke and Bunting are remarkable. Neither opposed Catholic Emancipation in 1829, because they saw it as the last act of an old drama, not the beginning of a new one. Both resisted the Irish national education experiment because it was too favourable to Irish Catholics, yet both subsequently accepted government money on more favourable terms despite cries of hypocrisy from their opponents. Neither had much time for the ecclesiastical trappings of Anglicanism with its Bishops, social privileges and financial exactions, but both could see that the future of Protestantism in Ireland, and of Christianity in England, might well depend on state support for established religion. As a result both were unrelenting opponents of voluntaryism. Both placed such confidence in Peel that the disappointments of his administration damaged their political credibility and exposed them to malicious counter-attacks from enemies within their own denominations. Finally, both Bunting and Cooke emerged from humble beginnings to become important religious and political figures in the second quarter of the nineteenth century. The close relationship between religion and politics in this period is something that neither desired, yet both profited from it, at least in terms of personal notoriety. Both acquired the label 'pope' from their denominational adversaries, but more for their autocratic style than for the degree of control they achieved.

Thus Bunting's policies were neither unique nor universally accepted within his own denomination. They could not however be ignored, and connexional conflict was particularly acute in the second quarter of the nineteenth century.

Opposition and secession

Convulsed from within and pressurized from without, Wesleyan Methodism in the second quarter of the nineteenth century suffered a series of controversies and secessions from which Methodism in Britain never fully recovered. The Leeds Protestant Methodists broke away in 1828, the Wesleyan Methodist Association seceded in 1836, and they were joined by the Wesleyan Reformers to form the United Methodist Free Church in 1857. Since Methodism is still a living Christian tradition in an avowedly ecumenical age, no subject has received as much attention from Methodist historians as its 'age of disunity'.[84] There are benefits as well as dangers in this emphasis, because the point of division often distils the essence of otherwise indistinct problems. Although each secession had a unique context, many of the same themes reappear. As Wesleyanism left behind its societary origins and acquired more formal denominational characteristics, those who disliked the trend dug in their heals at moments of symbolic significance. In Leeds the installation of an organ, with all its overtones of wealth, ritualism and formalism, provoked those with more serious grievances to make a stand. In the mid 1830s it was the spark of the proposed theological institution that lit the highly combustible fuel of anti-clericalism, local particularism and personal jealousies. By the time of the famous Flysheet controversy in the late 1840s, the objects of attack were the metropolitan location, bureaucratic centralization, and lack of spiritual energy of Bunting and his ministerial supporters. Moreover, each controversy had a domino effect. Malcontents were given precedents and inspiration. Conservatives reinforced discipline, dusted down the rule book, and constructed new ideological fortresses to repel the attacks. In this way, protest hardened the system that provoked it.

What made the disputes so intractable was the interconnected nature of the problems and of the Methodist system. Individual strands could not be separated and dealt with; rather the whole rope was showing signs of fray. Lurking within each of the controversies were deep-seated divisions between ministers and laymen, rich and poor, conservatives and radicals, supporters of central administration and upholders of local courts, and at the bottom of it all, fundamental disagreements about the nature of virginal Methodism. While ministers worked out more elevated concepts of the pastoral office, discontented laymen developed a Wesleyan version of Norman Yoke ideology, declaring that Wesley's flexible and pietistic Methodism had been corrupted by an unholy alliance of clerical bureaucrats and wealthy laymen. With so much ill-informed abuse flowing from both sides, the elaborate Wesleyan legal system for solving disputes proved to be too ambiguous, and too susceptible of manipulation by the powerful, to be of much use. Thus, practical problems soon became constitutional problems and they in turn became theological problems, and all these were laced with frustrated ambition and social cleavage. No wonder the Wesleyan system could not contain them, for that system depended for its operation on goodwill and Christian values. From that perspective, Methodist secessions in this period were not just crises of connexional governance, but were also departures from those spiritual and ethical principles to which both sides laid claim.

A judicious account of the constitutional and theological issues at stake in the Methodist secessions already exists,[85] but their social and political dimensions are even more important. In Leeds, for example, the organ dispute was superimposed on other tensions. Methodist radicals in the town had already opposed Conference policy on control of the Sunday schools, cottage prayer meetings, and circuit divisions. These radical upholders of 'low Methodism' were also of a lower social status than the trustees and patrons of the great Brunswick chapel who requested the organ, and demonstrated the fact by worshipping in a different chapel, and by taking up radical causes such as the abolition of church rates. Bunting described the radical faction as a species of 'Methodistical Luddism' in 'revolt against the first principles of our existing Church Government'.[86] Disputes running to first principles are not easy to resolve, especially since Bunting's first principle – the power and authority of Conference – soon became the crux of the problem. The resultant secession split the Leeds circuit in two, and the shockwaves were transmitted through the connexional system, causing further trouble in Liverpool, Sheffield and South London.[87] The preachers responded with pamphlets on the authority and responsibility of the pastoral office, which in the light of the problems they were designed to meet, proved utterly counter-productive. Once mutual charity had foundered on the rocks of social tension, no peace could be found through a further assertion of rights.

The dust from the Leeds case had barely settled when another agitation erupted over the introduction of a theological institution for the education of preachers. The project was opposed by those who wanted to retain the primitive simplicity of the ministry, and by those who objected to yet another extension of Bunting's power and influence. Connexional offices had been showered upon Bunting throughout his career, and in 1834 he was about to add the presidency of the new institution to the secretaryship of foreign missions he already held. Bunting's position in the 1830s, therefore, was not too dissimilar to Walpole's in the 1730s: he had become too powerful for his own good, and no appeal to constitutional principles nor the Wesleyan tradition could deflect those motivated by frustrated ambition. Dr Samuel Warren, an ageing classical scholar who probably hoped for a post in the new institution, led the attack on Bunting. He alleged that Methodism was in danger of falling into the hands of a 'dominant episcopal faction'.

From hence the connexion must prepare itself to receive a liturgical Service, a splendid Ritual, an illegitimate Episcopal Ordination, a cassocked race of Ecclesiastics, and whatever else may render this new – this improved edition of Methodism, imposing and magnificent in the eyes of the world.[88]

Such eloquence hardly befitted a man who later entered the Anglican ministry, but Warren's protest set fire to tinder that neither he nor anyone else could control. The resultant secession and the progress of 'Free Methodism' in its Lancashire stronghold has been the subject of an excellent local study.[89] Once again, behind the constitutional questions of Conference authority, ministerial power and local rights, there was an important social and political context which requires a town-by-town analysis.

In Manchester, for example, it has been shown that members of the Wesleyan Methodist Association were of a lower and more fragile social status than their Wesleyan counterparts. Most belonged to a 'Dickensien shabby genteel class' of shopkeepers and small tradesmen. As such they felt themselves to be above factory work but fell far short of entrepreneurial success. They had no direct contact with working-class politics, but experienced a religious form of political excitement in the meetings up to secession.[90] Their lack of material prosperity was translated into what John Kent has described as 'that nagging narrowness of the Protestant tradition, which is always eager to credit the spiritual deadness of everybody except the members of the critic's tiny clique'.[91] These emotions were easily channelled into resentment at the way in which the Wesleyan hierarchy, itself a beneficiary of upward social mobility, appeared to discriminate against their interests.[92] A like tale could be told of Liverpool, where a similar social constituency threw up an array of unsavoury characters whose spiritual claims were scarcely matched by their actions. Indeed, some aspects of Nonconformist culture in South Lancashire seemed to confirm the worst fears of the Wesleyan hierarchy. It was full of quirky, self-opinionated leaders. Some fired bullets at the Wesleyan Conference before leaving its jurisdiction, while others canvassed support for their own religious ventures. Jumpers, Ranters, Free Gospellers, Town Missions and Mormonism all attracted support from religious pilgrims in search of spiritual authenticity. Wesleyan Conference preachers, whether of conservative or liberal orientation, were not at home in this religious territory, but they were not above using the terrors which it inspired to strengthen discipline in the ranks.

The development of 'Free Methodism' in Rochdale was markedly different from that of Manchester and Liverpool. Rochdale's prosperity had come later than in either of the other towns, and its benefits had been appropriated by a predominantly Wesleyan Nonconformity. Neither Anglicanism nor Roman Catholicism made much of an impact on the town, so that by the early Victorian period it had become a citadel of Nonconformist Liberalism. Secure in its own local strength and prosperity, the Rochdale Methodist leadership saw no need to placate either the Established Church or its own hierarchy. This provincial, radical, and self-confident middle class sat loosely to connexional government, and eventually opted out to build its own memorial in the shape of Baillie Street chapel. From thence came leaders of the local Anti-Corn Law League, the Literary and Philosophical Society, the Religious Freedom, Peace, and Temperance Societies and the Good Samaritans. It would be hard to find a more representative sample of Nonconformist Liberalism than this. Paradoxically – and there is a warning here against viewing all

Methodist conflicts in terms of rich Wesleyans versus poor freedom fighters – Rochdale Wesleyanism retained more working-class members and primitive Methodist practices than its secessionist rival. The Baillie Street leadership replaced class meetings with mutual improvement societies, and left evangelism to the unexacting but productive efforts of professional revivalists like the American James Caughey.[93]

Along with the Free Methodist rejection of Wesleyan authority, there was a corresponding rejection of Wesleyan political loyalties. Whereas official Wesleyanism with its Tory bias resisted teetotalism, educational voluntaryism, and attacks on the Established Church, Association Methodists took the opposite side on each matter. Such a programme not only thrust them into the Whig-Liberal camp alongside their Dissenting allies, but also made them pioneers in the wider Methodist advance towards the Nonconformist Conscience. One interesting sidelight on the political differences between Wesleyan and Free Methodism is that although the latter took a rich haul of Sunday schools from the main connexion, its voluntaryist policy on daily education was a financial disaster.[94] Bunting and his supporters may have made many mistakes in the early Victorian period, but the pursuit of state money for day schools was not one of them.

The most serious internal upheaval in Methodist history began as a reform movement in the late 1840s, and culminated in the formation of the United Methodist Free Churches in 1857. Most of the characteristic elements of earlier Methodist disharmony surfaced again. This time the catalyst was a series of anonymous Flysheets attacking Bunting's whole system of connexional government. So damaging were the allegations, and so prolific was the ensuing propaganda, that Conference could ill afford to ignore the challenge. James Everett, the most likely author of the Flysheets, and his two closest supporters, William Griffith and Samuel Dunn, were expelled from the Wesleyan ministry by their peers at the annual Conference of 1849. Their guilt lay in refusing to deny their guilt, and such a judicial process by a private court of ministers was seized upon by *The Times*, and the predominantly Dissenting English provincial press, as evidence of Laud's ghost at work.[95] Wesleyanism had got itself into another legal muddle because its supreme court, the ministerial Conference, was also the nub of the problem. With justice not being seen to be done, the agitators gladly expanded the theatre of conflict. Their own ministerial credentials were feeble and their policies were confused, but as with Warren before them, their rhetoric exposed raw nerves in the socially divided Methodist circuits.[96] Although they always claimed to represent the majority of Wesleyans, the scale of the disruption took the agitators by surprise. In response conservative Wesleyans cranked their bureaucracy and propaganda organs into gear,[97] appealed once more to the pastoral office[98] and talked in terms of purges and clearances. But such remedies were of no avail in a dispute that burst the banks of connexional politics to take in a broader liberal revolt against Wesleyan Conservatism in all its internal and external manifestations.[99] Even Bunting could not resist the march of English provincial culture. Methodism had come in with the tide of social change in the decades after the French Revolution, but from the 1840s the tide was on the way out – and the Wesleyans were not the only Methodists to suffer.

When the storms subsided after the reform agitation, the most serious result was a reduction in Wesleyan Methodist numbers.[100] Membership losses ran to about 50,000, all in the first few years of disruption, and were mostly picked up by the Wesleyan reformed communities. But the battering which the whole episode gave to the connexion's morale meant that the Wesleyans did not recruit new members at the usual rate for several more years. The results of this were quickly apparent in the total membership of the community, which had always recruited rapidly at the bottom, and lost members less rapidly at the other end. As a result the number of Wesleyan Methodists in 1849 was not surpassed until 1875. Moreover, although the number of Methodists of all types continued to grow in absolute terms in the late-Victorian period, Methodism never again grew as fast as the English population. Ironically, the Church of England, which Methodism had challenged so effectively in the period 1780–1830, managed to hold its ground more successfully in the second half of the nineteenth century, at least among the sub-urbanized middle classes.

Methodist electoral behaviour[101]

The quarter century after the Reform Act is a particularly difficult period for students of English electoral behaviour. With the politics of influence only slowly giving way to the politics of opinion, any analysis of the post-1832 electorate must take into account an intricate combination of national, regional and local circumstances. While it is true that national swings from one party to another are dis-

cernible in early Victorian elections, and while it is also true that
regions acquired specific political characteristics,[102] the full complexity
of voting patterns can only be explored in the localities.[103] Even here
the relative weight one gives to occupation, influence, religion, age,
and opinion is difficult to judge, especially since these are not
independent variables. Although research on the formid.ble pollbooks
is still at an early stage, a number of tentative conclusions have been
offered. It appears that there is little correlation between voting and
class (in the Marxist sense), though there is a high correlation between voting and occupation.[104] In the north-east, for example, the
core of the Radical-Liberal party was the shopkeeping and artisan
class, the Whigs were predominantly the party of the upper and professional classes, and the Tories drew most of their support from the
upper classes, the older free trades, the Church, and the shipping
interest. In Oldham, Whig strength was located in the cotton and
engineering industries, and among small employers and large shopkeepers, whereas Tory strength lay in the coal industry and in the
Church of England.[105] But occupation and economic interests were
not the only determinants, because influence was still the most important factor in county elections. Even the age of voters has to be taken
into account, since those who became politically conscious for the
first time during the constitutional changes of 1828–32 were liable to
vote Liberal for the rest of their lives.

While no one doubts that religion is an important piece in the electoral jigsaw, its exact place is uncertain due to the nature of the
evidence. Apart from laboriously researching local church membership lists, it is impossible to be sure of the relative strength of
Anglicans and Dissenters among *voters*, because the 1851 religious
census dealt with the population as a whole. It is, moreover, difficult
to decide if religious motives were more important than others. For
example, did a Nonconformist employee vote with his Nonconformist employer out of economic self-interest, deference or a common
religious allegiance? Membership of a religious denomination did not
necessarily imply any political or social preferences. Nevertheless, it
is true that the enlarged Dissenting borough electorate after 1832
generally voted Liberal, while Anglicans, though not as solidly, voted
Conservative.[106] The fact that on average a third, and in 1847 more
than half, of the Anglican clergy in the Durham cathedral close voted
Liberal in elections between 1832 and 1871, shows that Anglican
voting was less monochrome than that of Dissenters.[107]

Such difficulties as exist in assessing the electoral behaviour of

Anglicans and Dissenters are compounded when the Methodists are taken into account. Not only were there many Methodist denominations in existence by the mid 1830s, but the political characteristics of the Wesleyans, who were by far the most numerous, are more complicated than those of any other nineteenth-century denomination. Essentially this was because the influence of preachers and wealthy laymen did not usually harmonize with the personal interests of Wesleyan voters. Thus Tory preachers and laymen found it difficult to influence Methodist voters, despite a virtual monopoly of connexional information. There were several reasons for this. First, Buntingite Tories were themselves conscious of the Wesleyan 'no politics' rule, which made them more concerned about opposing Liberal and Dissenting pressure groups within the connexion than in actively campaigning on behalf of the Tory party. Nevertheless, there were times in the 1830s when they sailed close to the wind. In 1830 both Bunting and Robert Newton canvassed against Lord John Russell, and Russell himself blamed the Methodists for his one-vote defeat at Bedford, thereby causing him the temporary inconvenience of supporting parliamentary reform from the family's pocket borough in Tavistock.[108] Similarly, Bunting was unapologetic about publicly supporting Tory candidates at Liverpool in 1832 and at Finsbury in 1834.[109] In these circumstances old Wesleyan principles were put under strain, as in 1837, when the electioneering of three Sheffield preachers was investigated by Conference. Bunting effectively absolved the preachers by stating that they were wrong 'to speak in committees and meetings preparatory to nominations' but 'not in having appeared upon the hustings in favour of a party candidate'. Thus the new principle, as far as anyone understood it, was that preachers were wrong to participate in the machinery of an election, but not wrong to influence the result of it.[110] Although inevitably Bunting produced a Wesleyan precedent, such convoluted arguments show that Conference Tories were becoming both more political and more uneasy.

A second reason for the electoral ineffectiveness of Conference Toryism is the fact that not all preachers were Tory supporters. Thus, even allowing for the obvious bias, a Wesleyan electoral agent for Lord Morpeth in Manchester was probably not far wrong when he wrote that

Our ministers, as a body, meddle not with politics. The great majority belong to no party; are fearful of sweeping changes, yet friendly to sound and gradual reforms. Their dislike to popery, derived rather from its portraiture as existing in times of universal bigotry and intolerance, than from a candid observation of its modified form and softened aspect in this age and this country, is, perhaps, not a little tinged with the prejudice they condemn. Here and there one meets with a genuine tory, and now and then with a sturdy radical; more frequently, however with such as are of a somewhat whiggish complexion. The first talk most, and most loudly – the second seldom, and in a subdued tone: for Dr Bunting . . . and a few other influential preachers, are avowed admirers of the Peel and Stanley policy; and they are men whose frown is not without its terrors. Rigorous is the discipline to which the corps ecclesiastic is subjected.[111]

Even if the Wesleyan preachers *en bloc* had set out to act as political canvassers, the nature of the Methodist polity was against them. A combination of itinerancy (however diluted), a deeply entrenched lay leadership in the localities, and the high ratio of laymen to preachers, meant that the connexion could not be politically manipulated on a regular basis. The occasional extra-parliamentary crusade for a limited objective was quite a different matter from the exercise of long-term electoral control.

With these structural qualifications in mind it is possible to arrive at some conclusions, albeit based on fragmentary evidence, about the nature of Wesleyan voting in the years 1832–50. Northern local studies show that Wesleyans were numerous among the same social groups as benefited from the Reform Act, including respectable, middle and lower middle-class shopkeepers, tradespeople and merchants.[112] Not surprisingly, these Methodists voted for the party that enfranchised them. In the first post-reform election, Manchester Wesleyans voted most commonly for the Whig-Liberal candidates Mark Phillips and Poulett Thompson.[113] There are many other documented examples of Methodist preachers and laymen voting Liberal, especially in areas dominated by other Dissenters,[114] but the most revealing, though also the most dangerous, piece of evidence is a voting survey carried out by the Liberal Methodist newspaper, the *Wesleyan Chronicle*.[115] Based on detailed returns from twenty-nine cities and boroughs and seven counties in the 1841 election, the paper alleged that out of 1843 Wesleyan voters, 1370 (74.3 per cent) voted Liberal, 308 (16.7 per cent) voted Tory, 46 (2.5 per cent) split their votes and 119 (6.5 per cent) abstained. Not only was this information collected by a Liberal paper, but it dealt with only one election and ignored the areas in which Wesleyan Tories were strongest, Manchester and Liverpool.

Nevertheless, all the fragments of evidence suggest that in this period most Wesleyans normally voted Liberal for occupational, social and religious reasons.

There were however occasions in the 1830s when Whig Irish and ecclesiastical policies caused a conservative reaction within Wesleyanism, though its electoral significance depended on local circumstances. For example, in the Bradford election of 1835, Wesleyans played a leading part in the victory of Hardy, a moderate Conservative, over Hadfield, a radical disestablishment candidate from Manchester. Hadfield's extremism forced a split in the alliance between moderate Whigs and Dissenting Radicals, and Hardy's 'Church in Danger' cry won the day.[116] Two years later the Liberals chose a safer candidate, improved their local organization, kept religion out of it, and romped home to a convincing victory.

The most determined attempt by Wesleyan Tories to influence the voting of the Methodist rank-and-file came in the period 1837–41. Throughout 1837, the *Watchman* stirred the religious prejudices of its evangelical readership by dwelling on Whig concessions to Irish Catholics, and once the election was declared, passionate appeals were made to Wesleyan voters: 'It is for you to decide whether Protestantism shall still be the polar star of our Senators.'[117] Politically astute Liberals within the connexion knew that anti-Catholic propaganda was a serious threat to Whig electoral interests, and responded accordingly. Morpeth's agent addressed the Wesleyan electors through the columns of the *Manchester Guardian*. He appealed to the old Whiggish Methodist tradition of religious and civil liberty as embodied in connexional patriarchs like Adam Clarke and Richard Watson. He called for justice to Ireland on generous principles, and for a pure and efficient Church of England. He declared his opposition to Catholicism on religious not political grounds, and concluded with the Whiggish refrain that it was foolish to resist the irresistible – Irish Catholics and English Dissenters could no longer be denied their civil and religious rights.[118]

The election itself was a disappointment for Wesleyan Tories because, apart from Dublin, where Wesleyans organized a tough, though unsuccessful campaign against O'Connell, Methodists seem to have ignored 'the baits of Tory ingenuity'.[119] According to the *Manchester Times*, Methodists in Salford, Sheffield and Leeds ignored Conference pressure and voted Liberal, but in Liverpool, where sectarian politics were strongest, the pollbooks disclose solid Wesleyan support for the Tory candidates.[120]

The most remarkable switch in Wesleyan electoral behaviour came in the Manchester election of 1839, when the Liberal complexion of earlier Methodist voting was converted into true-blue Conservatism. This was partially due to the successful application of no popery slogans to voters made receptive by Irish immigration, Whig educational policy, and vigorous pulpit politics. (Wesleyan Tories were also helped by the Whig-Liberal selection of a Unitarian candidate.) But perhaps most important of all was the fact that Methodist Liberals were now catered for by the Wesleyan Methodist Association, whose members voted solidly Liberal throughout the north of England. In this way political tensions both exacerbated, and were reflected in, the development of more homogenous chapel communities. Like-minded people of similar social status now banded together to express their distinctiveness through denominational and political conflicts.[121]

The no popery cry reached its peak in Manchester Wesleyanism in 1839 (though it survived considerably longer in Liverpool), and then began to obey a law of diminishing returns.[122] In any case Peel, by endowing Maynooth College, temporarily undermined its party significance, if not its local influence. The shattering impact of Peel's administration and the death or decline of Wesleyan Tory stalwarts in Manchester and Liverpool opened the way for less partisan politics within the connexion. Civic duty replaced the Protestant Constitution in the political creed of Wesleyan worthies. It would be a mistake, however, to underestimate the importance of sectarian politics in northern England after 1850. Despite a widespread rejection of formal religion, popular Protestant political culture continued to thrive in Victorian Lancashire. Stimulated by the Papal Aggression crisis and by post-famine Irish immigration, Orange politics enjoyed an Indian summer. Religion and ethnicity interacted with English class antagonisms to produce a peculiar kind of Tory populism.[123]

The tentative conclusions of this brief survey of Methodist electoral behaviour in the boroughs are that non-Wesleyans voted solidly Whig-Liberal, whereas Wesleyans displayed a more complicated pattern. Their social, occupational, and religious status led them to vote Liberal, unless local circumstances or candidates brought religious issues to the forefront. Then their evangelicalism, their distant loyalty to the Church of England, and their deference to preachers and wealthy laymen within their own connexion would influence them against pro-Catholic, Unitarian, or radical disestablishment candidates.

In the countryside, where Methodist membership lists are often lacking, it is difficult enough to work out Methodist voting patterns, whatever the beliefs and convictions behind them. Obelkevich's study of South Lindsey shows that Wesleyans, who constituted the great majority of Methodist electors in rural areas, voted along with other tenants for the party of their landowners. Thus the percentage of Whig and Tory voters among Wesleyans corresponds almost exactly with the wider electoral constituency.[124] This pattern is unlikely to be modified by other local studies, at least up to mid century.

Methodism and popular politics

The campaign to end slavery in the British colonies was another important influence on Methodist voting, but it was also of much wider political significance. Many Methodist leaders, from John Wesley to Richard Watson, the distinguished theologian, had written against slavery,[125] but it was not until the early 1830s that Methodists in large numbers committed themselves to political action. There were several reasons for this transformation. The most important was the dramatic expansion of Wesleyan missions in the first third of the nineteenth century. Problems of mission, including the ignorance of slaves and the preaching restrictions imposed by the planters began to occupy more space in denominational publications by the late 1820s. Tales of imprisoned missionaries and of persecuted slave converts added emotional excitement to the annual meetings of the Wesleyan Missionary Society. The frequency of violent incidents, culminating in the Jamaican slave rising in 1831, brought a new sense of urgency to traditional Wesleyan sympathies. Some of this excitement had radical implications. Richard Watson told the anniversary gathering of the Wesleyan Missionary Society in 1830 that 'all our Missionary enterprises, all our attempts to spread Christianity abroad, do, in point of fact, tend to increase our sympathies with the external circumstances of the oppressed and miserable of all lands. It is impossible for men to care for the souls of others without caring for their bodies also. . . . We cannot care for the salvation of the negro, without caring for his emancipation from bondage'.[126] Not many Wesleyan preachers were prepared to face the domestic extension of such views.

At the beginning of the 1830s, Methodist anti-slavery sentiment, which had been largely confined to denominational publications and missionary meetings, became more public and more political. The

Wesleyan Conference called for petitions against slavery in 1830, and a year later it recommended Methodists to give paramount importance to the slave question in their exercise of the franchise.[127] The scale of Methodist petitioning in the critical year of 1833 was impressive. There were 1953 Wesleyan petitions with 229,426 signatures, at a time when the official Wesleyan membership stood only at 260,491. Although Seymour Drescher has shown that in 1833 there were more signatures on community petitions than on those sent by religious denominations, the contribution made by the Wesleyans, in the light of their customary political quietism, was quite remarkable. Indeed, the whole of evangelical Nonconformity was mobilized against slavery.[128]

While the Methodist rank-and-file lent their considerable weight to the anti-slavery agitation, the Wesleyan leadership was more circumspect. Bunting, although a member of the Anti-Slavery Society's Corresponding Committee, refused to vote for an abolitionist candidate in the Liverpool election of 1832, because he was a Unitarian and a radical. Bunting advised his fellow preachers to remain neutral, while he voted for Lord Sandon, the Tory candidate. Inevitably, Bunting was attacked in the local press for allowing 'party feelings and politics' to overcome his commitment to the 'cause of humanity and religion'. The Methodist leader defended himself by stating that he had obtained an adequate pledge from Lord Sandon, and that Unitarians could not be trusted.[129]

The Liverpool election was an embarrassment for Bunting, but a few months later there were more serious matters to be considered. In February 1833, John Beecham, one of the secretaries for foreign missions, told Bunting that plans were advanced for sending ruled petitions to all Methodist circuits. Bunting thought that such action was not only precipitate (ministers had not yet declared their intentions), but politically undesirable.

A measure of this sort just now, no necessity being proved or proveable, would injuriously distract the thoughts and conversation of our people, and might so divert them from the best things to subjects much mixed up, in this time of excitement, with the politics of this world, as to injure the work of God. Our duty, and our policy too, require us to be the 'quiet in the land', as far and as long as we innocently can. I decidedly think that the holy cause of Anti-Slavery has already been disgraced and prejudiced in some quarters by the system of 'agitation', after the fashion of Irish Papists and Repealers, which has been employed to promote it. The wrath of man worketh not the righteousness of God. . . . Whether we ought, *as a Missionary Society*, to meddle with the *merely civil* or *political* part of the subject, I very much doubt.[130]

As with the Peace Societies in an earlier period, Bunting realized that Wesleyans were rubbing shoulders with undesirable allies, and he had no desire to see radicalism or liberalism advance on the back of legitimate evangelical concern for the negro. Moreover, both he and Beecham wanted the Wesleyans to conduct a dignified campaign so that they could extract missionary favours from the government should emancipation be granted.[131]

Apart from these tactical debates among Wesleyan leaders, the anti-slavery agitation had two main consequences for the development of Methodist political attitudes. First, the libertarian rhetoric employed throughout the anti-slavery campaign further eroded the ability of Wesleyan conservatives to keep political control of the connexion. Some Methodist societies even resorted to the ideology of the rights of man in petitions, which would probably have provoked their expulsion at the time of Peterloo.[132] More concretely, Roger Anstey has shown how the anti-slavery movement's policy of asking for pledges from parliamentary candidates worked to the advantage of the Whig-Liberal party. He calculated also that Wesleyans comprised 8.4 per cent of the electorate in 1832, and that the majority of them voted for Liberal anti-slavery candidates.[133] Although the suppositions upon which these calculations were based are dubious, the general direction of Anstey's argument is correct. The Wesleyan commitment to anti-slavery after the Reform Act benefited the Whigs more than the Tories.

Second, the style and techniques of the anti-slavery agitation served as models for subsequent religio-political crusades. Asking candidates for pledges, petitioning Parliament, and bringing religious zeal to bear on politics were all characteristics of Victorian Nonconformity.[134] By these means, evangelical Nonconformists, who were suspicious of politics, were able to enter the political arena with reasonably clear consciences. By the same token, religious denominations, including the Methodists, became more susceptible to internal disputes about politics.

The heat had scarcely gone out of the anti-slavery agitation when other extra-parliamentary campaigns got under way. This time the source of concern was not West Indian slaves but English workers. Despite the scale of popular political activity, however, the years

1837–48 posed fewer problems of control for the Wesleyan leadership than the period 1815–19. Partly because the job of expulsion had been done so professionally in the earlier period, and partly because of the enhanced social status of early Victorian Wesleyans,[135] Chartism had few contacts with mainstream Wesleyanism. There were, of course, ritual warnings against entering the 'arena of political controversy' in Conference addresses to the societies, but generally speaking references to Chartism are conspicuous by their absence from connexional correspondence.[136] Graham's educational proposals and the Maynooth grant by comparison attracted much more attention from the connexion's political machinery. Within Chartism itself, anti-Anglican slogans such as 'More Fat Pigs and less Fat Parsons'[137] had their Methodist counterparts in rhymes against 'The Hundred Popes of England's Jesuitry'[138] (the Wesleyan Conference). On his return from a missionary tour of Cornwall, Abram Duncan told the Chartist Convention that if J. R. Stephens 'was five months in Cornwall, he would rout all the Methodist parsons from the country'.[139]

The relationship between Methodism and Chartism was, of course, more complex than mere slogans can convey. Since Robert Wearmouth's work on the nineteenth century there has been widespread agreement that Chartism based some of its organizational structures on Methodist precedents. Class meetings, weekly subscriptions, hymns, camp meetings, and Love Feasts were all employed by Chartists, especially in areas of longstanding Methodist influence.[140] More recent work on Chartist organization has, however, refined some of these ideas. Eileen Yeo, for example, shows that some Chartist forms owed their origin to the age-old parish system of local government with its quarterly meeting of the vestry.[141] Moreover, structures borrowed from Methodism were skilfully democratized to guard against a Wesleyan-style oligarchy. Chartist class leaders were elected, not appointed, and there were sophisticated checks on the power and duration of local offices and officials.[142]

New light has been shed too on the contribution of Methodist personnel to the Chartist Movement. A few rebellious Wesleyans, a few more expelled Wesleyans, and considerably more Primitive Methodists, secessionist Methodists and ex-Methodists all played a major role in Chartism in the regions of South Lancashire, the West Riding, the north-east, Staffordshire, Leicestershire, and Nottinghamshire. The backgrounds and future careers of such men were as varied as Chartism itself, but they brought with them sufficient moral earnestness, discipline, and organizational and public speaking skills to thrust themselves into positions of leadership. Many were influenced initially by Rayner Stephens's type of Chartism which was low on political ideology and high on the mutual obligations of rich and poor. Caring little for the means and ends of mainstream Chartism, Stephens was teased into the movement on the basis of an Old Testament crusade against the New Poor Law. Stephens's critique of early Victorian society was not so much political and structural as moral and ethical. In a comparison between Stephens and Harney, Schoyen states that 'to the passionate exponent of resistance to the New Poor Law [Stephens], political change was incidental – the real remedy for distress lay in the spiritual regeneration of the upper classes. To Harney, the seizure of the state was primary'.[143] Nevertheless, through men like Stephens, Chartism appropriated religious forms and biblical radicalism to its own cause, thereby broadening its appeal.

If Stephens was influential in early Methodist recruitment to Chartism, there were other more profound causes to be discovered in working-class autobiographies.[144] Many are pilgrimages from an early conversion experience (usually between 14 and 17) accompanied by a serious Methodist commitment to a more radical and politicized Christianity on the one hand or, less commonly, to complete secularism and infidelity on the other. Many of the most intellectually gifted travelled this path through private reading, which exposed weaknesses in either the Bible or church structures and practices. 'Too much emphasis on book knowledge', according to Dr Vincent, 'threatened to upset the fragile balance between rational inquiry and anti-intellectual revivalism which lay at the heart of the Methodist approach to Christian faith.'[145] Thus Christopher Thomson, who attended a Methodist Sunday school, was threatened with frightening religious sanctions to prevent him becoming too smart for his own good. For men like Thomson self-improvement went hand in hand with political consciousness, resulting in a new kind of secularized Christianity. So too, John Skevington, a Primitive Methodist preacher at the age of 14, and later the leader of Loughborough Chartism, wrote that 'though a man may be a Chartist and not a Christian, a man cannot be a Christian and not a Chartist unless through ignorance'.[146] Similarly, Joseph Barker, a somewhat erratic New Connexion Methodist, wrote that

Formerly I thought it wrong for a Christian to meddle in political matters. Formerly I thought it the duty of Christians to unite themselves together in churches, to shut themselves out from the world, to constitute themselves a little exclusive world, and to confine their labours to the government of their little kingdom and to the increase of the numbers of its subjects. I now think differently. I have no faith in church organizations. I believe it my duty to be a man; to live and move in the world at large; to battle with evil wherever I see it, and to aim at the annihilation of all corrupt institutions and at the establishment of all good, and generous, and useful institutions in their places.[147]

There is here a powerful mixture of meliorism, worldly Christianity and deep-seated ecclesiastical frustration.

It would be foolish to build too much on examples, but if, as recent statistics indicate,[148] most active Chartists were aged between 30 and 40, and if, as Susan Budd has shown, that this was precisely the age when many religious men drifted away from their faith,[149] Methodism through the Chartists, may have reaped the bitter crop of its earlier successes. The fact that mainstream Wesleyanism was run by a closed clerical élite simply added a potent anti-clericalism to the general level of popular frustration with organized religion.

Along with structures and personalities, the relationship between Methodism and Chartism can be investigated on yet another level; that is their interaction within a local community. A particularly valuable example is James Epstein's study of Chartism in the industrial villages of Nottinghamshire, which were also centres of Primitive Methodism.[150] Primitive Methodists brought much needed crusading zeal to Chartism, but against that, writes Epstein, 'Methodists constituted a community which to a large degree had turned in upon itself, separated and sheltered from the working-class at large through a sense of moral superiority.' By contrast, 'Chartism was essentially a non-sectarian inclusive movement which sought to appeal to a larger sense of class solidarity.' Epstein argues that the Methodists opposed Chartism's convivial activity – 'the tavern culture, the men and women making pipes before meetings, the country dancing on the common, [and] the balls and political preaching on the sabbath'. In 1841 one Nottingham Primitive Methodist was expelled on the grounds that he was 'a bad man, fond of ale, a desperate tobacco smoker, and a great Chartist'. On the other side, New Testament warnings against the rich, like the more traditional appeal to England's ancient constitution, 'served as a powerful source of legitimation for Chartist action'. Thus in areas of mutual strength, the relationship between Methodism and Chartism was both complex and dynamic. Neither emerged from the experience unscathed.

Methodism and Chartism must be investigated, therefore, at different social, geographical and structural levels. Between the upper reaches of Anglicanism and Wesleyanism, and Chartism, there was a yawning gap which Chartists at first tried to bridge by marching *en masse* to Anglican churches or by setting up churches of their own, but before long the gap was both acknowledged, and seen to be irrelevant.[151] As Ward has it, 'Urban Chartists were not much hurt by the thunderbolts of Church or Conference, and felt relatively little need for a religious bulwark against them.'[152] Within more rural and non-Wesleyan Methodist environments, where Conference writ did not run, the gap was considerably narrower, and sparks jumped across.

The same pattern is discernible in Methodism's relationship with trade unionism, though here there is even greater need for the historian to be faithful to the local cultural setting. In that respect we are well served by three recent studies of popular religion and society in centres of agricultural and mining trade unionism. Robert Moore and Robert Colls have studied the effects of Methodism in the mining communities of the north-east, while Nigel Scotland has concentrated on the agricultural trade unionism of East Anglia.[153] Though different in method, Moore's sociological approach and Colls's focus on working-class experiences have, nevertheless, produced similar conclusions. They agree that the most important feature of village Methodism in mining communities was not so much the politics of its leaders and members, as its sense of community and reassurance for people experiencing profound social and economic changes.[154] Colls, in particular, shows how Primitive Methodism was almost tailor-made for pit communities. In villages that were intimate and conforming, yet subject to scarcity and disaster, Methodism fulfilled many needs. It helped explain, and took the sting out of, suffering and death. It provided a moral and religious framework for the education of the young. Its individualistic conversionism and corporate expectancy in prayer meetings added drama and a sense of importance to otherwise humdrum lives. Its emphasis on music and song, even to the extent of appropriating local tunes and dialects, both chimed in with, and created a religious alternative to, the local tavern culture. For women who were largely excluded from that culture, Methodism offered new opportunities for service and social intercourse outside the domestic tedium of home.[155] Finally, Methodism seemed to strike a particularly successful balance between individual and corporate requirements. Whereas the associated disciplines of choir, class and chapel taught people to worship together, there was within the Methodist structure ample scope for individual self-improvement to find institutional expression.

It was through the opportunities afforded by chapel culture that Methodists were able to hold places of influence in local trade unions out of all proportion to their numerical strength.[156] Although Methodists were generally a minority in north-east mining villages, they were a serious disciplined minority. According to Colls

The chapel had taken these men [Primitive Methodist trade unionists] out of the mainstream of village life and nurtured civic abilities in them: some vision of Man's significance, some rhetoric of justice, some reading and a lot of speaking. Most importantly, Methodism had been a cocoon of seriousness in a pub and coursing-path world of careless enjoyment and self-mockery. The cocoon provided its own reason and reward for self-improvement so dearly won by the miner.[157]

In the mining districts the chief problem lies not in explaining why a high percentage of trade union leaders were Methodists, but in understanding what kind of trade unionism they led. Moore is helpful here because he shows how Methodists divided their society into the saved and the unsaved, or the good and the bad, but not into middle and working classes. Thus, 'while Methodism did produce political leaders amongst working men it did not produce leaders who would articulate and pursue class interests as such'.[158] Since most Durham mining companies were paternalist and Nonconformist in varying degrees, Methodists identified themselves as much with the employers, who shared their religious and moral outlook, as with the wider working-class community, which exhibited a mixture of respect and disdain for Methodist religion and morality. Paternalism, of course, was no answer to the industrial problems of 1831 and 1844, when over-capacity and increasing competitiveness resulted in wage reductions and lay-offs. In the strikes that followed, Primitive Methodist trade unionists showed they had the capacity to set aside accommodation in the light of Old Testament wrath against the oppressors of the people.[159] Strike ditties exemplify, therefore, a curious mixture of biblical and enlightenment idealism laced with patriotism and hatred of the rich.

The impact of Methodism on the mining communities of the north-east was largely responsible for the region's reluctance to abandon Liberalism for labour politics at the beginning of the twentieth century. Theirs was a Liberalism based on the acceptance of a market economy, opposition to Anglican educational privileges, dislike of the Tory brewing interest, and an emphasis on mutual obligations as against class conflict.[160] Thus whether one concentrates on the immediacy of local Methodist mining culture or on the long-term impact of religion on class politics, the conclusion is much the same; Methodism both fostered radicalism and opposed it, and the roots of this paradox are to be found in the religious mind itself, with its acceptance of authority on the one hand, and its desire to have justice and fair play on the other. The urgency of the economic and social problems determined the respective weight given to each.

In the agricultural unionism of East Anglia, where the Methodist contribution was equally important, many of the same themes reappear, though with one major difference. In north-eastern pit communities the Anglican ethos had limited appeal, with the result that Methodist radicalism was rarely directed against the Established Church despite the enormous wealth of the Durham hierarchy. In East Anglia, however, the process of enclosure raised many parsons to gentry status and effectively separated them from the village poor.[161] Not only was Primitive Methodism the main beneficiary of such changes, but also its character was shaped by social protest right from the start. 'Emerging initially as a form of religious protest', writes Scotland, Primitive Methodism 'became also the basis of a social protest against the harsher realities of labouring life.'[162] Yet there is need for care here. It would be a mistake to view rural Methodism solely in terms of religious and social *protest*, when its most important achievement was to create an *alternative* religious culture. While a reformed Anglicanism put its faith on clergy, churches, parsonages, rites and sacraments, Methodists – both Wesleyan and Primitive – placed theirs on a corporate and zealous religious community at the same time as rural cohesion came under severe stress.[163] In meeting the Methodist challenge, therefore, Anglicans were not short of energy but they were deficient in social and religious understanding.

In conclusion, two points need to be made about Methodism and popular politics. The first is that the relationship between them is a good deal more complicated – and more colourful – than the rather sterile debates surrounding the Halévy thesis would indicate. Second, proper attention must be paid to the local economic, religious and social setting. The fact that Methodism, in structural and theological terms, is more identifiable than early modern Puritanism is no reason to treat it as a monolith. Reality is usually more complex than historians suppose.

References

1 A. P. Stanley, *The Life of Thomas Arnold* (London 1901), p. 278.

2 E. J. Whately, *Life and Remains of Archbishop Whately*, 2 vols. (London 1866), vol. 1, p. 159.

3 W. R. Ward, *Religion and Society in England 1790–1850* (London 1972), pp. 130–4; Owen Chadwick, *The Victorian Church*, 2 vols. (London 1966), vol. 1, pp. 46–7; and E. J. Hobsbawm and George Rudé, *Captain Swing* (London 1970), pp. 112–13, 153–4, 229–32.

4 For a list of names, see Ward, *Religion and Society*, p. 211.

5 Donald Southgate, *The Passing of the Whigs 1832–1886*, 2nd edn (London 1965), pp. 45–50; and Norman Gash, *Reaction and Reconstruction* in *English Politics 1832–1852* (Oxford 1965), pp. 33–4.

6 G. I. T. Machin, *Politics and the Churches in Great Britain 1832–1868* (Oxford 1977), pp. 54–6.

7 See Patricia Hollis (ed.), *Pressure from Without in early Victorian England* (London 1974).

8 T. Arnold to J. Marshall, 23 January 1840, in Stanley, pp. 534–7.

9 Matthew Arnold, *Culture and Anarchy* (London 1869), pp. 26–31.

10 Ward, *Religion and Society*, p. 179; and T. J. Nossiter, *Influence, Opinion and Political Idioms in Reformed England* (Brighton 1975), pp. 131–43.

11 *Watchman*, 3 August 1836.

12 J. S. North, 'The rationale – why read Victorian periodicals?', in J. D. Vann and R. T. VanArsdel (eds.), *Victorian Periodicals* (New York 1978), pp. 3–20; and P. Scott, 'Victorian religious periodicals: fragments that remain', in Derek Baker (ed.), *Sources, Methods and Materials of Ecclesiastical History* (London 1975), pp. 325–39.

13 *Wesleyan Methodist Magazine* (1835), pp. 151–3.

14 W. R. Ward, *Early Victorian Methodism* (London 1976), pp. 48–51, 73–4, 83–4.

15 Benjamin Gregory, *Side Lights on the Conflicts of Methodism 1827–1852* (London 1898), pp. 150–64.

16 D. A. Gowland, *Methodist Secessions: The origins of Free Methodism in three Lancashire towns* (Manchester 1979), p. 121.

17 *Watchman*, 7 January 1835.

18 *Speech of the Rev. Dr Bunting delivered in London, on Monday June 10th 1839 in reference to the Government Scheme of National Education recently abandoned and to the Government New Scheme just proposed* (Manchester 1839), p. 14. For another example see *Watchman*, 29 May 1839, in reply to the *Patriot*'s accusation that the Wesleyans were augmenting the Conservative opposition to the plan.

19 Gregory, p. 160.

20 Gash, p. 166.

21 John Russell, *Memoirs of the Affairs of Europe from the Peace of Utrecht*, 2 vols. (London 1824–9), vol. 2, p. 584.

22 *Watchman*, 13 January 1836.

23 For a stimulating reappraisal of Peel's politics in the 1830s see Ian Newbould, 'Whiggery and the dilemma of reform: Liberals, Radicals and the Melbourne administration, 1835–9', *Bulletin of the Institute of Historical Research*, **53** (1980), pp. 229–41, and 'Sir Robert Peel and the Conservative party1832–1841: A study in failure?', *English Historical Review*, **98** (July 1983), pp. 529–57.

24 *Watchman*, 29 July 1835, and 6 January 1836.

25 *Watchman*, 15 February 1837.

26 *Watchman*, 22 March 1837.

27 *Watchman*, 12 December 1838.

28 Ward, *Religion and Society*, pp. 241–3; and A. J. Hayes and D. A. Gowland (eds.), *Scottish Methodism in the Early Victorian Period* (Edinburgh 1981), pp. 43–7, 88–9, 92–3.

29 Thomas Chalmers, *Lectures on the Establishment and Extension of national Churches; delivered in London from April 25th to May 12th, 1838* (Glasgow 1838).

30 Gregory, pp. 155–7.

31 Ward, *Early Victorian Methodism*, pp. 59–60. *Watchman*, 1 March 1837.

32 Ward, *Early Victorian Methodism*, pp. 89–93.

33 ibid., pp. 124, 182. Anon, *How will Wesleyan Electors Vote?* (letters reprinted from the *Manchester Guardian* 1837).

34 *The Times*, 6 January 1835, 26 November 1836.

35 *Hansard*, 3rd series, **XXV**, c. 860. See also *Quarterly Review*, **53** (February 1835), p. 193.

36 *Coningsby*, Book 2, ch. 2. In fact Disraeli overestimated the Toryism of the Wesleyans – see R. F. Foster, 'Political novels and nineteenth-century history', *Winchester Research Papers in the Humanities*, no. 10 (Winchester 1981).

37 *Watchman*, 14 July, and 4 August 1841. Also Ward, *Religion and Society*, pp. 251–2.

38 Hayes and Gowland, pp. 14–21; Machin, pp. 112–47; and Ward, *Religion and Society*, pp. 239–44.

39 Chalmers, p. 20.

40 Machin, p. 142.

41 Gregory, p. 349.

42 George Turner, *The Constitution and Discipline of Wesleyan Methodism* (London 1841), pp. 64–83.

43 Gregory, p. 350.

44 See Ward, *Religion and Society*, p. 243; and Hayes and Gowland p. 16.

45 Ward, *Religion and Society*, p. 242.

46 Machin, p. 141.
47 This seems to be the plain reading of Bunting's speech to Conference, recorded in Gregory, p. 350.
48 ibid., p. 348.
49 Ward, *Religion and Society*, p. 243. See also the letter from William Vevers to Bunting, 14 March 1843 in *Early Victorian Methodism*, p. 283.
50 *Watchman*, 31 January 1844.
51 *Watchman*, 22 May 1844; Hayes and Gowland, p. 17; Ward, *Early Victorian Methodism*, p. 300. See also R. F. Holmes, *Henry Cooke* (Belfast 1981), pp. 158–60.
52 *Watchman*, 12 June, and 17 July 1844.
53 *Watchman*, 21 August 1844.
54 *Watchman*, 8 January 1845. There is a more detailed treatment of the Maynooth issue in my 'Methodism and anti-Catholic politics 1800–46' (unpublished PhD thesis, University of St Andrews 1977), pp. 269–89.
55 See printed resolutions of a meeting on 28 March 1845 in Minutes of the Committee of Privileges.
56 *Watchman*, 2 April 1845.
57 A revealing Ms. diary of the Rev. Charles Prest is in the private possession of John Prest, Balliol College, Oxford. I am indebted to him for letting me read it.
58 M.C.A. Mss., C. Prest to J. Bunting 7 April, and 27 May 1845.
59 Speech reprinted in the *Watchman*, 30 April 1845.
60 M.C.A. Mss., J. Bunting to D. O'Connell, 22 October 1845.
61 A. S. Thelwall, *Proceedings of the Anti-Maynooth Convention* (London 1845) p. 87.
62 For an explanation of the various denominational positions see G. I. T. Machin, 'The Maynooth grant, the Dissenters and disestablishment, 1845–1847', *English Historical Review*, **82** (1967), pp. 61–85; Machin, *Politics and the Churches*, pp. 169–80; and E. R. Norman, *Anti-Catholicism in Victorian England* (London 1968), pp. 23–51.
63 See *New Methodist Magazine* (1845), pp. 259–62; and *Wesleyan Association Magazine* (1845), pp. 158–61, 215–17.
64 *Watchman*, 2 April 1845.
65 Thelwall, pp. 18–204.
66 ibid., p. 127.
67 ibid. p. xliii.
68 *Hansard*, 3rd series, **LXXIX**, c. 459; *Watchman*, 30 April 1845.
69 *Watchman*, 9 April 1845.
70 M.C.A. Mss., C. Prest to J. Bunting, 27 May 1845; and T. Waugh to Bunting, 9 June 1845.
71 Thelwall, p. 126; *Belfast Newsletter*, 20 May 1845; and *The Annual*

Address of the Conference to the Societies in Ireland (Cork 30 June 1845).

72   Chadwick, vol. 1, p. 223.

73   *Watchman*, 11 June 1845.

74   Norman, p. 25.

75   *Watchman*, 10 October, and 7 November 1838.

76   J. Bunting to T. Chalmers, 5 April 1840, in Hayes and Gowland, pp. 88–9.

77   See *Watchman*, 24 May 1843, and Prest's diary. The names are listed in my doctoral dissertation, p. 303.

78   *Brief Statement of the Proceedings of the Conference in Liverpool for promoting Christian Union and of the object of the proposed Evangelical Alliance* (Liverpool 1845).

79   Ward, *Early Victorian Methodism*, pp. 332–8.

80   *Evangelical Alliance: Report of the Proceedings of the Conference held at the Freemason's Hall, London, from August 19 to September 2, 1846* (London 1847), pp. 248–9, 507–9.

81   Calculations are based on the membership lists of both Conferences. Because of the Methodist system of itinerant preaching, some well known Wesleyan Tories who had cut their teeth in South Lancashire were stationed elsewhere in 1845–6.

82   Bunting was a regular speaker at Alliance gatherings in 1846. See, for example, *Report of the Speeches delivered at the Public Meeting, held in the Free Trade Hall, Manchester, for the purpose of explaining the principles and objects of the proposed Evangelical Alliance* (Manchester 1846).

83   See Holmes, and Peter Brooke, 'Controversies in Ulster Presbyterianism 1790–1836' (unpublished PhD thesis, University of Cambridge 1980).

84   The most recent are Gowland; Ward, *Religion and Society*, pp. 236–78; John Kent, *The Age of Disunity* (London 1966); Robert Currie, *Methodism Divided* (London 1968); and J. T. Wilkinson, 'The rise of other Methodist traditions', in R. Davies, A. R. George and G. Rupp (eds.), *A History of the Methodist Church in Great Britain* (London 1978), vol. 2, pp. 276–329.

85   J. C. Bowmer, *Pastor and People* (London 1975).

86   W. R. Ward, *The Early Correspondence of Jabez Bunting 1820–1829* (London 1972), pp. 165–6.

87   Ward, *Religion and Society*, pp. 147–53.

88   Gowland, p. 36.

89   ibid.

90   Gowland, p. 66, quotes an excellent example from the *Christian Advocate*, 16 February 1835.

91   Kent, p. 70.

92   Gowland, p. 65.

93 For the impact of Caughey on Methodism see Richard Carwardine, *Trans-atlantic Revivalism: Popular Evangelicalism in Britain and America 1790–1865* (Westport, Connecticut 1978), pp. 102–33. Ward, *Early Victorian Methodism*, pp. 314–15, 339–41, 419–20.

94 Gowland, pp. 148–9.

95 Bowmer, p. 155.

96 Ward, *Religion and Society*, pp. 264–73.

97 See, for example, the letter from F. J. Jobson to Bunting, 25 September 1849, in Ward, *Early Victorian Methodism*, pp. 383–4.

98 Bowmer, p. 157.

99 This is the argument of E. R. Taylor, *Methodism and Politics 1791–1851*, 2nd edn (New York 1975), pp. 165–95. For similar contemporary assessments see Ward, *Early Victorian Methodism*, pp. 391–3.

100 R. Currie, A. Gilbert and L. Horsley, *Churches and Churchgoers: Patterns of Church Growth in the British Isles since 1700* (Oxford 1977), pp. 139–46; A. D. Gilbert, *Religion and Society in Industrial England* (London 1976), pp. 30–9; and Ward, *Religion and Society*, p. 266.

101 Research on this topic is still at an early stage, and most of the important local studies, upon which this section is based, are from the north of England. Only time will reveal their typicality or otherwise.

102 Nossiter, pp.177–207. Also, J. P. D. Dunbabin, 'British elections in the nineteenth and twentieth centuries, a regional approach', *English Historical Review*, **95** (1980), pp. 241–67.

103 J. P. Parry, 'The state of Victorian political history', *Historical Journal*, **26** no. 2 (1983), pp. 469–84. He states that 'local historians have demonstrated conclusively that financial hard-headedness and religious affiliation and prejudice, together with local landlord or employer pressure, were infinitely more likely to influence voting than assessments of the performance of governments. . . .'

104 J. R. Vincent, *Pollbooks: How Victorians Voted* (Cambridge 1967), pp. 1–33; Nossiter, p. 167.

105 John Foster, *Class Struggle and the Industrial Revolution*, 2nd edn (London 1977), p. 199.

106 Machin, pp. 40–2.

107 Nossiter, p. 123.

108 John Prest, *Lord John Russell* (London 1972), p. 37; *The Times*, 1 May 1835; and Gregory, p. 202.

109 Ward, *Early Victorian Methodism*, pp. 28–9, 76.

110 Gregory, p. 236.

111 *How will Wesleyan Electors vote?*, pp. 4–5; Vincent, p. 69.

112 Nossiter, pp. 17–18; Foster, pp. 166–74.

113 Gowland, p. 121 and note 6. For more details on Manchester see his 'Political opinion in Manchester Wesleyanism 1832–1857', *Proceed-*

ings of the Wesley Historical Society, **36** (1968), pp. 93–104.

114 *How will Wesleyan Electors vote?*; and Foster, pp. 198–9.

115 Reproduced by Vincent, pp. 69–70.

116 D. G. Wright, 'A radical borough: Parliamentary politics in Bradford 1832–41', *Northern History*, **4** (1969), p. 141.

117 *Watchman*, 19 July 1837.

118 *How will Wesleyan Electors Vote?*

119 *Watchman*, 9 August 1837; Ward, *Religion and Society*, p. 253.

120 Gowland, p. 128.

121 ibid., pp. 131–3.

122 ibid., p. 133.

123 Patrick Joyce, *Work, Society and Politics*, 2nd edn (London 1982), pp. 240–67.

124 James Obelkevich, *Religion and Rural Society: South Lindsey 1825–1875* (Oxford 1976), p. 211.

125 Bernard Semmel, *The Methodist Revolution* (London 1974), pp. 94–6, 147–51, 178–80.

126 Roger Anstey, 'Religion and British slave emancipation', in David Eltis and James Walvin (eds.), *The Abolition of the Atlantic Slave Trade* (Madison, Wisconsin 1981), p. 47.

127 Ward, *Early Victorian Methodism*, p. 28.

128 For details about Wesleyan and Nonconformist petitioning, see Anstey, p. 51; Seymour Drescher, 'Public opinion and the destruction of British Colonial Slavery', in James Walvin (ed.), *Slavery and British Society, 1776–1846* (London 1982), pp. 22–48; and E. F. Hurwitz, *Politics and the Public Conscience* (London 1973), p. 144.

129 Ward, *Early Victorian Methodism*, pp. 27–8.

130 ibid., p. 29.

131 ibid., pp. 23–5. See also, M.C.A. Mss., Zachary Macaulay to Jabez Bunting, 14 December 1829, and 30 November 1833.

132 James Walvin, 'The public campaign in England against slavery, 1787–1834', in Eltis and Walvin (eds.), p. 73.

133 Anstey, pp. 51–3.

134 The best treatment of this subject is by D. A. Hamer, *The Politics of Electoral Pressure: a study in the history of Victorian Reform Agitations* (Hassocks, Sussex 1977).

135 There is a warning against exaggerating the bourgeois nature of early Victorian Methodism by C. D. Field, 'The social structure of English Methodism: eighteenth-twentieth centuries', *British Journal of Sociology*, **28** no. 2 (1977), pp. 199–225.

136 R. F. Wearmouth, *Some Working-Class Movements of the Nineteenth Century* (London 1948). There are, however, very few references to Chartism in Ward's edition of the Bunting correspondence in *Early Victorian Methodism*.

137 James Epstein, 'Some organisational and cultural aspects of the Chartist movement in Nottingham', Epstein and D. Thompson (eds.), *The Chartist Experience* (London 1982), pp. 221–68.

138 H. U. Faulkner, *Chartism and the Churches*, 2nd edn (London 1970), p. 30.

139 T. M. Kemnitz and F. Jacques, 'J. R. Stephens and the Chartist movement', *International Review of Social History*, **19** (1974), p. 225.

140 Wearmouth, pp. 85–231.

141 Eileen Yeo, 'Some practices and problems of Chartist democracy', in Epstein and Thompson (eds.), p. 353.

142 ibid., pp. 353–60.

143 Kemnitz and Jacques, p. 213.

144 David Vincent, *Bread, Knowledge and Freedom: A Study of Nineteenth-Century Working Class Autobiography* (London 1981); and Susan Budd, *Varieties of Unbelief* (London 1977).

145 Vincent, p. 179.

146 J. F. C. Harrison, 'Chartism in Leicester', in Asa Briggs (ed.), *Chartist Studies* (London 1959), p. 131.

147 Faulkner, p. 27.

148 Christopher Godfrey, 'The Chartist prisoners, 1839–41', *International Review of Social History*, **24** (1979), pp. 189–236; and Epstein, p. 232.

149 Budd, pp. 105–6.

150 Epstein, p. 250.

151 Faulkner, pp. 35–41. Also, Patricia Hollis (ed.), *Class and Conflict in nineteenth-century England 1815–1850* (London 1973), pp. 257–8.

152 Ward, *Religion and Society*, p. 202.

153 Robert Colls, *The Collier's Rant* (London 1977); Robert Moore, *Pit-Men, Preachers and Politics* (Cambridge 1974); and Nigel Scotland, *Methodism and the Revolt of the Field* (Gloucester 1981).

154 Moore, p. 96. I am indebted to Robert Colls for sharing some of these ideas at the Religion and Society History Workshop in London, 1983.

155 In the 1840s Primitive Methodists shuffled women to the margins in the same way as happened in Wesleyanism half a century before.

156 Colls, p. 101; and Moore, pp. 68–70.

157 Colls, p. 100.

158 Moore, p. 27.

159 Colls, pp. 97–116; and Wearmouth, pp. 300–5.

160 Moore, pp. 159–68.

161 Scotland, p. 21; and Obelkevich, pp. 112–14, 117.

162 Scotland, p. 9.

163 Obelkevich, pp. 103–258.

Conclusion

That after-glow [of the early Wesleyan mission to the poor] has long faded away; and the picture we are apt to make of Methodism in our imagination is not an amphitheatre of green hills, or the deep shade of broadleaved sycamores, where a crowd of rough men and weary-hearted women drank in a faith which was a rudimentary culture, which linked their thoughts with the past, lifted their imagination above the sordid details of their own narrow lives, and suffused their souls with the sense of a pitying, loving, infinite Presence, sweet as summer to the houseless needy. It is too possible that to some of my readers Methodism may mean nothing more than low-pitched gables up dingy streets, sleek grocers, sponging preachers, and hypocritical jargon. . . . [1]

George Eliot's romantic and nostalgic comparison between the early Methodist world of 'miracles, instantaneous conversions', with 'revelations by dreams and visions', and its seedy mid Victorian successor, is not without parallel in Methodist correspondence. When James Anderson, an old Methodist preacher, paid a return visit to the Inverness circuit in 1829 after a forty-year absence, he found nothing but decline and discouragement. In response he remembered the time when Methodists eschewed 'ease and convenience' and were prepared to 'preach wherever we could find an open door'. As he dwelt on early missionary experiences of swallowing snow and dry bread on desolate hillsides, he reflected bitterly on the new preachers and the expensive new chapels 'which broke the spirit of the people'. [2] Nostalgia for the golden age of virginal Methodism is prevalent also in many of the radical critiques of Bunting's hegemony. One suspects, however, that some of those most desirous of primitive simplicity would have found its demands too much for them. The cry was nevertheless a good one, for it had piety on its side.

But there could be no going back. There were after all not many 'broad-leaved sycamores' in the centre of Manchester or Leeds in the early nineteenth century. The problem for Wesley's successors was managing a connexion that grew beyond all expectations in a period of international warfare and political unrest. The most important thing to emerge from the voluminous correspondence of Methodist preachers in the 1790s was their uncertainty about what to do next. Of course, like any growing organization, it had its fair share of ambitious men and windbags, but even the well-intentioned were squeezed between the demands of the people and pressure from a nervous established order. Methodist leaders knew they were making ground against 'carnal Anglicanism', but, following Wesley's example, most of them had no desire to erode social and political stability at the same time. They were caught, therefore, between the spiritual and social exhilaration of mounting a successful challenge to the establishment, and the nagging fear that this could easily get out of control. This accounts for some quite dramatic shifts in opinion at the first sign of radicalism from within, or government pressure from without.

The real problem for the Methodists was that the British state in the eighteenth century was expertly designed to protect landed property and Anglican privileges through a political and legal system that was itself subject to aristocratic control. No brick could be taken out of this edifice without weakening the rest of the building. Such was the basis of most of the correspondence about Methodism which appeared on the desks of English Cabinet Ministers at the turn of the century, and which prompted Sidmouth to take repressive action in 1811. The best example is from North Wales, where the growth of Dissent in general and Calvinistic Methodism in particular so alarmed Lord Bulkeley that he wrote at length to the then Prime Minister, Lord Grenville.

I cannot help attempting to draw your attention to the growth and increase of Methodism and Sectarism of every description and denomination in the Principality of Wales. The evil is of great magnitude inasmuch as their principles have a strong republican democratic bias, and they are certainly undermining the Church Establishment with all the industry possible, preparatory to other objects of an equally dangerous tendency. They have a sort of Synod or Meeting House government, which regulates the taxing of each other for building new meeting houses and paying their Preachers as well as for resistance to any legal process against any one of their own persuasion, whether it be of a criminal nature or the holding out against a landlord's ejectment, or any other similar process. The Petty Juries are now mostly composed of Sectaries, and woe be to the cause of a Churchman that comes to their decision against a Methodist. . . .

The King's health which had used to be the first toast in farmer's houses when they were all Churchmen is now the last, and of Lords they say they must soon come to hedge and ditch as well as they; in short they hate all superiority of rank or super eminence. With all this I cannot say they are disloyal as far as we are committed with Bonaparte and the French Government, but I am convinced their attachment to the Monarchy and the aristocracy of the country is very considerably weakened. Many however still like the King personally. . . . I mention this to show your Lordship the evil attending itinerant Sectarian preachers, and the necessity of confining their preachers to residence in districts, for many . . . go to Ireland and even to America and return again to their rounds. Should not some legal check be put to this overindulgence. As the law now stands the Sectaries must completely undermine and ruin the Established Church, the main pillar and prop of the State, and I assure your Lordship they are very sanguine in their expectations. A fig for the Parsons they say, they are all good for nothing, and they may think themselves very lucky if they get their tythes, which is all they care for, but we hope to see the day when we shall have neither Parsons nor tythes. . . .[3]

Letters like this highlight the Wesleyan dilemma at the turn of the century. However conservative they claimed to be in social and political terms, they were seen by the established order in Church and State as a radical challenge to its control. This was all the more problematic for connexional leaders, because episodes like the Kilhamite secession and the bizarre tales of revivalistic excesses brought them face to face with their own limited control over English popular religion. Some older or less well-educated Methodist preachers, whose desire for saving souls outstripped their sensitivity to its political consequences, were not too put out by these problems, but young men like Bunting, who had their teenage conversions in the 1790s, were confronted by them for the next twenty years.

Bunting's career is particularly instructive. Born the son of a radical Manchester tailor and a Derbyshire country girl, his early revivalistic enthusiasm was dampened by bad experiences.[4] Like many another educated and thoughtful evangelical, Bunting, in his 20s, became embarrassed by the religious culture in which he had earned his reputation. This was exacerbated by his first taste of Methodist administration and evangelical high society in London, and after that he put as much distance as possible between himself and Methodism's interface with popular enthusiasm, whether religious or political. He was helped on his way by a plethora of administrative jobs and by Sidmouth's bill in 1811, which forced all Methodist leaders to reassess the connexion's role in English society. Bunting's opinion, expressed through the resolutions of the Manchester Wesleyans, was crystal clear:

That the facilities, which have thus been afforded for religious worship and instruction [by the Methodists] have powerfully contributed to the improvement of public morals, and to the promotion of industry, subordination, and loyalty, among the middle and inferior orders of the community; and that to this high degree of Religious Liberty, under the blessing of Divine Providence, the preservation of this happy country from the horrors of that revolutionary frenzy, which has so awfully desolated the nations of the Continent, is principally to be ascribed.[5]

Thus, Sidmouth's bill, for all its political incompetence and ultimate failure, succeeded beyond the most sanguine expectations of its supporters in harnessing Methodism to the forces of stability and order. Of course, this was no easy task in a decade of peace societies, Luddism and Peterloo, but a united front of preachers and wealthy laymen, using expulsion as the ultimate weapon, made substantial inroads into Methodist radicalism. In popular and historical mythology, Bunting is held responsible for this crusade as if he had personally drafted, supervised and executed the master plan of what is called 'Buntingite Methodism'. But this is far from being the case. Certainly Bunting was an enthusiastic advocate of conservative policies, but so too was virtually everyone else of importance within the connexion. Even Thomas Allan, who had more reason than most to distrust ministerial pretensions, was unswerving in his opposition to Methodist radicals. Divisions of opinion within the Wesleyan élite were common in the 1790s and again after 1820, but unless the surviving evidence is misleading, this was not true of the period in between. The reason was that the 'no politics' rule inherited from Wesley seemed to provide a pious and logical answer to a most inconvenient problem. But the price was heavy. By 1820 Wesleyanism had largely purged itself of popular radicalism and unrestrained revivalism, but in so doing it lost contact with the working classes in town and country.

No sooner had one set of political problems eased when another took their place. This time the stimulus came from Catholic Ireland, radical Dissent, and a rebellious Methodism unhappy with connexional government. These challenges, although in some respects separate, interacted with one another to make the Wesleyan élite more Tory and its critics more Liberal. The use of party labels is, however, a distortion of the fundamentally religious basis of Methodist attitudes to politics in the nineteenth century. Even Bunting, who had more to do with parliamentary politics and politicians than most Methodists, was more of a churchman than a politician. E. R. Taylor states that Bunting

took the lead in all matters of public concern to Wesleyans, and acted as their representative in questions affecting Missions, Slavery Abolition, Roman Catholic Emancipation, Sabbath Observance, Disestablishment, and Education. On questions affecting Parliamentary Reform, the Corn Laws, and Free Trade, he was, for so prominent a public man, strangely quiet. . . . He was not a politician. His approach to public questions was that of a Churchman, not that of a man interested in the relation between religion and politics. He was comparatively unconcerned about the theoretical rights and wrongs of Disestablishment. . . . Other questions he regarded in a similar manner, and even education, which as an issue in the nineteenth century, deeply influenced Nonconformist politicians, was not, with Bunting, anything other than a fundamentally religious matter.[6]

Taylor's general argument is correct, but it is overstated. No one would deny that Bunting, like all Wesleyans, applied moral and religious values to politics, nor that there was an uneasy tension in many Methodist minds about the respective domains of religion and politics,[7] but one must not deduce from this that Bunting was a type of religious dinosaur thrashing around in an environment no longer congenial to him. Bunting was not unconcerned about 'Disestablishment', nor was he naïve about 'Education'; rather he was trying to protect the religious foundations of the state against secular and heterodox encroachment. Bunting, like Newman for that matter, knew that Nonconformist Liberalism, for all its self-confidence, would not save England from secularism. When the *Wesleyan Magazine* (1835) stated, with reference to a legal provision for Catholic clergy in Ireland, that 'what is morally and religiously wrong can never be politically right',[8] it was not declaring its lack of interest 'in the relation between religion and politics', but making a positive statement about the parameters within which early Victorian politics should function.

The real problem with Bunting's political views was not their religious foundation, but their strategic unsuitability for the Wesleyan connexion in the second quarter of the nineteenth century. In the first place, Bunting was operating within a Nonconformist population whose social aspirations in English provinces could not be satisfied by state-supported religion. Second, Bunting compounded the problem by branding deviant opinions as unWesleyan, and by refusing to admit the party political significance of his actions. Political disagreements were thereby unnecessarily transformed into crises of connexional governance. Thus, attempts to keep on the lid of political uniformity simply forced the steam to escape elsewhere. Finally, Bunting's political activities were in the ultimate sense unpolitical, in that he looked upon political pressure as a device for bringing home the pork with the Wesleyan community. To be successful, this strategy depended on Wesleyan muscle, or on what Methodists could offer governments in return for their favours. In the first quarter of the nineteenth century the Wesleyans offered their moderating influence on the politicized artisans of northern England, but in the second quarter of the century they had little to offer except an uninspired sectarianism, which was exploited by politicians in opposition, but which frustrated them when in power. Thus, in the more pluralistic religious climate of the nineteenth century the Wesleyans were just powerful enough to prevent political infringements of their liberties, but they had neither the voting strength nor the social prestige to wring special favours from Anglican politicians.

In any case most Wesleyans paid little attention to official Conference policies, unless an orchestrated denominational campaign thrust petitions under their noses. When the issue was explained from the pulpit they signed willingly enough, but this was not the same thing as exercising effective control over their political opinions. One preacher told Bunting that the Reform Act produced 'such a lust of power in a considerable number of our people, that it is becoming very difficult indeed, in some places, to exercise that pastoral authority . . . which is indispensable to order and good government'.[9] Convinced of the rectitude of their position, Wesleyan preachers relied more heavily on the authority of the pastoral office, but there was neither enough of them, nor enough people willing to listen, to make a decisive difference to lay opinion.[10]

A more popular aspect of Wesleyan Toryism was its anti-Catholicism. From a modern perspective, this element within Methodism appears to be in stark contrast to its more noble support for the abolition of negro slavery, but the contradiction is only apparent. From the Methodist viewpoint one was simply a physical, and the other a spiritual, expression of bondage. Moreover, both were serious obstacles to the Methodist missionary enterprise in Ireland and in the colonies.[11] It is difficult for the historian to recapture the sense of missionary excitement in the ranks of early nineteenth-century Methodism about what could be achieved in the world, if only error could be held in check. Five million slaves and about the same number of Catholic Irishmen were waiting to be set free from oppressive systems, before being Christianized by evangelical methods.[12] It was the threat to missionary effectiveness that forced Bunting into an apparent volte-face between his support for Catholic Emancipation in 1829 and his opposition to Irish national education in 1832. A few years later he made another appeal for scriptural education – this time in the West Indies.[13]

Methodist anti-Catholicism was occasioned by more than just missionary excitement; it was also an expression of English popular chauvinism. Reporting on Spanish political instability in 1840, Robert Alder, a secretary to the Methodist Missionary Society, stated that 'the leaders of the Spanish people do not appear to know what is meant by a state of freedom; and indeed how should they, seeing that they have been trained in the school of Popery or of Infidelity'.[14] Such chauvinism was easily politicized by Wesleyan leaders in the period from Catholic Emancipation to the Papal Aggression crisis. But outside areas of extensive Irish settlement or strike-breaking, it was a largely dormant emotion unless pricked by pulpit oratory or by electoral excitement.[15] However, even anti-Catholic sentiment fell victim to Methodist divisions, when the secession groups went voluntaryist over Maynooth. Buntingite Wesleyans took off in another direction, for while Maynooth did not convert them to Evangelical Alliance, it persuaded them that its hour had come.

Charting the course of Methodist politics from the written evidence of its main protagonists is one thing, assessing the impact of Methodism on British society in more general terms is quite another. The main problem, as outlined in the Introduction, is that there were many Methodisms in many places at many times. What linked the Methodist soldiers stationed in Ireland in 1798 to suppress the rebellion of the United Irishmen with the Methodist members of the Sheffield Society for Constitutional Information? What linked the austere and colourless Methodism of popular repute with the carnival atmosphere of Cornish revivalism? What had Durham miners in common with George Eliot's 'sleek grocers'? What had Methodist doctors of divinity to do with folk preachers like Gideon Ouseley and Billy Bray? Even in a single town in a single year, what linked the down-at-heel frequenters of primitive city centre chapels with the clientele of their imposing suburban counterparts? This is not to say, however, that Methodism, like Puritanism, is a term that has almost ceased to mean anything, for Methodists were distinguished by their evangelical Arminianism, connexional system, itinerant preachers, local chapel structure, pietism and hymnody. The point is that Methodism is not a static entity to be brought out of the cabinet of English historical exhibits, dusted and examined, and then put back again. It was a living religious movement which changed and was changed by the social context in which it took root. Perhaps too much has been written about Methodism's impact on society and not enough about society's impact on Methodism. Insights from the second approach would assuredly shed some light on the dominant social theory of Methodism – that it was a conservative and stabilizing force in English society during the Industrial Revolution.

This theory is built with many different materials. According to Halévy, the evangelical movement imbued 'the élite of the working class, the hard-working and capable bourgeois, . . . with a spirit from which the established order had nothing to fear'.[16] Such men married their cries for religious liberty with equal devotion to order and stability. To this, Thompson added the idea that Methodism served as a displacement of energy away from temporal objectives into the demands of the chapel community, or else into the psychic release of revivalism. Moreover, Methodism's work discipline, a product of the insecure salvation offered by Wesley's Arminianism, was the perfect foundation for industrial capitalism. Any remaining chinks in the conservative armour of Wesleyanism were sealed by the indoctrination of children, Bunting's preachers, and the expulsion of dissidents. Hence, any contribution Methodism may have made to popular politics through education and organization was incidental to its main role in the experiences of working people.[17]

The complex relationship between Methodism and popular politics has been dealt with already, but the link between Methodist ideology and industrial capitalism is urgently in need of fresh attention. Most of the pioneer work was done by Wellman J. Warner, upon whom Thompson relied for detailed examples to support his own thesis.[18] Warner in turn acknowledged his debt to Max Weber and R. H. Tawney. By using eighteenth-century pamphlets and nineteenth-century local histories of Methodism he uncovered an impressive array of material in support of the Protestant ethic. Warner was all too aware of the difficulty of his undertaking.

Any inquiry into social psychology is, of course, an elusive project. In the present instance it seemed best to make a study of the bearing of the Wesleyan movement upon the creation of a social mentality, in the form of a detailed analysis with contemporary documentation.[19]

Some of Warner's contemporary documentation needs to be handled with care. He drew, for example, on deliberate Methodist propaganda designed to stave off Anglican criticism, and on the biographies of successful Methodists. Many of the Methodist local studies available to him were written in the mid Victorian period when bourgeois values were especially admired. Methodist economic failures, like Davenport in Mrs Gaskell's *Mary Barton*, would not surface in this kind of literature.[20]

There are other objections to fitting Methodism too neatly into the mould of the Protestant ethic. Warner recognized that Wesley's teaching on economic matters was hardly a model of industrial capitalism. After providing for necessities Wesley urged Methodists to give away the rest, otherwise they would be guilty of robbing God and the poor, corrupting their own souls, wronging the widow and the fatherless, and of making themselves 'accountable for all the want, affliction, and distress which they may, but do not remove'.[21] In addition Wesley told his followers to think nothing of the future, to demand no more than a fair price, and to make sure that excessive wealth was not passed on to their children. Even his acceptance of the prevailing economic order should not be interpreted to mean that he acquiesced in its perversions. For example, he wrote approvingly of mob action in 1758 because 'their business was only with the forestallers of the market, who had brought up all the corn far and near to starve the poor, and load a Dutch ship, which lay at the quay'.[22] For Wesley, the justice of their claim and the peacefulness of their protest overrode his scruples about direct action by the poor. Wesley's view that poverty was caused either by indolence (of all classes, not just the poor) or by the selfishness and greed of the rich infused his economic teaching with a stern morality. All was underpinned by a straightforward appeal to the judgement of God.

I charge you, in the name of God, do not increase your substance! As it comes daily or yearly, so let it go: otherwise you lay up treasures upon earth; and this our lord as flatly forbids, as murder and adultery. By doing it, therefore, you would treasure up to yourselves wrath against the day of wrath, and revelation of the righteous judgment of God. But suppose it were not forbidden, how can you, on principles of reason, spend your money in a way, which God may possibly forgive, instead of spending it in a manner which He will certainly reward? You will have no reward in heaven, for what you lay up: you will for what you lay out. Every pound you put into the earthly bank is sunk; it brings no interest above. But every pound you give to the poor is put into the bank of heaven.[23]

This aspect of Wesley's economic teaching has been buried beneath layers of English social history dominated by the Protestant ethic, but it has been recently excavated by John Walsh. He has drawn attention to Wesley's conviction that all great spiritual movements surged from the poor, and to his advocacy of the early Christian practice of sharing goods and property in Methodist societies.[24] Such teaching occasioned contemporary attacks for its communism, and embarrassed Wesley's followers into reinterpreting it along more conventional lines.[25] According to Walsh, Wesley was a traditionalist Catholic, rather than a Protestant individualist, in his social teaching on poverty.

There was, of course, another side to Wesley's teaching. He preached thrift and hard work as daily Christian duties, and stated that 'without industry we are neither fit for this world, nor for the world to come'.[26] Such teaching was easily appropriated by the Methodists as they experienced the benefits of an expanding economy. Not surprisingly, the majority of them paid more attention to Wesley's plea for industry than to his example of holy charity. Methodist philanthropy did not die with the onset of industrialization, but it became less urgent, and came to be seen as an instrument of social control, rather than as an expression of Christian grace. Wesley knew what was happening, and tried to stop it, but, according to Warner, Wesley's attempt to marry industriousness and charity was 'impossible of mass realization'.[27] The result was that Wesley, who was no believer in the Protestant ethic himself, made an unintended contribution to its extension in England during the Industrial Revolution. Another aspect of Wesley's economic teaching which did not survive his death, was his belief that economic distress was caused by human failure which defeated divine purpose. Thus, 'the consolations of a future recompense as a soporific for present suffering were not brought into the foreground by Wesleyans until the period of the French Revolution'.[28]

Research is still too incomplete to make a proper judgement on the economic contribution made by Methodists to English industrial growth. It is assumed too easily that masters welcomed Methodist employees with open arms, especially in the early stages of industrialization when Methodists were thought to be peculiar, and employer's hiring policy seems to have worked more within kinship than religious networks.[29] In addition, Methodists were sometimes unpopular with other workers, and had greater independence conferred upon them by chapel membership. In any case most employers had more terrible weapons available to them than mere religious deference.[30] However these problems are resolved, one must be careful not to exaggerate the importance of the Methodists. Even on Gilbert's most optimistic figures, evangelical Nonconformists comprised only a small minority of English workers, and Methodism never became the religion of the factory proletariat.[31]

It is, therefore, quite unrealistic to build large-scale social theories on the relationship between popular evangelicalism, and industrial capitalism. As far as Methodism is concerned, the most that can be said is that its theology, chapel culture, and opportunities for lay initiative were peculiarly suited to those smaller industrial towns that made up the infrastructure of England's industrial society. It drew little support from major entrepreneurs or from the labouring poor. John Foster's local study of Oldham has shown that Methodists, by the early Victorian period, were particularly well represented among tradesmen and craftsmen. In Oldham, at least, Methodists serviced industrial growth and traded on its benefits, but generally speaking, they were not engaged in large manufacturing enterprises, either as captains of industry or as troops in the factories.[32] In this kind of environment, Methodism was at once a statement of lower middle-class independence from Anglican and gentry control, and the creator of an alternative synthesis of work, community and religious experience.

Apart from Halévy's thesis and its subsequent refinements, the most common interpretation of Methodism's impact on English society is that it sowed the seeds of individual responsibility and religious liberty which eventually bore fruit in Victorian Liberalism. Thus Methodism, whether consciously or unconsciously, eroded the English confessional state and prepared the way for a more pluralistic and liberal society. In this scheme, an early Wesleyan Toryism was gradually replaced by a more progressive ideology, as evidenced in Methodism's contribution to Gladstonian Liberalism and the Nonconformist Conscience. There is just enough truth in this interpretation to make it worth exposing the accompanying myths. There is no doubt that the growth of evangelical Nonconformity made it more difficult for the Church of England to maintain its social, legal and political privileges, or that the late Victorian state was more liberal than its late eighteenth-century predecessor. Methodism, by presenting a peaceful yet radical religious challenge to the Church of England, played a major part in the transition. But it is in marrying this social reality with political ideology that myths are created.

In particular, both the Toryism of the Bunting era and the Liberalism of late nineteenth-century Wesleyanism have been exaggerated.[33] Indeed, there are some striking similarities between the two periods. By the end of the century, Wesleyans were still employing the old no politics rule to stop their chapels being used for political purposes. Similarly, although rural Wesleyans were repeatedly irritated over Anglican policy on burials, the connexion as a whole did not support the Liberation Society, nor did it approve of the disestablishment sentiment in the Free Church councils. When it came to specific matters like the removal of Nonconformist grievances over marriage ceremonies, Wesleyans still preferred to act through their own Committee of Privileges rather than join with other Nonconformists. Over Irish Home Rule, the old anti-Catholic sentiment surfaced again in an extraordinary way. Not only did Irish Methodists lobby their English counterparts to oppose Home Rule, but there were electoral swings away from Liberalism in the Methodist strongholds of Lincolnshire, Devon and Cornwall. In fact, according to Dr Bebbington, Wesleyans were specially responsive to ultra-Protestantism and Imperialism at the end of the nineteenth century.[34] Even over educational matters Wesleyans could still be strongly particularist, as they fought against Anglican privileges, secularist encroachment and Unitarian schemes. They could, of course, still unite with the rest of evangelical Nonfonformity for moral crusades like the Contagious Diseases affair but, on the whole, Wesleyans were a law unto themselves. The majority of them still voted Liberal, and all Wesleyan MPs between 1868 and 1886 were Liberal, but theirs was a peculiar sort of Liberalism. Stephen Koss states that 'the Wesleyan commitment to the Liberal Party evolved slowly, and had no sooner been proclaimed than it showed definite signs of retreat. While it lasted, theirs was a Liberalism of a distinctly different hue, stoutly opposed to the secularist and egalitarian tendencies of the party's Radical wing'.[35] Moreover, Wesleyan Conservatism did not die with Bunting. Men like Sir George Hayter Chubb, the leading figure in the Nonconformist Unionist Association, and a renowned military philanthropist, continued the Conservative tradition, even if its earlier strength could never be recaptured. This is not to deny that come election time in areas of Methodist (especially non-Wesleyan) strength, the chapel could still be Liberalism at prayer, for Nonconformity offered 'an alternative establishment whose attitudes it articulated'.[36]

The most satisfactory way of analysing the relationship between Methodism and politics in English society *c.* 1750–1850 is to root Methodism as firmly as possible in its religious, social, geographical and chronological context. As Obelkevich wrote of South Lindsey, religious life 'cannot be "reduced" to its social foundations, but it is unintelligible without them'.[37] After all, men and women who were Methodists were also people who worked, lived in a particular area, had aspirations, and thought about their relationship to the world in many different ways. Moreover, they were people who took their religion seriously, and generally brought a religious gloss to their political behaviour. This applies as much to Bunting as to his most severe critics. It applies also to Irish Methodists, Cornish miners and Nottinghamshire Chartists. To add to the complexity, Methodism did not fit easily into the traditional English division of Church and Dissent. It had, therefore, fewer established interests to defend, and only a short history to draw upon. This made Methodists more malleable and more vulnerable to external pressures. Moreover, Methodism, which was composed of a range of social groups in town and country, was not immune to the class animosities that characterized English society after 1780. The half century after 1780 was, therefore, the most important period in the history of British Methodism, for it was in this period that Methodism failed to sink deep roots into working-class culture. Victorian Methodism was, of course, far from moribund. Even the much-abused Wesleyans had their religious successes, and Methodists of all types held their own in English society, at least until the 1880s, when the signs of decline were unmistakable.[38] But it was in the earlier period that class and sectarian conflicts shaped Wesleyan Methodism into a distinctive denomination, and provoked a number of Methodist secessions. In the generation overshadowed by the French Revolution, Wesleyan leaders, as with historians ever since, found it impossible to separate religion from its complex social and political setting. This emerges clearly from the official Wesleyan circular sent out in the aftermath of Peterloo.

Finally, dear Brethren, let us intreat you, in reference to the subject now under consideration, to be careful that your conversation be as becometh the Gospel of Christ. And be in nothing terrified by your enemies, who may threaten you for your loyalty to your Religion, to your Government, and the Institutions of our beloved Country; for even on the supposition that such threats should ever be executed against any of you, it would only follow that unto you it would be given on the behalf of Christ, not only to believe on his name, but also to suffer *for his sake*. If there be therefore any consolation in Christ, if any comfort of love, if any fellowship of the Spirit, if any bowels and mercies, fulfil ye our joy, that ye be like minded, having the same love, being of one accord, of one mind blameless and harmless, the sons of God without rebuke, in the midst of a crooked and perverse Nation, among whom shine ye as lights in the world.[39]

References

1 George Eliot, *Adam Bede* (1859) Everyman edn (London 1960), pp. 38–9.
2 A. J. Hayes and D. A. Gowland (eds.), *Scottish Methodism in the Early Victorian Period* (Edinburgh 1981), p. 62.
3 Lord Bulkeley to Lord Grenville, Baronhill, Anglesey, 1 October 1806. I am grateful to Dr Peter Jupp for this transcript from the Grenville Mss. in the British Museum.
4 W. R. Ward, *The Early Correspondence of Jabez Bunting 1820–1829*, Camden 4th series, **11** (London 1972), pp. 9–12.
5 T. P. Bunting, *The Life of Jabez Bunting* (2 vols., London 1859, 1887), vol. 1, p. 371.
6 E. R. Taylor, *Methodism and Politics 1791–1851*, 2nd edn (New York 1975), pp. 134–5.
7 B. S. Turner and M. Hill, 'Methodism and the pietist definition of politics: Historical development and contemporary evidence', in M. Hill (ed.), *A Sociological Yearbook of Religion in Britain*, vol. 8 (1975), pp. 159–80.
8 ibid., p. 166.
9 W. R. Ward, *Early Victorian Methodism* (Oxford 1976), p. 125.
10 Perhaps the most important part of the debate about the nature of the pastoral office in nineteenth-century Wesleyanism is not whether Wesley authorized it or not, but when and for what reason its authority was pressed into action.
11 For a fuller treatment of evangelical theology and its application to slavery see Roger Anstey, *The Atlantic Slave Trade and British Abolition 1760–1810* (London 1975), pp. 157–99.
12 Slave numbers are deliberately taken from John Beecham to Jabez Bunting, 1 December 1832, in Ward, *Early Victorian Methodism*, p. 22.
13 ibid., pp. 52–8.
14 ibid., pp. 250–1.
15 There has been little study of religious bigotry as a social phenomenon in Britain. A preliminary report of research in progress was presented to the History Workshop (London 1983) by C. King and C. Brown (Preston

Polytechnic). For an example of anti-Catholic rioting at election time, even in a small isolated community see B. J. Biggs, 'Methodism in a rural society: North Nottinghamshire, 1740–1815' (unpublished PhD thesis, University of Nottingham 1975) p. 522 (1826 election).

16   Élie Halévy, *A History of the English People in the Nineteenth Century*, vol. 1, *England in 1815*, paperback edn (London 1970), p. 425.

17   E. P. Thompson, *The Making of the English Working Class* (London 1963), pp. 350–400.

18   ibid., p. 355.

19   W. J. Warner, *The Wesleyan Movement in the Industrial Revolution* (London 1930), Preface.

20   Elizabeth Gaskell, *Mary Barton* (1848), ch. 6.

21   Warner, p. 210.

22   ibid., p. 150.

23   Luke Tyerman, *The Life and Times of the Rev. John Wesley, M.A.*, vol. 3, 3rd edn (London 1876), p. 519.

24   John Walsh, 'Methodism and the common people', in Raphael Samuel (ed.), *People's History and Socialist Theory* (London 1981), pp. 354–62. Dr Walsh is preparing a more substantial treatment of this theme.

25   Warner, p. 156.

26   ibid., p. 141.

27   ibid., p. 152.

28   ibid., p. 163.

29   These elements are not, of course, mutually exclusive. For recent surveys and bibliographies on industrialization and the family see, Michael Anderson, 'Sociological history and the working-class family: Smelser revisited', *Social History*, part 3 (1976), pp. 317–34, and D. Brown and M. J. Harrison (eds.), *A Sociology of Industrialisation* (London 1978), pp. 72–87.

30   Sidney Pollard, 'Factory discipline in the industrial revolution', *Economic History Review*, 2nd series, **16** (1964), pp. 254–71.

31   A. D. Gilbert, 'Methodism, Dissent and political stability in early industrial England', *Journal of Religious History*, **10** (1978–9), pp. 381–99.

32   John Foster, *Class Struggle and the Industrial Revolution: Early Industrial Captialism in Three English Towns*, paperback edn (London 1977), pp. 161–202.

33   See, for example, B. S. Turner and M. Hill, 'Methodism and the pietist definition of politics: historical development and contemporary evidence', in M. Hill (ed.), *A Sociological Yearbook of Religion in Britain*, vol. 8 (1975), pp. 159–80.

34   This section is based largely on D. W. Bebbington, *The Nonconformist Conscience* (London 1982). I am grateful to Dr Bebbington for showing me his forthcoming article in the *Historical Journal* called 'Noncon-

formity and electoral sociology, 1867–1918'. He has unearthed considerable evidence to show that Wesleyan anti-Catholicism weakened its electoral commitment to the Liberal Party. For clarification of Irish Methodist opposition to Home Rule, see 'A grave crisis – an appeal to the Methodists of Great Britain from ministers of the Methodist Church in Ireland', printed resolutions (1892), in the Methodist Archives, Northern Ireland PRO. For Methodist attitudes to imperialism see Stephen Koss, 'Wesleyanism and Empire', *Historical Journal*, **18** (1975), pp. 105–18.

35 Stephen Koss, *Nonconformity in Modern British Politics* (London 1975), p. 19. Also, Ian Sellers, *Nineteenth-Century Nonconformity* (London 1977), pp. 65–91; and J. H. S. Kent, 'Hugh Price Hughes and the Nonconformist conscience', in G. V. Bennett and J. D. Walsh (eds.), *Essays in Modern English Church History* (London 1966).

36 Clyde Binfield, *So Down to Prayers: Studies in English Nonconformity 1780–1920* (London 1977), p. 132.

37 James Obelkevich, *Religion and Rural Society: South Lindsey 1825–1875* (Oxford 1976), p. 313.

38 R. B. Walker, 'The growth of Wesleyan Methodism in Victorian England and Wales', *Journal of Ecclesiastical History*, **24** no. 3 (July 1973), pp. 267–84.

39 M.C.A., 'To the Societies in the Connexion established by the late Rev. John Wesley, A.M.', Printed circular, 12 November 1819.

Appendix

(COPY OF

To *the Right Honourable t.*
in Parlia

THE humble Petiti
founded by the
signed, attendi
in the County o

SHEWETH,

THAT, if a Bill, intituled, " An Ac
" Year of the Reign of King William and Queen Mary
" so far as the same relate to Protestant Dissenting
into a Law, it will be a great infringement of the L
valuable Rights and Privileges which your Petitioners

Your Petit
may not

Thomas Blanshard, Preacher.	Francis Kent.
William Jones.	Thomas Scott.
Edward Smith.	Edward Brown.
John Gifford.	Francis Smith.

ETITION.)

—

ds Spiritual and Temporal,
ssembled.

undersigned Persons, being Members of Societies,
erend JOHN WESLEY, and of other Persons under-
ngregation at

in and render more effectual, certain Acts of the First
e Nineteenth Year of the Reign of his present Majesty,
," now depending before your Lordships, be carried
ligious Toleration, and will be subversive of the most

refore humbly pray your Lordships, that the said Bill
a Law.

William Cooper.	Ely Cole.
ohn Taylor.	Thomas Heap.
rancis Collin.	Thomas Brown.

HOMAS CORDEUX, AGENT.

London, May 18, 1811.

DEAR BROTHER,

BY this or to-morrow night's coach we intend to transmit you the Form of a Petition to the House of Lords, against Lord Sidmouth's Bill, which, we hope, will be *instantly* signed by all the Men in our Societies, and by all the Men who attend our Congregations. We do *not* think it advisable for women to sign, and no young man is to sign who is under sixteen Years of Age.

We intend to send you a number of Petitions ready written. We wish to have a Petition from every Chapel in your Circuit, as our object is to have as many Petitions as possible, and to be signed by as many persons as possible; but we would much rather have a great number of Petitions, than to have the friends who attend different Chapels, to join in one Petition.

But be sure keep all the Petitions distinct, and as there may be several Sheets of Parchment to each Petition, let them be sewed together at *each* Chapel *before* they are brought to the head of the Circuit, or else the signatures will get mixed, and those sheets of signatures which belong to one Petition, will, if there be any confusion, become mixed with others. Therefore, give particular directions that the sheets of signatures be all sewed together at each Chapel, before they are brought away; then collect and send the whole by the first coach. Let the number of Names to each Petition be accurately counted, and send to Mr. Butterworth a list of all the Petitions, and the number of Signatures to each.

The Parcels containing the Petitions must be all directed to Mr. Joseph Butterworth, 43, Fleet-Street, London; and they must all be in London at the latest, by twelve o'clock on Tuesday next, the 21st instant. Pray write by post to Mr. Butterworth, when you send the List, and say by what conveyance the Petitions are returned, and write on the outside of the Parcel where it comes from. We must not be disappointed of receiving the Petitions on Tuesday next, if it can be avoided. Keep the Petitions as clean and neat as you can, and desire the people not to be in a hurry to sign their names. Let all things be done decently and in order.

You will observe that all the Sheets belonging to each Petition should be so fastened together as to form one Roll. They are only to be written on one side of the Parchment. Persons who cannot write will *not* make their marks. All persons must sign their own names.

No Preacher, or any other Person must, on any account, sign more than one Petition.

In order that every person who signs the Petition, may know what the Petition is, we send a printed Copy of it sewed to each Skin of Parchment, which printed Copy must be taken away before you sew the several skins together.

ment we could obtain, rather than have the names improperly crowded together.

You will be sure to fill up, very neatly, the Blanks in all the Petitions, describing the Chapel and County, before you send them off to the respective Chapels or Societies in your Circuit for Signature, and you may as well fill up the Blanks in the printed Forms also, in order that every Petitioner may see precisely what he signs.

No person need mention his trade, or place of abode. The travelling Preachers may as well add the word Preacher to their names.

Let us again entreat, that the whole of this affair be conducted in the fear of God, and let not a word be spoken or *written* but in a way which will shew the utmost Honor and respect to our afflicted Sovereign Lord the King.—To His Royal Highness the Prince Regent—and to the Government of our Country.

Signed, by order of the Committee,

THOMAS BLANSHARD.

Have steady Messengers to be ready to go off to each Station in the Circuit, the instant the Petitions arrive.—Our respectable Friends the Stewards and Leaders will do this, when they are told, that the London Committee are at work night and day.

You will keep all the Parchment you do not use, as you may hereafter want to use them for a Petition to the House of Commons, if the Bill should pass the Lords.

All the Petitions that *can* be sent back by Tuesday next, send them, but such as cannot, will be in time for other stages of the Bill in the House of Lords.

We recommend you to Copy the following Notice, and let it be read in all our Chapels:

The Form of a Notice, to be read from the Pulpit, immediately after Service :

" A Petition to Parliament will be ready to be signed against a Bill now before the House of Lords, which, if passed into a law, it is to be greatly feared would materially affect the Laws of Toleration, and our religious Privileges.—The Petition to be signed by all the Men who are present, who are upwards of sixteen Years of Age, whether they are Members of our Society, or who only attend our Chapels. The Petition will also remain, for the Signatures of our absent Friends, at   till   o'clock.

Bibliography

Primary sources

Manuscripts
Printed sources
Newspapers and periodicals
Pamphlets

Secondary sources

Books
Articles
Unpublished theses

Primary sources

Manuscripts

1 *Irish Wesleyan Historical Society Archives*
   Stored temporarily in the Northern Ireland Public Record Office A large
   collection of uncatalogued letters. Particularly useful is the correspondence of Jabez Bunting, Adam Clarke, Gideon Ouseley, William Stewart,
   and Matthew Tobias.
2 *Methodist Church Archives* in the John Rylands University Library
   of Manchester

Thomas Allan Papers
Charles Atmore Papers
John Barber Papers
Joseph Benson Papers
Samuel Bradburn Papers
Jabez Bunting Papers
Joseph Butterworth Papers
Adam Clarke Papers
Thomas Coke Papers
George Cubitt Papers

Henry Deery Papers
James Dixon Papers
Joseph Entwistle Papers
Abraham Farrar Papers
Edmund Grindrod Papers
Thomas Jackson Papers
Alexander Kilham Papers
John Mason Papers
Gideon Ouseley Papers
John Pawson Papers
Charles Prest Papers
John Scott Papers
William Stewart Papers
John Stuart Papers
William Thompson Papers
Richard Treffrey jun. Papers
William Vevers Papers
Thomas Waugh Papers

Journal of Joseph Entwistle

Thomas Jackson Lectures: Lecture on Popery
          Religious Education
          The Signs of the Times
          Church and State
          State of Religious Parties abroad
          Duke of Wellington

Minutes of the Book Committee
Minutes of the Committee of Privileges (1803–22 and 1835–45). Intervening years are missing.

3 *Methodist Missionary Society Archives*, in Marylebone Road, London when consulted, but now in the School of Oriental and African Studies. Three folders of uncatalogued letters from Irish missionaries dating from 1799. They also include the reports of the agents of the Missionary Committee responsible for Irish schools: Thomas Bewley, Thomas Edwards, Valentine Ward, and Elijah Hoole.

4 Diary of the Rev. Charles Prest in private possession of John Prest, Balliol College, Oxford.

Printed sources

Bunting, Jabez, *Sermons*, 2 vols., London 1861
Hansard's *Parliamentary Debates*, vols. XVII to 3rd series LXXX
Journals of the House of Commons
Minutes of the Methodist Conferences, vols. I–IX
Minutes of the Methodist Conferences in Ireland, 3 vols., Dublin 1864–7

O'Leary, Arthur, *Miscellaneous Tracts*, 2nd edn, Dublin 1781

Osborn, G. (ed.), *The Poetical Works of John and Charles Wesley*, 13 vols., London 1868–72

Wesley, John:

    The Journal of John Wesley, Nehemiah Curnock (ed.), 8 vols., London 1909–16

    The Letters of John Wesley, John Telford (ed.), 8 vols., London 1931

    Sermons, 2 vols., London 1825

    Works, Thomas Jackson (ed.), 14 vols., London 1831

    The Oxford edition of the *Works of John Wesley* (editor-in-chief Frank Baker, 34 vols. projected): vol. 11, G. R. Cragg (ed.), *Appeals to Men of Reason and Religion*, Oxford 1975; and vol. 25, Frank Baker (ed.), *Letters, 1, 1721–1739*, Oxford 1980.

Wesleyan Education Reports, London 1837–47

Wesleyan Education Resolutions, 21 May 1839; 6 April, 10 May, 20 June 1843

Wesleyan Methodist Missionary Society Reports, vol. 1, 1789–1820

Wesleyan Methodist Printed Circulars (on political matters), attached to the Minutes of the Committee of Privileges

Newspapers and periodicals

Annual Register

Arminian Magazine (1778–97), continued as the *Methodist Magazine* (1798–1821), continued as the *Wesleyan Methodist Magazine*

Belfast Newsletter

British Critic

Congregational Magazine

Eclectic Review

Gentleman's Magazine

Illuminator

Monthly Repository

New Methodist Magazine (1812–33), continued as the *Methodist New Connexion Magazine*

Northern Star

Pamphleteer

The Times

Watchman

Watchman's Lantern

Wesleyan Association Magazine

Wesleyan Protestant Methodist Magazine

Pamphlets

Aitken, Rev. R., *An address to the Preachers, office-bearers; and members of the Wesleyan Methodist Societies, London 1835*

Allan, Thomas [Sosia, Pseud.], *A Letter to a Protestant Dissenter in answer to the question 'shall the dissenters join with the Roman Catholics in their petitions to Parliament for what is called Catholic emancipation?'*, London 1812

Allen, Rev. James (speech by), *At a meeting held in the Town Hall, at Windsor, on the subject of Church Rates. As reported in the Oxford Journal, March 25, 1837, Buckingham, 1837*

Anon., *The Popery of Methodism or the Enthusiasm of Papists and Wesleyans compared*, with an appendix containing John Wesley's reasons against separating from the Church, Leeds 1839

Anon., *How will the Wesleyan Electors Vote?* (from the *Manchester Guardian*), Manchester 1837

Anon., *A Word to a Protestant Answered*, Whitby n.d.

Anon., *The Education Bill and the Wesleyans being Reasons for Having Declined to sign the Wesleyan Petition Against that Measure. Stated in a Letter to a friend.*, London 1843

Anon., *Remarks on Popery, and the impolicy of Granting any Further Concessions, to the Roman Catholics*, Bristol 1823

B. A., *Apostasy Developed: or, England's Shekinah Departing* (from the *Wesleyan Methodist Magazine*, July and August 1846), London 1846

Blackburn, John, *The Three Conferences held by the opponents of the Maynooth College Endowment, in London and Dublin, during the months of May and June 1845. Containing a Vindication of the author from the aspersions of the Dissenting Press*, London 1845

Blackburne, Archdeacon, *Considerations on the present state of the controversy between the Protestants and Papists of Great Britain and Ireland*, London 1768

Bunting, Jabez, *A Great Work Described and Recommended, in a Sermon, preached on Wednesday, May 15, 1805. . . . Before the Members of the Sunday School Union*, London 1812

Bunting, Rev. Dr (speech by), *Delivered in London, on Monday, June, 10, 1839 in reference to the Government Scheme of National Education recently abandoned and to the Government New Scheme just proposed*, Manchester 1839

Butler, Charles, *An Address to the Protestants of Great Britain and Ireland*, London 5 February 1813

Butterworth, Joseph (printed circular to Methodist preachers and others in Ireland requesting information on), *The State of Ireland and the real spirit and character of the Roman Catholics*, London 1812

Challoner, Richard, *A Caveat against the Methodists*, 5th edn, London 1803

Chalmers, Thomas, *On the Use and Abuse of Literary and Ecclesiastical Endowments*, Glasgow 1827

Chalmers, Thomas, *Lectures on the Establishment and Extension of National Churches*, Glasgow 1838

Colchester, Charles Abbot, *The Fifth of November or Protestant Principles Revived. In Memory of the Glorious Revolution by King William III. Including a correct and authentic copy of a speech on the Roman Catholic Relief Bill, delivered May 24, 1813*, London 1814

Consistent Whig, *Considerations on the late Disturbances* (Gordon riots), London *c*. 1780

Crowther, Jonathan, *Christian Order: or Liberty without Anarchy; Government without Tyranny; and every man in his proper place* (a reply to Kilham's Progress of Liberty), Bristol 1796

Cubitt, George, A *Speech delivered at the Town Hall, Sheffield, on Wednesday, February 18, 1829 at a Meeting convened for the purpose of petitioning against the Concession of Legislative and Political Power to the Roman Catholics*, Sheffield 1829

Cubitt, George, *The Rev. G. Cubitt's Reply to O'Connell's Two Letters Addressed to the Wesleyan Methodists*, London 1839

Cubitt, George, *Strictures on Mr. O'Connell's Letters to the Wesleyan Methodists*, London 1840

Dixon, James, *Letters on the Duties of Protestants with regard to Popery*, Sheffield 1839

Dixon, James, *The Present Position and Aspects of Popery and the duty of Exposing the Errors of Papal Rome. A Lecture first delivered in Sheffield, Dec. 12th, 1839*, London 1840

Dunn, Samuel, *Recollections of Thomas Jackson and his Acts*, London 1873

Dunn, Samuel, *An Exposure of the Mummeries, Absurdities and Idolatries of Popery*, Newcastle n.d.

Epaphras, *The Church of England compared with Wesleyan Methodism*, Bristol 1836

Evangelical Alliance

   Brief Statement of the Proceedings of the Conference in Liverpool for Promoting Christian Union and of the object of the Proposed Evangelical Alliance, 1845

   Report of the speeches delivered at the Public Meetings, held in the Free Trade Hall, Manchester, on Friday Evening, January 16th, 1846 for the purpose of explaining the principles and objects of the Proposed Evangelical Alliance, Manchester 1846

   Brief Summary of Facts in relation to the Proposed Evangelical Alliance, London 14 April 1846

   Proposed Evangelical Alliance, London June 1846

   Report of the Conference. Held at Freemason's Hall, London from August 16th to September 2nd, 1846

Fish, Henry, *Jesuitism traced in the Movements of the Oxford Tractarians*, London 1842

Fish, Henry, *The Workings of Popery: or the Effects which Popery has a tendency to Produce, and the means which are employed to produce them; In which the question is briefly viewed in relation to the Maynooth Grant*, London 1845

Gentleman, A in Ireland, *An Extract of a Letter to Mr. William Thompson*, London 1798

Gilbert, Rev. N., *An Answer to the Rev. John Wesley's Misrepresentations of the Catholic Doctrines*, Whitby 1811

Hanby, Thomas, *An Explanation of Mr. Kilham's Statement of the Preacher's Allowance*, Nottingham 1796

Hibernian Society

> *Nineteenth Annual Report of the London Hibernian Society, for Establishing Schools, and Circulating the Holy Scriptures in Ireland: with Extracts of Correspondence* (includes letters from O'Connell), London 1825

> *Twentieth Annual Report* (includes split with Kildare Place Society), London 1826

> *Extracts of Correspondence*, July 1827–January 1829, London 1829

Holroyd, J. B., *Remarks and Illustrations on a Letter from the Rev., J. L., Roman Catholic Priest, at Scarborough to a member of the Methodist Society, in that town*, Scarborough 1827

Holroyd, J. B., *A Reply to Methodism Unmasked, by the Rev. J. L., Roman Catholic Priest, at Scarborough; in which the Abominations of the Church of Rome are further exposed*, Dewsbury 1828

Irish Methodist (Daniel McAfee), *O'Connell versus the Methodists. An Exposure of the Jesuitism of the Church of Rome*, Dublin 1839

Jackson, Rev. Samuel, *Religious Education in Responsible Hands; or, The Present Generation of Adults Providentially placed between Children and the Lord Jesus Christ*, London 1843

Jackson, Thomas, *A Letter to the Rev. Edward B. Pusey, D. D. Regius Professor of Hebrew in the University of Oxford. Being a Vindication of the Tenets and Character of Wesleyan Methodists, against his Misrepresentations and Censures*, London 1842

Jackson, Thomas, *An answer to the question Why are you a Wesleyan Methodist?*, 4th edn, London 1842

Jackson, Thomas, *The Wesleyan Conference, its Duties and Responsibilities with a Vindication of its recent acts of discipline*, London 1849

J. L., Rev., *A Refutation of Remarks and Illustrations by J. B. Holroyd (Wesleyan Methodist Minister) on a Letter to A Member of the Methodist Society in which his Glaring Blunders, and Total Ignorance of Canons, Councils, Bulls etc. are exposed*, Scarborough 1827

Kilham, Alexander [Paul & Silas, pseud.], *An Earnest Address to the Preachers assembled in Conference*, n.p. 1795

Kilham, Alexander, *The Progress of Liberty, amongst the people called*

Methodists. To which is added the Out-lines of a Constitution, Alnwick 1795

Kilham, Alexander, *A Candid Examination, of the London Methodistical Bull*, Alnwick 1796

Kilham, Alexander, *An Account of the Trial of Alexander Kilham, Methodist Preacher, before the General Conference in London*, Nottingham 1796 [T. Taylor and T. Coke, signed], *Minutes of the Examination of Mr. Alexander Kilham, before the General Conference in London, on the 26th, 27th, and 28th of July, 1796.*

Kilham, A. and Thom, W., *Out-lines of a Constitution; proposed for the examination, amendment and acceptance, of the Members of the Methodist New Itinerancy*, Leeds 1797

Langston, John, *An Essay on the Origin, Nature, and Tendency of Popery*, Marlborough 1829

Laurie, Alderman Sir Peter, *Puseyism: or, An Address to the Wesleyan Methodists*, London 1843

Leeds, Wesleyan Deputation, *A Letter to the Hon. J. Stuart Wortley and Edmund Beckett Denison, Esq. (Members of Parliament for the West Riding of the County of York)*, Leeds 26 April 1843

Leeds, Wesleyan Deputation, *A Second Letter to the Hon. John Stuart Wortley*, Leeds 9 June 1843

McAfee, Daniel, *Transubstantiation Refuted: A Discourse*, Belfast 1828

McAfee, Daniel, *The Calumnies, Falsehoods, and Religion of O'Connell Exposed, The Queries Proposed by his Son, Maurice, satisfactorily Answered, and Protestantism Defended in Seven Letters*, Cork 1839

McAfee, Daniel, *The Apostacy of the Rev. Richard Waldo Sibthorp, B. D., from Protestantism to Popery Demonstrated, in an Address to the Protestant Operatives of Great Britain*, Belfast 1842

McLean, Rev. J., *The Proposed Schemes of National Education Examined. A Sermon*, London 1839

McNeile, Hugh, *Lectures on the Church of England*, London 1840

Mason, J. A., *An Earnest Appeal to the People called Methodists and to the Nation at large*, London 1827

Mason, Rev. J. A., *Strictures on the Second part of Wesley's Pretended Roman Catechism. Addressed to the Methodists of Stourbridge and its Vicinity*, London 1828

Mather, A. and Pawson, J., *An Affectionate Address to the Members of the Methodist Societies*, London 1796

Mather, A., Pawson, J. and Benson, J., *A Defence of the Conduct of the Conference in the Expulsion of Alexander Kilham, addressed to the Methodist Societies*, n.p. c. 1796

Maynooth College, *Its Teaching and its Endowment. Being the Substance of a series of leading articles extracted from the "Watchman" Newspaper*, London 1945

O'Connell, Daniel, *Letter to the Ministers and Office-Bearers of the*

Wesleyan Methodist Societies of Manchester, London 6 July 1839

O'Connell, Daniel, *To the Ministers and Office-Bearers of the Wesleyan Methodist Societies of Manchester*, second letter, London 1 August 1839

O'Connell, Daniel, *A full Report of the proceedings of the Great Meeting of the Catholics of London held at Freemason's Hall, on the fifteenth day of July, 1839*

Osborn, George, *No Popery in Schools Supported by the State! An Address Delivered at the Wesleyan Chapel, Westminster on Tuesday May 28th, 1839; with reference to The Proposed Government Scheme of Public Education*, London 1839

Ouseley, Gideon, *The Substance of Two Letters to the Rev. John Thayer, Once a Presbyterian Minister, but now a Roman Catholic Priest and Missionary. In Consequence of his Public Challenge to all Protestants*, n.p. 1814

Ouseley, Gideon, *The Substance of a Letter to the Rev. Mr. Fitzimmons. Roman Catholic Priest on some Chief Pillars or Principal Articles of his Faith*, Glasgow 1816

Ouseley, Gideon, *Five Letters in reply to the Rev. Michael Branaghan, P.P.*, Dublin 1824

Ouseley, Gideon, *Letters to Dr Doyle on the Doctrines of his Church with an easy and effectual plan to obtain Immediate Emancipation*, Dublin 1824

Ouseley, Gideon, *Reply to Mr A. Morrison* (originally to the Editor of the *Morning Post*), 7 March 1827

Ouseley, Gideon, *Error Unmasked. Priest Walsh's Attack on Protestantism and its clergy defeated, His Professions proved vain, and his faith deeply erroneous*, Dublin 1828

Ouseley, Gideon, *Letters in Defence of the Roman Catholics of Ireland in which is opened the Real Source of their Many Injuries, and of Ireland's Sorrows; Addressed to D. O'Connell*, London 1829

Ouseley, Gideon, *A Review of A Sermon preached by Dr. Peter A. Baynes, Roman Catholic Bishop, at the Opening of the R. Catholic Chapel, in Bradford, Yorkshire*, Dublin 1829

Ouseley, Gideon, *Letters on Topics of Vast Importance to All Roman Catholics and the State in reply to Doctor Crolby's Letter to Lord Donegal*, Dublin 1832

Ouseley, Gideon, *An easy Mode of Securing Ireland's Peace* (to P. C. Crompton, Esq., solicitor-general), Dublin 1833

Ouseley, Gideon, *A Dreadful Conspiracy against The Church of Christ Developed*, Dublin 1837

Philopatris, Letters of, on Mr Plunkett's bill, reprinted from the *Morning Post*, March 1821

Protestant, A, *Answer to a Roman Catholic Bishop's Caveat against the Methodists*, n.p. 1810

Roberts, Joseph, *The Identity of Popery with Paganism*, London 1840

Scott, Abraham, *A Vindication of 'Popery Unmasked'. In answer to the Rev. Edward Daniels*, Hanley 1826

Scott, Abraham, *The Rise and Downfall of Popery predicted by St. Paul*, Hanley 1827

Slack, J., *Remarks upon the Rev. N. Gilbert's Vindication of Popery and Abuse of the Methodists; to R. Campion*, Stokesley 1811

Stanley, Rev. Jacob, *A Tract for the Times. Puseyite Artifice Detected and Wesleyan Methodists Vindicated*, Bristol 1842

Stanley, Rev. Jacob, *The Danger of Puseyism and High-Churchism. Being an answer to an Anonymous Pamphlet entitled 'The Danger of Dissent'*, London 1845

Telford, Rev. J., *The Allans of Old Jewry, and the Founder of the Allan Library*, from the *Wesleyan Methodist Magazine*, London 1887

Vevers, William, *Observations on the Members of the Church of Rome Giving security to a Protestant State*, Leeds 1829

Vevers, William, *An Essay on the National Importance of Methodism*, London 1831

Vevers, William, *A Summary of the Doctrines of the Papal and Protestant Churches*, London 1839

Vevers, William, *The Claims of the Clergy: A letter to the Reverend Hugh McNeile, being a Reply to his speech in the Amphitheatre, Liverpool, April 27th, 1843, addressed to the Wesleyan Methodists*, Derby 1843

Watson, Richard, *The Labyrinth or Popish Circle, Translated from the Latin of Simon Episcopus*, London 1826

Wesley, John, *A Word to a Protestant*, 8th edn, London 1745

Wesleyan, A, *Strictures on the Principle 'Religious Opinions are not a just ground for Exclusion from Civil Offices'*, n.p., n.d.

Wesleyan Methodist, *An Appeal to Wesleyan Methodists and all True Protestants on the Catholic Question*, London 1829

Wesleyan Tracts for the Times, published anonymously but the full list of authors and titles is as follows: Osborn, George, *'Why don't you come to Church?'*; Hannah, Dr J., *Wesleyan Methodism not a Schism*; Thornton, W. L., *Apostolical Succession – A Summary of Objections to the Present Claim*; Turner, George, *Wesleyan Ministers True Ministers of Christ*; Osborn, George, *Modern Methodism, Wesleyan Methodism*; Cubitt, George, *Justification by Faith an Essential Doctrine of Christianity*; Sandwith, Humphrey, *Lyra Apostolica, an Impious Misnomer*; West, F. A., *Baptism not Regeneration*; Barrett, Alfred, *Wesleyans have the true Sacraments*; McOwan, John, *A Letter to 'A Country Curate'*; all published by the Wesleyan Conference Office, London 1842

West W., *Observations and Reflections on what is styled Catholic Emancipation*, Liverpool 1812

Wright, Samuel, *A Reply to the Letters of Daniel O'Connell MP, addressed to the Ministers and Office-Bearers of the Wesleyan Methodist Society*, London 1839

Secondary sources

Books

Akenson, D. H., *The Irish Education Experiment*, London 1970
Allen, Richard, *History of Methodism in Preston and it Vicinity*, Preston 1866
Andrews, Stuart, *Methodism and Society*, London 1970
Anstey, Roger, *The Atlantic Slave Trade and British Abolition 1760–1810*, London 1975
Armstrong, Anthony, *The Church of England, the Methodists and Society, 1700–1850*, London 1973
Arthur, William, *The Life of Gideon Ouseley*, London 1876
Aspland, R. B., *The Rise, Progress and Present Influence of Wesleyan Methodism*, London 1831
Ayling, Stanley, *John Wesley*, London 1979
Baker, Frank, *John Wesley and the Church of England*, London 1970
Balleine, G. R., *A History of the Evangelical Party*, London 1909
Barratt, George, *Recollections of Methodism and Methodists in the City of Lincoln*, Lincoln 1866
Bebbington, D. W., *The Nonconformist Conscience*, London 1982
Beckett, J. C., *Protestant Dissent in Ireland 1687–1780*, London 1948
Beckett, J. C., *The Making of Modern Ireland 1603–1923*, London 1966
Bennett, G. V. and Walsh, J. D. (eds.), *Essays in Modern English Church History*, London 1966
Best, G. F. A., *Temporal Pillars*, Cambridge 1964
Binfield, Clyde, *So Down to Prayers*, London 1977
Black, E. C., *The Association: British Extraparliamentary Political Organization 1769–1793*, Harvard 1963
Bossy, John, *The English Catholic Community 1570–1850*, London 1975
Bowen, Desmond, *The Protestant Crusade in Ireland 1800–1870*, Dublin 1978
Bowmer, J. C., *Pastor and People*, London 1975
Bradley, Ian, *The Call to Seriousness*, London 1976
Brewer, John, *Party Ideology and Popular Politics at the Accession of George III*, Cambridge 1976
Brewer, John and Styles, John (eds.), *An Ungovernable People: The English and their law in the seventeenth and eightenth centuries*, London 1980
Briggs, Asa (ed.), *Chartist Studies*, London 1959
Briggs, J. H. Y. and Sellers, I., *Victorian Nonconformity*, London 1973

Brilioth, Y., *The Anglican Revival – studies in the Oxford Movement*, London 1925

Brown, F. K., *Fathers of the Victorians*, Cambridge 1961

Budd, Susan, *Varieties of Unbelief*, London 1977

Bunting, T. P., *The Life of the Rev. Dr. Jabez Bunting*, 2 vols., London 1859 and 1887

Butler, Charles, *Reminiscences of Charles Butler, Esq.*, 3rd edn, London 1822

Cannon, John (ed.), *The Whig Ascendancy*, London 1980

Carpenter, S. C., *Church and People 1789–1889*, London 1933

Carwardine, Richard, *Trans-atlantic Revivalism – Popular Evangelicalism in Britain and America, 1790–1865*, Westport, Connecticut 1978

Chadwick, Owen, *The Victorian Church*, 2 vols., London 1966 and 1970

Chaloner, W. H. (ed.), *Samuel Bamford* (autobiography), vol. 1, London 1967

Chew, Richard, *James Everett, a Biography*, London 1875

Chew, Richard, *William Griffith – Memorials and Letters*, London 1885

Church, L. F., *The Early Methodist People*, London 1948

Church, L. F., *More About the Early Methodist People*, London 1949

Clark, G. Kitson, *Churchmen and the Condition of England, 1832–85*, London 1973

Colls, Robert, *The Collier's Rant*, London 1977

Cookson, J. E., *The Friends of Peace. Anti-war liberalism in England, 1793–1815*, Cambridge 1982

Cornish, F. W., *History of the English Church in the Nineteenth Century*, 2 vols., London 1910

Crookshank, C. H., *History of Methodism in Ireland*, 3 vols., London 1885–8

Cunningham, Valentine, *Everywhere Spoken Against: Dissent in the Victorian Novel*, Oxford 1975

Currie, Robert, *Methodism Divided*, London 1968

Currie, R., Gilbert, A. and Horsley, L., *Churches and Churchgoers – Patterns of Church Growth in the British Isles since 1700*, Oxford 1977

Davies, R. E., *Methodism*, London 1963

Davies, R. E., George A. R. and Rupp, E. G., *A History of the Methodist Church in Great Britain*, vol. 2, London 1978, and vol. 3, London 1983

Davies, R. E. and Rupp, E. G., *A History of the Methodist Church in Great Britain*, vol. 1, London 1965

Davis, R. W., *Dissent in Politics – the Political Life of William Smith, MP*, London 1973

Dickinson, H. T., *Liberty and Property – Political Ideology in Eighteenth-Century Britain*, London 1977

Dimond, S. G., *The Psychology of the Methodist Revival; An Empirical and Descriptive Study*, Oxford 1926

Dowling, P. J., *A History of Irish Education*, Cork 1971

Duffy, Eamon (ed.), *Challoner and his Church*, London 1981

Dyos, H. J. and Wolff, M. (eds.), *The Victorian City: Images and Realities*, 2 vols., London 1973

Dyson, J. B., *A History of Wesleyan Methodism in the Congleton Circuit*, London 1856

Edwards, Maldwyn, *This Methodism*, London 1939

Edwards, Maldwyn, *Methodism and England: A Study of Methodism in its Social and Political Aspects, 1850–1932*, London 1943

Edwards, Maldwyn, *After Wesley: A Study of the Social and Political Influence of Methodism in the Middle Period (1791–1849)*, London 1948

Edwards, Maldwyn, *John Wesley and the Eighteenth Century: A Study of his Social and Political Influence*, 2nd edn, London 1955

Eltis, David and Walvin, James (eds.), *The Abolition of the Atlantic Slave Trade*, Wisconsin 1981

England, T. R., *The Life of the Rev. Arthur O'Leary*, London 1822

Entwistle, William, *Memoir of the Rev. Joseph Entwistle, by his son*, Bristol 1848

Epstein, James and Thompson, Dorothy (eds.), *The Chartist Experience: Studies in Working-Class Radicalism and Culture 1830–1860*, London 1982

Etheridge, J. W., *The Life of the Rev. Adam Clarke LL.D.*, London 1858

Everitt, Alan, *The Pattern of Rural Dissent: the Nineteenth Century*, Leicester 1972

Faulkner, H. U., *Chartism and the Churches*, 2nd edn, London 1970

Foster, John, *Class Struggle and the Industrial Revolution*, London 1974

Furneaux, Robin, *William Wilberforce*, London 1974

Gash, Norman, *Mr. Secretary Peel*, London 1961

Gash, Norman, *Reaction and Reconstruction in English Politics, 1832–52*, Oxford 1965

Gash, Norman, *Sir Robert Peel*, London 1972

Gash, Norman, *Aristocracy and People*, London 1979

Gay, J. D., *The Geography of Religion in England*, London 1971

Gilbert, A. D., *Religion and Society in Industrial England, 1740–1914*, London 1976

Gill, F. C., *The Romantic Movement and Methodism*, London 1937

Goodwin, Albert, *The Friends of Liberty: The English Democratic Movement in the age of the French Revolution*, London 1979

Gowland, D. A., *Methodist Secessions: The origins of Free Methodism in three Lancashire towns*, Manchester 1979

Green, R., *Anti-Methodist Publications Issued During the Eighteenth Century*, London 1902

Gregory, Benjamin, *Side-Lights on the Conflicts of Methodism 1827–52*, London 1898

Haire, Robert, *Wesley's One-and-Twenty visits to Ireland*, London 1947

Halévy, Élie, *A History of the English People in the Nineteenth Century*, vols. 1–4, London 1949–51

Halévy, Élie, *The Birth of Methodism in England*, translated by Bernard Semmel, Chicago 1971

Hammond, J. L. and B., *The Village Labourer*, London 1911

Hammond, J. L. and B., *The Town Labourer*, London 1917

Harrison, J. F. C., *The Early Victorians 1832–1851*, London 1971

Harrison, J. F. C., *The Second Coming: Popular Millenarianism 1780–1850*, London 1979

Hayes, A. J. and Gowland, D. A., *Scottish Methodism in the Early Victorian Period*, Edinburgh 1981

Healey, Rev. J., *Maynooth College: its Centenary History 1795–1895*, Dublin 1895

Henriques, Ursula, *Religious Toleration in England 1787–1833*, London 1961

Hobsbawm, E. J., *Primitive Rebels*, Manchester 1959

Hobsbawm, E. J., *Labouring Men: studies in the history of labour*, London 1964

Hobsbawm, E. J., *The Age of Revolution*, 2nd edn, London 1973

Hobsbawm, E. J. and Rudé, George, *Captain Swing*, London 1970

Hollis, Patricia (ed.), *Class and Conflict in Nineteenth-Century England 1815–1850*, London 1973

Hollis, Patricia (ed.), *Pressure from Without in early Victorian England*, London 1974

Holmes, R. F., *Henry Cooke*, Belfast 1981

Horn, Pamela, *The Rural World 1780–1850*, London 1980

Hughes, Philip, *The Catholic Question 1688–1829*, London 1929

Hunt, E. H., *British Labour History 1815–1914*, London 1981

Hurley, Michael (ed.), *John Wesley's Letter to a Roman Catholic*, Belfast 1968

Huston, Rev. Robert, *The Life and Labours of the Rev. Fossey Tackaberry*, London 1853

Inglis, K. S., *Churches and the Working Classes in Victorian England*, London 1963

Jackson, Thomas, *Recollections of my own Life and Times*, London 1873

Jeffery, Frederick, *Irish Methodism*, Belfast 1964

Jeffery, Frederick, *Methodism and the Irish Problem*, Belfast 1973

Jessop, Rev. William, *Methodism in Rossendale*, London 1880

Joyce, Patrick, *Work, Society and Politics: the culture of the factory in later*

Victorian England, Hassocks, Sussex 1980

Kendall, H. B., *The Origin and History of the Primitive Methodist Church*, 2 vols., London 1905; revised and enlarged 1919

Kent, J. H. S., *Jabez Bunting: The Last Wesleyan*, London 1955

Kent, J. H. S., *The Age of Disunity*, London 1966

Kent, J. H. S., *Holding the Fort: Studies in Victorian Revivalism*, London 1978

Kerr, D. A., *Peel, Priests and Politics*, Oxford 1982

Knox, R. A., *Enthusiasm: A Chapter in the History of Religion*, Oxford 1950

Koss, Stephen, *Nonconformity in Modern British Politics*, London 1975

Kreiser, B. R., *Miracles, Convulsions, and Ecclesiastical Politics in Early Eighteenth Century Paris*, Princeton 1978

Laqueur, T. W., *Religion and Respectability: Sunday Schools and Working Class Culture, 1780–1850*, London and New Haven 1976

Lecky, W. E. H., *A History of England in the Eighteenth Century*, 8 vols., London 1878

Lester, George, *Grimsby Methodism (1743–1889) and the Wesleys in Lincolnshire*, London 1890

Liddon, H. P., *Life of E. B. Pusey*, London 1894

McCann, Phillip (ed.), *Popular Education and Socialization in the Nineteenth Century*, London 1977

Machin, G. I. T., *The Catholic Question in English Politics 1820 to 1830*, Oxford 1964

Machin, G. I. T., *Politics and the Churches in Great Britain 1832 to 1868*, Oxford 1977

McLeod, Hugh, *Religion and the People of Western Europe 1789–1970*, Oxford 1981

Manning, B. L., *The Protestant Dissenting Deputies*, Cambridge 1952

Martin, David, *A Sociology of English Religion*, London 1967

Matthews, H. F., *Methodism and the Education of the People*, London 1949

Mills, A. J. F., *The History of the Riots in London in the year 1780, commonly called the Gordon Riots*, London 1883

Monk, R. C., *John Wesley: His Puritan Heritage*, London 1966

Moore, Robert, *Pit-Men, Preachers and Politics: The effects of Methodism in a Durham mining community*, Cambridge 1974

Murphy, James, *The Religious Problem in English Education: the Crucial Experiment*, Liverpool 1959

Newman, J. H., *Essays Critical and Historical*, vol. 1, London 1871

Newsome, David, *The Parting of Friends*, London 1966

Norman, E. R., *Anti-Catholicism in Victorian England*, London 1968

Norman, E. R., *Church and Society in England, 1770–1970*, Oxford 1976

Nossiter, T. J., *Influence, Opinion and Political Idioms in Reformed*

England: Case Studies from the North-east 1832–74, Hassocks, Sussex 1975

Obelkevich, James, *Religion and Rural Society: South Lindsey 1825–1875*, Oxford 1976

Oliver, W. H., *Prophets and Millennialists*, Auckland 1978

Outler, A. C. (ed.), *John Wesley* (A Library of Protestant Thought), New York 1964

Overton, J. H., *The Evangelical Revival in the Eighteenth Century*, London 1886

Overton, J. H., *John Wesley*, London 1891

Palmer, R. R., *The Age of the Democratic Revolution*, 2 vols., Princeton 1959

Parker, C. S. (ed.), *Life and Letters of Sir James Graham, Bt.*, 2 vols., London 1907

Paz, D. G., *The politics of working-class education in Britain, 1830–50*, Manchester 1980

Pellew, G., *The Life and Correspondence of Henry Addington, First Viscount Sidmouth*, 3 vols., London 1847

Perkin, Harold, *The Origins of Modern English Society, 1780–1880*, London 1969

Phillips, R. C., *Irish Methodism*, London 1897

Piette, Maxim, *John Wesley in the Evolution of Protestantism*, London, 1937

Pilkington, W., *The Makers of Preston Methodism and the Relation of Methodism to the Temperance Movement*, London 1890

Port, M. H., *Six Hundred New Churches*, London 1961

Porter, Roy and Teich, Mikulas (eds.), *The Enlightenment in National Context*, Cambridge 1981

Prest, John, *Lord John Russell*, London 1972

Reynolds, J. A., *The Catholic Emancipation Crisis in Ireland, 1823–1829*, Yale 1954

Robson, R. (ed.), *Ideas and Institutions of Victorian Britain: essays in honour of G. Kitson Clark*, London 1967

Royle, Edward, *Victorian Infidels: The Origins of the British Secularist Movement, 1791–1866*, Manchester 1974

Rupp, Gordon, *Just Men*, London 1977

Samuel, Raphael (ed.), *People's History and Socialist Theory*, London 1981

Savage, M. W. (ed.), *Sketches, Legal and Political by The Late Right Honourable Richard Lalor Sheil*, 2 vols., London 1855

Scotland, Nigel, *Methodism and the Revolt of the Field*, Gloucester 1981

Sellers, Ian, *Nineteenth-Century Nonconformity*, London 1977

Semmel, Bernard, *The Methodist Revolution*, London 1974

Senior, H., *Orangeism in Ireland and Britain, 1795–1836*, London 1966

Shaw, Thomas, *A History of Cornish Methodism*, Truro 1967

Simon, J. S., *John Wesley and the Methodist Societies*, London 1923

Simon, J. S., *John Wesley and the Advance of Methodism*, London 1925

Snyder, H. A., *The Radical Wesley and Patterns for Church Renewal*, Downers Grove, Illinois 1980

Soloway, R. A., *Prelates and People: ecclesiastical social thought in England*, 1783–1852, London 1969

Southey, Robert, *The Life of Wesley; and the Rise and Progress of Methodism*, 2 vols., London 1820

Southgate, Donald, *The Passing of the Whigs, 1832–1886*, London 1962

Stanley, A. P., *The Life and Correspondence of Dr Arnold*, 2 vols., London 1844

Stevenson, John, *Popular Disturbances in England, 1700–1870*, London 1979

Storch, R. D. (ed.), *Popular Culture and Custom in Nineteenth-Century England*, London 1982

Sykes, Norman, *Church and State in England in the Eighteenth Century*, Cambridge 1934

Sykes, Norman, *The English Religious Tradition*, London 1953

Taylor, E. R., *Methodism and Politics 1791–1851*, Cambridge 1935

Taylor, George, *A History of the Rise, Progress and Suppression of the Rebellion in the County of Wexford in the year 1798*, Dublin 1829

Telford, John, *Two West-End Chapels: Sketches of London Methodism from Wesley's Day*, London 1886

Thomas, H. F. and Keller, R. S. (eds.), *Women in New Worlds*, Nashville 1981

Thomis, M. I., *Politics and Society in Nottingham, 1785–1835*, London 1969

Thomis, M. I., *The Town Labourer and the Industrial Revolution*, London 1974

Thompson, D. M. (ed.), *Nonconformity in the Nineteenth Century*, London 1972

Thompson, E. P., *The Making of the English Working Class*, London 1963

Thompson, K. A., *Bureaucracy and Church Reform: the organisational response of the Church of England to social change, 1800–1965*, Oxford 1970

Todd, J. M., *John Wesley and the Catholic Church*, London 1958

Townsend, W. J., Workman, H. B. and Eayrs, George (eds.), *A New History of Methodism*, 2 vols., London 1909

Tuttle, R. G., *John Wesley: His Life and Theology*, Exeter 1979

Twiss, Horace, *Life of Lord Chancellor Eldon*, 3 vols., London 1844

Tyerman, Luke, *The Life and Times of the Rev. John Wesley, M.A., Founder of the Methodists*, 3 vols., London 1890

Vickers, John, *Thomas Coke: An Apostle of Methodism*, London 1969

Vidler, A. R., *The Church in an Age of Revolution*, London 1961

Vincent, David, *Bread, Knowledge and Freedom: A Study of Nineteenth-Century Working Class Autobiography*, London 1981

Vincent, J. R., *Pollbooks: How Victorians Voted*, Cambridge 1967

Vincent, J. R., *The Formation of the British Liberal Party 1857–1868*, Hassocks, Sussex 1976

Walvin, James (ed.), *Slavery and British Society 1776–1846*, London 1982

Ward, W. R., *Religion and Society in England 1790–1850*, London 1972

Ward, W. R. (ed.), *The Early Correspondence of Jabez Bunting, 1820–1829*, London 1972

Ward, W. R. (ed.), *Early Victorian Methodism: the Correspondence of Jabez Bunting, 1830–58*, Oxford 1976

Wardle, David, *Education and Society in Nineteenth-Century Nottingham*, Cambridge 1971

Warner, W. J., *The Wesleyan Movement in the Industrial Revolution*, London 1930

Watkin, E. I., *Roman Catholicism in England from the Reformation to 1850*, Oxford 1957

Wearmouth, R. F., *Methodism and the Working-Class Movements of England, 1800–1850*, London 1937

Wearmouth, R. F., *Methodism and the Common People of the Eighteenth Century*, London 1945

Wearmouth, R. F., *Some Working-Class Movements of the Nineteenth Century*, London 1948

Wickham, E. R., *Church and People in an Industrial City* [Sheffield], London 1957

Wilberforce, R. I. and S., *The Life of William Wilberforce*, 5 vols., London 1838

Wilkinson, J. T., *Hugh Bourne 1772–1852*, London 1952

Williams, G. A., *Artisans and Sans-Culottes*, London 1968

Wood, A. S., *The Inextinguishable Blaze: Spiritual Renewal and Advance in the Eighteenth Century*, London 1960

Yeo, Stephen, *Religion and Voluntary Organisations in Crisis*, London 1976

Young, D. T., *Robert Newton – the Eloquent Divine*, London 1907

Young, Kenneth, *Chapel*, London 1972

Articles

Baker, Frank, 'Methodism and the '45 rebellion', *The London Quarterly and Holborn Review* (October 1947), pp. 325–33

Baxter, John, 'The great Yorkshire revival 1792–6: a study of mass revival among the Methodists', in M. Hill (ed.), *A Sociological Yearbook of Religion in Britain*, vol. 7 (1974), pp. 46–76

Best, G. F. A., 'The religious difficulties of national education in England, 1800–70', *Cambridge Historical Journal*, **12** (1956), pp. 155–73

Best, G. F. A., 'The Protestant Constitution and its supporters, 1800–1829', *Transactions of the Royal Historical Society*, 5th series, **8** (1958), pp. 105–27

Best, G. F. A., 'The Evangelicals and the Established Church in the early nineteenth century', *Journal of Theological Studies*, **10** (1959), pp. 63–78

Best, G. F. A., 'The constitutional revolution, 1828–32, and its consequences for the Established Church', *Theology*, **62** (1959), pp. 226–34

Best, G. F. A., 'The Whigs and the Church Establishment in the age of Grey and Holland', *History*, **45** (1960), pp. 103–18

Best, G. F. A., 'Popular Protestantism in Victorian Britain', in R. Robson (ed.), *Ideas and Institutions of Victorian Britain*, London 1967

Best, G. F. A., 'Evangelicalism and the Victorians', in A. Symondsen (ed.), *The Victorian Crisis of Faith*, London 1970

Bradley, J. E., 'Whigs and Nonconformists: "Slumbering Radicalism" in English politics, 1739–1789', *Eighteenth Century Studies*, **9** no. 1 (1975), pp. 1–27

Burgess, J., 'The growth and development of Methodism in Cumbria: the local history of a denomination from its inception to the union of 1932 and after', *Northern History*, **17** (1981), pp. 133–52

Cahill, G. A., 'The Protestant Association and the anti-Maynooth agitation of 1845', *Catholic Historical Review*, **43** (1957), pp. 273–308

Cahill, G. A., 'Irish Catholicism and English Toryism', *Review of Politics*, **19** (1957), pp. 62–76

Currie, Robert, 'A micro-theory of Methodist growth', *Proceedings of the Wesley Historical Society*, **36** (1967), pp. 65–73

Dick, Malcolm, 'The myth of the working-class Sunday school', *History of Education*, **9** no. 1 (1980), pp. 27–41

Dreyer, Frederick, 'Faith and experience in the thought of John Wesley', *The American Historical Review*, **88** no. 1 (1983), pp. 12–30

Edwards, M. S., 'The resignation of Joseph Raynor Stephens', *Proceedings of the Wesley Historical Society*, **36** (1967), pp. 16–21

Field, C. D., 'The social structure of English Methodism: eighteenth-twentieth centuries', *British Journal of Sociology*, **28** no. 2 (1977), pp. 199–225

Gilbert, A. D., 'Methodism, Dissent and political stability in early industrial England', *Journal of Religious History*, **10** (1978–9), pp. 381–99

Gilley, Sheridan, 'The Roman Catholic mission to the Irish in London', *Recusant History*, **10** (1969–70), pp. 123–41

Gilley, Sheridan, 'Protestant London, No-Popery and the Irish poor, 1830–60', part 1, *Recusant History*, **10** (1969–70), pp. 210–30; part 2 *Recusant History*, **11** (1971–2), pp. 21–46

Gilley, Sheridan, 'Christianity and Enlightenment: an historical survey', *History of European Ideas*, **1** no. 2 (1981), pp. 103–21

Godfrey, Christopher, 'The Chartist prisoners, 1839–41', *International Review of Social History*, **24** (1979), pp. 189–236

Gowland, D. A., 'Political opinion in Manchester Wesleyanism, 1832–57', *Proceedings of the Wesley Historical Society*, **36** (1968), pp. 93–104

Greaves, R. W., 'Roman Catholic relief and the Leicester election of 1826', *Transactions of the Royal Historical Society*, 4th series, **22** (1940), pp. 199–223

Griffin, A. R., 'Methodism and trade unionism in the Nottinghamshire-Derbyshire coalfield, 1844–1890', *Proceedings of the Wesley Historical Society*, **37** (1969), pp. 2–9

Hempton, D. N., 'The "Watchman" and religious politics in the 1830s', *Proceedings of the Wesley Historical Society*, **42** (1979), pp. 2–13

Hempton, D. N., 'Wesleyan Methodism and educational politics in early nineteenth century England', *History of Education*, **8** no. 3 (1979), pp. 207–21

Hempton, D. N., 'The Methodist crusade in Ireland', *Irish Historical Studies*, **22** no. 85 (1980), pp. 33–48

Hempton, D. N., 'Evangelicalism and eschatology', *Journal of Ecclesiastical History*, **31** no. 2 (1980), pp. 179–94

Hempton, D. N., 'Bickersteth, bishop of Ripon: the episcopate of a mid-Victorian evangelical', *Northern History*, **17** (1981), pp. 183–202

Hempton, D. N., 'Thomas Allan and Methodist politics 1790–1840', *History*, **67** no. 219 (1982), pp. 13–31

Hennell, Michael, 'Evangelicalism and worldliness, 1770–1870', *Studies in Church History*, **8** (1972), pp. 229–36

Hexter, J. H., 'The Protestant revival and the Catholic question in England, 1778–1829', *Journal of Modern History*, **8** (1936), pp. 297–319

Inglis, K. S., 'Patterns of religious worship in 1851', *Journal of Ecclesiastical History*, **11** (1960), pp. 74–86

Itzkin, E. S., 'The Halévy thesis – a working hypothesis?' *Church History*, **44** no. 1 (1975), pp. 47–56

Kemnitz, T. M. and Jacques, F., 'J. R. Stephens and the Chartist movement', *International Review of Social History*, **19** (1974), pp. 211–27

Kent, J. H. S., 'M. Élie Halévy on Methodism', *Proceedings of the Wesley Historical Society*, **29** (1953), and **34** (1964)

Kiernan, V., 'Evangelicalism and the French Revolution', *Past and Present*, no. 1 (1952), pp. 44–56

Koss, Stephen, 'Wesleyanism and Empire', *Historical Journal*, **18** (1975), pp. 105–18

Machin, G. I. T., 'The Maynooth grant, the Dissenters and Disestablishment, 1845–7', *English Historical Review*, **82** (1967), pp. 61–85

Machin, G. I. T., 'Gladstone and Nonconformity in the 1860s: the formation of an alliance', *Historical Journal*, **17** (1974), pp. 347–64

McLeod, Hugh, 'Recent studies in Victorian religious history', *Victorian Studies*, **21** no. 2 (1978), pp. 245–55

Martin, R. H., 'Missionary competition between Evangelical Dissenters and Wesleyan Methodists in the early nineteenth century: a footnote to the founding of the Methodist Missionary Society', *Proceedings of the Wesley Historical Society*, **42** part 3 (1979), pp. 81–6

Meacham, Standish, 'The church in the Victorian city', *Victorian Studies*, **11** (1968), pp. 359–78

Miller, D. W. 'Presbyterianism, and "Modernization" in Ulster', *Past and Present*, no. 80 (1978), pp. 66–90

Money, J., 'Birmingham and the West Midlands, 1760–1793: politics and regional identity in the English provinces in the later eighteenth century', *Midland History*, **1** no. 1 (1971), pp. 1–19

Moore, Robert, 'The political effects of village Methodism', in M. Hill (ed.), *A Sociological Yearbook of Religion in Britain*, vol. 6 (1973)

Newbould, Ian, 'Whiggery and the dilemma of reform: Liberals, Radicals and the Melbourne administration, 1835–9', *Bulletin of the Institute of Historical Research*, **53** (1980), pp. 229–41

Newbould, Ian, 'Sir Robert Peel and the Conservative party 1832–1841: a study in failure?', *English Historical Review*, **98** (1983), pp. 529–57

Norman, E. R., 'The Maynooth question of 1845', *Irish Historical Studies*, **15** (1966–7), pp. 407–37

Parry, J. P., 'The state of Victorian political history', *Historical Journal*, **26** no. 2 (1983), pp. 469–84

Piggin, Stuart, 'Halévy revisited: the origins of the Wesleyan Methodist Missionary Society: an examination of Semmel's thesis', *The Journal of Imperial and Commonwealth History*, **9** no. 1 (1980), pp. 17–37

Pollard, Sidney, 'Factory discipline in the industrial revolution', *Economic History Review*, 2nd series, **16** (1964), pp. 254–71

Rack, H. D., 'Domestic visitations: a chapter in early nineteenth century evangelism', *Journal of Ecclesiastical History*, **34** (1973), pp. 357–76

Rack, H. D., 'Wesleyanism and "the world" in the later nineteenth century', *Proceedings of the Wesley Historical Society*, **42** part 2 (1979), pp. 35–54

Rupp, E. G., 'John Wesley's Toryism and our present discontents', *The Presbyter*, (February 1945), pp. 3–12

Salter, F. R., 'Political Dissent in the 1830s', *Transactions of the Royal Historical Society*, 5th series, **3** (1953), pp. 125–43

Sanderson, Michael, 'Social change and elementary education in industrial Lancashire 1780–1840', *Northern History*, **3** (1968), pp. 131–54

Scott, Patrick, 'Zion's trumpet: evangelical enterprise and rivalry 1833–35', *Victorian Studies*, **13** (1969), pp. 199–203

Scott, Patrick, 'Victorian religious periodicals: fragments that remain', in D. Baker (ed.), *Sources, Methods and Materials of Ecclesiastical History*, London 1975

Stigant, P., 'Wesleyan Methodism and working-class radicalism in the North, 1792–1821', *Northern History*, **6** (1971), pp. 98–116

Thompson, D. M., 'The 1851 Religious Census – problems and possibilities', *Victorian Studies*, **11** (1967), pp. 87–97

Thompson, D. M., 'The churches and society in nineteenth-century England: a rural perspective', *Studies in Church History*, **8** (1972), pp. 267–76

Thompson, E. P. T., 'The moral economy of the English crowd in the eighteenth century', *Past and Present*, no. 50 (1971), pp. 76–136

Thompson, E. P. T., 'Anthropology and the discipline of historical context', *Midland History*, 1 no. 3 (1972), pp. 41–55

Thompson, E. P. T., 'Patrician society, plebeian culture', *Journal of Social History*, 7 no. 4 (1974), pp. 382–405

Turner, B. S. and Hill, M., 'Methodism and the pietist definition of politics: historical development and contemporary evidence', in M. Hill (ed.), *A Sociological Yearbook of Religion in Britain*, vol. 8 (1975), pp. 159–80

Turner, J. M., 'Of Methodists and Papists compar'd', *Procedings of the Wesley Historical Society*, **41** part 2 (1977), pp. 37–8

Unwin, R. W., 'Tradition and transition: market towns of the Vale of York, 1660–1830', *Northern History*, **17** (1981), pp. 72–116

Walker, R. B., 'Religious changes in Cheshire 1750–1850', *Journal of Ecclesiastical History*, **17** (1966), pp. 77–94

Walker, R. B., 'Religious changes in Liverpool in the nineteenth century', *Journal of Ecclesiastical History*, **19** (1968), pp. 195–211

Walker, R. B., 'The growth of Wesleyan Methodism in Victorian England and Wales', *Journal of Ecclesiastical History*, **24** (1973), pp. 267–84

Walsh, J. D., 'Origins of the Evangelical Revival', in G. V. Bennett and Walsh (eds.), *Essays in Modern English Church History*, London 1966

Walsh, J. D., 'Methodism and the mob in the eighteenth century', *Studies in Church History*, **8** (1972), pp. 213–27

Walsh, J. D., 'Elie Halévy and the birth of Methodism', *Transactions of the Royal Historical Society*, 5th series, **25** (1975), pp. 1–20

Ward, J. T. and Treble, J. H., 'Religion and education in 1843: reaction to the Factory Education Bill', *Journal of Ecclesiastical History*, **20** (1969), pp. 79–110

Ward, W. R., 'The Tithe Question in England in the early nineteenth century', *Journal of Ecclesiastical History*, **16** (1965), pp. 67–81

Ward, W. R., 'The religion of the people and the problem of control, 1790–1830', *Studies in Church History*, **8** (1972), pp. 237–57

Ward, W. R., 'The relations of enlightenment and religious revival in Central Europe and in the English-speaking world', *Studies in Church History*, subsidia 2 (1979), pp. 281–305

Ward, W. R., 'Power and Piety: the origins of religious revival in the early eighteenth century', *Bulletin of the John Rylands University Library of Manchester*, **63** no. 1 (1980), pp. 231–52

Wiener, C. Z., 'The beleaguered isle: a study of Elizabethan and early Jacobean anti-Catholicism', *Past and Present*, no. 51 (1971), pp. 27–62

Wood, A. Skevington, 'The eighteenth century Methodist revival reconsidered', *Evangelical Quarterly*, **53** part 3 (1981), pp. 130–48

Wright, D. G., 'A radical borough: parliamentary politics in Bradford 1832–41', *Northern History*, **4** (1969), pp. 132–66

Unpublished theses

The most comprehensive guide to theses on Methodism and popular religion is to be found in the annual bibliographies of Methodist historical literature in the *Proceedings of the Wesley Historical Society*. Since March 1963, the same periodical has, from time to time, constructed lists of academic theses alone. See, for example, vol. 39 part 6 (1974), pp. 184–5; vol. 41 part 3 (1977), pp. 93–4; and vol. 41 part 5 (1978), pp. 162–3. Non-Methodist or comparatively recent theses, which do not appear in the above lists, have been footnoted in the usual way.

Index

Postscript

In the realm of historical reconstruction there is never an ideal time to finish a book. Both in the development of one's own ideas and, more particularly, through the work of others the subject is advanced even before the book is published. Since it is exactly three years since the ink dried on the last page of manuscript, the aim of this short postscript is to bring the reader up to date on recent developments in the writing of Methodist history.

Many reviewers have drawn attention to the central importance I have given to Ireland in the evolution of Methodist political attitudes – at least among the Wesleyan élite – in the first half of the nineteenth century. Although this is not an argument I would wish to modify, it became increasingly apparent to me that Irish Methodism, in its own right, was deserving of more serious treatment than was possible in this volume. That deficiency has now been remedied, at least in part.[1] What was most striking from this research was the way in which Methodism grew most rapidly in the so-called frontier areas of Southern and South Western Ulster where economic competition between Catholics and Protestants was most acute in the period 1770–1830. In such places vital religion served important ethnic, cultural and political functions, the utility of which was quickly spotted by Anglo-Irish landowners of evangelical outlook. When viewed against this background of increased economic and political competition, Methodism was both the beneficiary of, and the contributor to, the growing sectarian tensions of Northern Irish society at the end of the eighteenth century.

What happened in Ireland was regionally distinctive, but far from unique, as recent work on Welsh Nonconformity, Cornish revivalism and Methodist growth in other parts of England has made clear. E. T. Davies has shown, for example, how much of nineteenth-century Welsh Nonconformity had its roots in the religious and social protest of tenant farmers and small holders in the countryside, and among the proto-industrial workers of Glamorgan and Monmouthshire, against predominantly Anglican landowners and entrepreneurs.[2] Here was a powerful mixture of ethnicity, class and religion which formed the basis of one of Britain's most remarkable religious cultures. In early nineteenth-century Wales one Nonconformist chapel was built every eight days, and the chapel attendance figures for some Welsh regions recorded in the 1851 religious census were astonishingly high. Nineteenth-century Welsh society, economy and politics is therefore incomprehensible without reference to the fundamental division between Church and chapel. As Davies has it 'the demands made by nonconformists in Wales throughout the century and the pressures exerted by them arose out of the nature of nonconformity itself and the social, political and economic grievances to which most of them were subjected'.[3]

Cornish Methodism also had a strong anti-Anglican tradition, but its most distinctive characteristic in the nineteenth century, as David Luker's work has shown, was its recurrent bursts of intense revivalism.[4] Part of the explanation for this pattern lies in Cornwall's Celtic isolation from the rest of England and in its tightly knit mining and fishing communities. Many other exogenous factors could be cited in support of this line of argument, but there is also a need 'to focus on internal developments within the churches' since that is where the combustible enthusiasm was ignited. Luker also emphasizes the importance of community solidarity in the transmission of revivalistic energy, and this is corroborated by J. M. Turner in his treatment of the Primitive Methodist revivalism which swept through the rural and industrial villages of the Trent valley in the aftermath of the Napoleonic Wars.[5] Methodist growth throughout the British Isles, it seems, was most spectacular in areas where religious enthusiasm offered tangible benefits of emotional reassurance to transitional communities in the early stages of Britain's industrial revolution.[6]

An important attempt to uncover the 'sacred world view' of labourers in such communities has been made by Deborah Valenze in *Prophetic Sons and Daughters: Female Preaching and Popular Religion in Industrial England*.[7] With understandable impatience with the dominance of men, chapels and politics in Methodist historiography, Dr Valenze's chosen terrain is the cottage-based religion, primarily Methodist, which 'flourished during a specific pre-industrial phase of popular evangelicalism, when public and private converged within the domestic framework of labouring life'.[8] Such religion was genuinely popular because it was rooted in the home and was therefore more resilient to the external controls imposed by industrial entrepreneurs on the one hand, and the institutionally religious on the other. Instead cottage religion brought forth its own sturdy independent leadership, the most striking aspect of which was the relatively high proportion of women. They owed their emergence from obscurity to the domestic setting of popular religion, the sense of autonomy they gained from labouring experiences and the receptivity of men to female leadership when profound social and economic changes threatened families and kinship networks. Acquainted with grief and hardship from an early age, and made even more independent by geographical mobility and late marriage, women preachers were surprisingly young – about 18 – when they began their preaching ministry, and were remarkably unsubmissive to all kinds of authority.

Apart from establishing the importance of cottage religion and women preachers in the popular evangelicalism of early industrial England, Dr Valenze also makes a valuable contribution to the much debated issue of religion and social class.[9] By selecting a number of regional case studies, including some with rapidly growing industrial villages, she shows how popular evangelicalism could serve as an alternative loyalty for rural migrants set free from the old social controls of squires and parsons, but unwilling to submit to new ones imposed by employees and 'respectable' denominations. Initially Wesleyan Methodism served this function, but by the beginning of the nineteenth century its increasing formalism and notorious connexional discipline alienated some of its more humble supporters. Thereafter a multifaceted sectarian Methodism became the dominant expression of cottage-based religion. Indeed the subtle ways in which official Wesleyanism adapted itself to the upward aspirations of 'the improving sort' are splendidly reproduced in the author's case study of Belper in Derbyshire. It was left to the Primitives to re-create 'the world of cottage industry, village familiarity and household unity' in response to the dominant factory paternalism of the Strutt family.[10] Dr Valenze's book makes an important, if understandably not definitive, contribution to our understanding of popular religion in early industrial Britain and is deserving of a wide readership.[11]

Under the broad canopy of popular culture, revivalism and popular religion in nineteenth-century Britain has attracted almost as much attention as the study of law and society in the eighteenth century.[12] Here too I soon became aware of the inadequacies of my own treatment of Methodism and the law in the half century before Wesley's death. So persistent was mob violence against the Methodists – at least before the 1760s – and so fragile was the protection offered by the law in English localities that eighteenth-century Methodists were repeatedly involved in legal disputes. The nub of the problem, according to Bishop Gibson, the Church of

England's most eminent ecclesiastical jurist, was that the Methodists were in open defiance of the laws of the land by posing as Anglicans but acting as Dissenters.[13] Gibson alleged that the Methodists undermined the Anglican parochial system and its pastoral control, yet refused to seek legal protection within the terms of the Toleration Act. Gibson considered this position to be an example of antinomianism – a legal manifestation of the doctrinal heresies of early Methodism.

Wesley, of course, rejected this intepretation, but there was more than a hint of disingenuity in his argument that Methodists were not Dissenters. Many of them were, and were encouraged to remain so, if that was their denominational provenance when they joined Methodist societies. Wesley therefore had it both ways, arguing (when it suited him) that Methodism as a whole was impeccably Anglican, but also that it was an undenominational society displaying 'a catholic spirit'. By requesting toleration while refusing Dissenting status, Wesley pushed the existing laws to the limit and beyond. Since the Methodists were sometimes confused about their own legal status, and the law was itself confused by ambiguities in seventeenth-century statutes, toleration of Methodism in English localities depended upon the urgency of the social situation and the discretion of Anglican magistrates.[14] This was an unsatisfactory position for all concerned, but it was not intolerable, at least until the revolutionary pressures of the period 1790–1820, when the existing laws could no longer cope with the strains placed upon them. As a result a new Toleration Act was passed in 1812. But for the first half century of Methodism's existence, Wesley coped with legal uncertainties by keeping firm control of his own societies, and by steadfastly resisting both patrician and plebeian violence against his followers. His strategy was to take as many of these cases as possible to metropolitan courts where local prejudices were not so important.

In the eighteenth century legal ambiguities and the novelty of the Methodist system proved to be a double-edged sword for the Methodists. On the one hand they were relatively free from effective restraints imposed by parliament, Quarter Sessions and ecclesiastical courts; but on the other, they were wide open to mob violence, which was winked at by the civil and ecclesiastical authorities and from which no effective legal redress was available in the localities. With this background in mind it is perfectly understandable that Methodist political activities in the quarter century after Wesley's death were dominated by a desire to protect their rights before the law. Even into the late nineteenth century the niggling limits of religious toleration exacerbated the dissidence of Dissent and kept Church and chapel rivalry to the forefront of the political stage.[15]

It is tempting to conclude by taking into account the helpful criticisms and suggestions of reviewers, but it is difficult to do so without capitulating to either special pleading or unhelpful polemics. Suffice to say that it is a weakness in my book that Wales was not given more serious treatment, not because it would have undermined the central arguments as has been suggested, but because it would have strengthened them.[16] Second, the relationship between religion and social class is infinitely complex – more so than I properly indicated – and subject to subtle local and chronological changes over the period. Only more local or congregational studies can fully explore such complexities; but undergraduates will already know that the historical rush to the localities in recent times has done as much to obfuscate as to clarify the important *international* themes in the study of popular religion. As for the rest of the book, it must stand as it is, for print, once set, is a remarkably unforgiving medium of communication.

David Hempton
November 1986

References

1 David Hempton, 'Methodism in Irish Society, 1770–1830', *Transactions of the Royal Historical Society*, 5th series, **36** (1986), pp. 117–42.
2 E. T. Davies, *Religion in the Industrial Revolution in South Wales* (Cardiff 1965); and *A New History of Wales: Religion and Society in the Nineteenth Century* (Llandybïe, Dyfed 1981), p. 16.
3 Davies, *A New History*, p. 17.
4 David Luker, 'Revivalism in theory and practice: the case of Cornish Methodism', *Journal of Ecclesiastical History*, **37** no. 4 (1986), pp. 603–19.
5 J. M. Turner, *Conflict and Reconciliation: Studies in Methodism and Ecumenism in England 1740–1982* (London 1985), pp. 82–8.
6 A. D. Gilbert, *Religion and Society in Industrial England: Church, Chapel and Social Change 1740–1914* (London 1976), p. 114.
7 D. M. Valenze, *Prophetic Sons and Daughters* (Princeton 1985).
8 ibid., p. 11.
9 See also Hugh McLeod, *Religion and the Working Class in Nineteenth-Century Britain* (London 1984); and his 'New perspectives on Victorian working-class religion: the oral evidence', *Oral History*, **14** no. 1 (1986), pp. 31–49.
10 Valenze, *Prophetic Sons and Daughters*, pp. 159–83.
11 I deal more comprehensibly with this subject in 'Popular religion and irreligion in Victorian fiction', in T. Dunne (ed.), *The Writer as Witness: Literature as historical evidence* (Cork 1987); and 'Popular religion in Britain 1800–1985', in T. Thomas (ed.), *The British: their Religious Beliefs and Practices* (London 1987).
12 See, for example, J. Brewer and J. Styles (eds.), *An Ungovernable People: the English and their law in the seventeenth and eighteenth centuries* (London 1980).
13 E. Gibson, *Observations upon the Conduct and Behaviour of a Certain Sect usually distinguished by the Name of Methodists* (London 1744), pp. 4–13.
14 Lambeth Palace Library Mss., Secker Papers, vol. 8 (Methodists). This includes the Lavington correspondence, parts of which are reproduced by O. A. Beckerlegge in *Proceedings of the Wesley Historical Society*, **42** (1980), pp. 101–11, 139–49 and 167–80.
15 See J. M. Turner, *Conflict and Reconciliation*, pp. 14–19 and 113–45 for helpful comments on the relationship between Methodism and the law.
16 Davies, *A New History*, pp. 16–25, 42–6 and 61–77.